David James Burrell

The Golden Passional

And Other Sermons

David James Burrell

The Golden Passional
And Other Sermons

ISBN/EAN: 9783337116934

Printed in Europe, USA, Canada, Australia, Japan

Cover: Foto ©Lupo / pixelio.de

More available books at **www.hansebooks.com**

The Golden Passional

BY THE SAME AUTHOR

THE SPIRIT OF THE AGE
AND OTHER SERMONS
12mo, cloth, 381 pages

"FOR CHRIST'S CROWN"
AND OTHER SERMONS
12mo, cloth, 370 pages

WILBUR B. KETCHAM, Publisher
2 Cooper Union -   -   New York

THE GOLDEN PASSIONAL

AND OTHER SERMONS

BY

DAVID JAMES BURRELL, D.D.

Pastor of the Collegiate Church at Fifth Avenue and 29th Street,
New York

NEW YORK
WILBUR B. KETCHAM
2 COOPER UNION

COPYRIGHT, 1897,
By WILBUR B. KETCHAM.

CONTENTS

	PAGE
THE GOLDEN PASSIONAL	5
THE SERE AND YELLOW LEAF	18
YE SERVE THE LORD CHRIST	27
PROGRESS IN OLD PATHS	37
THE MISSION OF AMERICA TO THE WORLD	48
SEARCH THE SCRIPTURES	60
JOHN THE BAPTIST	71
THE OUTSIDE OF THE PLATTER	81
THE KENOSIS	91
IN NO WISE	101
LUTHER AND THE REFORMATION	110
THE STAR OF BETHLEHEM	121
ONE THING	132
CAIN	141
THE ELOQUENT SILENCE OF JESUS	151
I. IN THE PORCHES OF BETHESDA	161
II. IN THE PORCHES OF BETHESDA	172
WANTED: A NEWSPAPER	183
FISHERS OF MEN	197
BEHOLD, THY KING COMETH UNTO THEE	207
CITIZEN GEORGE WASHINGTON	220
THE SIGN OF THE PROPHET JONAS	234

CONTENTS.

	PAGE
To Thine Own Self Be True	243
The Creed of the Mount	253
The Church	263
In the Fields at Eventide	277
"Shibboleth"	286
"Son, Remember"	296
Sunday Pleasures	306
Our Confidant	318
Vandals in the Temple	329

THE GOLDEN PASSIONAL.

"When thou shalt make his soul an offering for sin, he shall see his seed, he shall prolong his days, and the pleasure of the Lord shall prosper in his hand."—ISA. liii., 10.

The people called Isaiah "a bird of ill-omen," because he denounced their sins. He lived in degenerate times. The nation was enervated by wealth and luxury. The altars of Baal smoked on every hill top. People sauntered to the groves to mingle in the orgies of the unclean Astarte. A form of worship was kept up in Jehovah's temple, but it was purely external. The hands that ministered at the altar were "full of blood." Then Isaiah stood by the pillars of the temple, and cried, "Hear, O heavens, and give ear, O earth, for the Lord hath spoken: I have nourished and brought up children, and they have rebelled against me. The ox knoweth his owner and the ass his master's crib; but Israel doth not know, my people doth not consider. Ah, sinful nation, a people laden with iniquity; they have forsaken the Lord!"

Then retribution. Plague, famine, hostile incursions and spoliations to the very gates of the city. "Unmerciful disaster followed fast and followed faster." Again the prophet stood by the temple pillars, and cried, "Why should ye be stricken any more?

The whole head is sick, the whole heart is faint. From the sole of the foot even unto the crown of the head there is no soundness, but wounds and bruises and putrefying sores. Your country is desolate, your cities are burned; and the daughter of Zion is left as a cottage in a vineyard, as a lodge in a garden of cucumbers. Come, now, and let us reason together, saith the Lord: though your sins be as scarlet, they shall be as white as snow; though they be red like crimson, they shall be as wool!"

Then the scene changes. The Miserere becomes a Gloria. The prophet presents a series of panoramic visions, beginning with the eternal generation of divine love and ending in the consummation of redeeming grace.

The first of the visions introduces us into the councils of the ineffable Trinity, where the Persons of the Godhead are represented as moved and troubled by the cry of the distressed people and saying, one to another, "Whom shall we send, and who will go for us?" A voice replies, "Here am I, send me."

Then in the stable at Bethlehem. A cradle scene. Great is the mystery of godliness, God manifest in flesh! The Son of God is bound with swathing bands and laid in the manger. The world knows not that its Redeemer has come; but the key-note of the gladsome song is struck: "For unto us a child is born, unto us a Son is given, and his name shall be called Wonderful, Counsellor, The Mighty God, The Everlasting Father, The Prince of Peace!"

Again, at the crossing of the ways. The Lord of redemption stands like a merchant vending his wares, and crying to the passers-by, "Ho, every one that thirsteth, come ye to the waters, and he that hath no money; come ye, buy, and eat; yea, come, buy wine and milk without money and without price. Incline your ear and come unto me: hear, and your soul shall live."

Again, on the mountains of Israel: "He feedeth his flock like a shepherd; he gathereth the lambs with his arm; he carrieth them in his bosom, and gently leadeth those that are with young."

Then on the heights of the Jordan. A man of war approaches in the distance, travelling in the greatness of his strength. "Who is this," cries the prophet, "that cometh from Edom with garments dyed in blood?" "I, that speak in righteousness, mighty to save." "And wherefore art thou red in thine apparel?" "I have trodden the wine-press alone, and of the people there was none with me. I looked and there was none to help; and I wondered that there was none to uphold; therefore mine arm hath brought salvation."

Again, at the temple gate. The king draws near; the voice of his herald is heard: "Prepare ye the way of the Lord, make straight in the desert an highway for our God." The prophet responds, "O Zion, get thee up into the high mountain; O Jerusalem, lift up thy voice with strength, and be not afraid. Say unto the cities of Judah, Behold your God!"

And finally on Via Dolorosa. A mysterious figure is seen borne down under an intolerable burden. His face is marred more than any man's. He hath no form nor comeliness. There is no beauty that we should desire him. There are scourge marks on his back. He walks like a pariah, bending under his burden, and the multitudes on either side hide their faces from him. He is despised and they esteem him not. He groans under his burden and pours out his soul unto death.

Thus the series of prophetic visions ends in the Golden Passional.* It is a foregleam, clear as the morning star before the sun, of the Lord's own saying, "God so loved the world that he gave his only begotten son, that whosoever believeth in him, should not perish, but have everlasting life." With reference to this vision there are certain enquiries which suggest themselves, and which it behooves us to answer as sinners seeking to return to God.

I. *Who is this mysterious burden bearer, and how does his strange labor concern us?*

It was seven hundred years after this vision when Philip, the evangelist, heard the voice of the Spirit saying: "Go down to Gaza by the desert road." At the time a great revival was going on in Samaria and this man seemed necessary to that work. But God's voice was ultimate law to him. So he arose, without questioning or murmuring, and journeyed down the desert road. Staff in hand, he trudged on, wondering why God should have imposed this task upon him. He heard the rumbling of a chariot behind him, and presently the chancellor of Candace, the Queen of Ethiopia, rode by. He had an open scroll upon his knees and was reading aloud from this Golden Passional.

Philip heard him: "*He is despised and rejected of men; a man of sorrows and acquainted with grief: and we hid as it were our faces from him; he was despised, and we*

---

* This is the name given by Polycarp to Isaiah's prophecy of the vicarious pain of Christ.

esteemed him not. Surely he hath borne our griefs, and carried our sorrows; yet we did esteem him stricken, smitten of God, and afflicted. But he was wounded for our transgressions, he was bruised for our iniquities: the chastisement of our peace was upon him; and with his stripes we are healed. He was oppressed and he was afflicted, yet he opened not his mouth: he is brought as a lamb to the slaughter, and as a sheep before her shearers is dumb, so he openeth not his mouth. And he made his grave with the wicked and with the rich in his death; because he had done no violence, neither was any deceit in his mouth. Yet it pleased the Lord to bruise him; he hath put him to grief: when thou shalt make his soul an offering for sin, he shall see his seed, he shall prolong his days, and the pleasure of the Lord shall prosper in his hand."

And the voice said to Philip, "Go near and join thyself to this chariot." He hurried on and spoke to the Ethiopian: "Understandest thou what thou readest?" "How can I," he answered, "except some one shall teach me?" He gave his hand to the wayfarer and helped him into the chariot. Then Philip expounded to him the prophecy of sorrow. And the chancellor asked, "I pray thee of whom speaketh the prophet this? Of himself or of some other man?" And Philip told him that the mysterious burden-bearer was none other than the long-prophesied and hoped-for Messiah, who by his vicarious suffering, should deliver the world from its sin. As they rode on, they heard the rippling of a fountain and the Ethiopian said: "Here is water. What doth hinder me to be baptized?" And Philip said, "If thou believest with all thine heart thou mayest." He answered "I believe that Jesus is the Christ of God." And when they were come up from the water the Spirit of the Lord caught away Philip, and the chancellor of Queen Candace went on his way rejoicing. He had found the great life-giving truth. He had discovered the personality of the central figure of the Passional. O friends, he who has discovered that, has learned the life-giving power of truth. He who finds Christ, finds all.

II. *And what is this burden?*

It is the sin of the world. The soul of this burden-bearer was made an offering for sin.

Sin is a tremendous fact. Not sin in the abstract, but in the concrete; your sin and mine. There is not a man or woman among us who does not feel the shame and torture of it. Paint it as black as you may, our hearts and consciences must say "Yea" and "Amen" to the indictment.

> " The other shape,
> If shape it might be call'd that shape had none
> Distinguishable in member, joint or limb;
> Or substance might be call'd that shadow seem'd,
> For each seemed either; black it stood as night,
> Fierce as ten furies, terrible as hell,
> And shook a dreadful dart; and from his seat
> The monster, moving onward, came as fast
> With horrid strides; hell trembled as he strode."

And Death also is a tremendous fact — death following sin as surely as the night the day. We may reason as we will against the truth of retribution, we cannot dispossess ourselves of a profound belief in the law of moral cause and effect. A liberal writer has said, "We have managed in the progress of these last times to fill hell up." O, would that it were possible! But the great gulf is fixed; fixed not merely by a divine decree recorded in Holy Writ, but also in the reason of man. We know that beneath the awful words that fell from the merciful lips of Christ respecting the outer darkness, the worm that gnaws and gnaws and never dies, the fire that burns and burns and is never quenched, there is an irrefutable truth: "The soul that sinneth it shall die!"

> "There is a death whose pang
> Outlives this fleeting breath.
> O, what eternal horrors hang
> Around the second death!"

And then the problem. On the one hand: How shall a man be just before his God? On the other: How shall God be just and yet the justifier of the ungodly? How to punish the sin, and yet save the sinner; how to vindicate the law and yet deliver the man who has violated it; this is the question. The only answer is in Substitution. Here is the key of the problem. The innocent must suffer for the guilty, the just for the unjust. Here is the rationale of every sacrifice that ever was laid upon an altar. There is no meaning in the death of all the lambs and bullocks which have been offered the world over since the beginning of time, except as they point to substitution. The innocent for the guilty; the just for the unjust; the Lamb slain from the foundation of the world.

We observe a clear suggestion of this truth in the Greek fable of Prometheus, who was chained to the rock of the Caucasus with the vulture tearing at his vitals, crying out in his pain, "I must needs endure this until one of the gods perchance shall bear it for me."

The fulfillment of all such hopes and reasonings is found on Calvary. Here Jesus, the only begotten

Son of the Father, expiates the world's sin in vicarious pain. Justice and love are met together, righteousness and peace have kissed each other. The law is satisfied and the guilty are delivered. God is just and can justify the ungodly: for the soul of Jesus has been made an offering for sin.

There is a profound significance in that word "soul" in this connection. The pain of our Redeemer was not mere physical pain. The driven nails, the fevered pulse, the gangrene, were mere accessories of a deeper and more unspeakable anguish. Why else did this sufferer shrink and tremble in view of his approaching death? Have the martyrs been braver than he? Alice Driver, drawing near to Smithfield, touched the chain and cried, "This is a goodly neckerchief; God be praised for it!" John Bradford, facing the fagots said, "Now shall I ascend in a fiery chariot to sup with my Lord in his kingdom this night." Archbishop Cranmer, who had recanted and then recovered himself, thrust his right hand into the flame and cried, "O, thou unworthy hand, burn first; I will be avenged on thee for subscribing to that damnable scroll." Castilia, standing on a dizzy height from which she was to be thrust to her death, said to her executioners, "Cast my body down if you will; my soul cannot fall, but like an eagle shall ascend to God." Brave martyrs these who, smiling and triumphant, faced their death!

Not so Jesus. He shrank from the purple draught, saying, "O, my Father, if it be possible, let this cup pass from me!" He cried under the chill shadow of the cross, "Now is my soul troubled, and what shall I say; Father, save me from this hour." Let it be remembered, however, that the physical pain of Jesus was but an inferior factor in his awful sacrifice; he gave his soul an offering for sin. The noble army of martyrs kept their consciences sweet and pure. The fire, the gleaming axe might shrivel their flesh and rack their bones, but could not reach their inmost souls which were possessed by a peace that passeth understanding. No such peace was possible to Jesus; for in exchanging places with those for whom he died, he took into his own heart and conscience their conviction of sin. He so exchanged personalities with those for whom he died, that he lost his own consciousness of innocency and felt himself the chief of sinners in their stead. He made their iniquity his own; so it is written, "He was made a curse for us;" and again, "He that knew no sin was made sin for us that we might be made the righteousness of God in him."

The cry of Cain, as he looked upon his red hands, was, "My burden is greater than I can bear." The lament of David was, "Have mercy upon me, O God, for I have sinned and done evil in thy sight." And Paul cried out, "O, wretched man that I am! Who shall deliver me from the body of this death?" Thus all sinners, honest with themselves, have been mourning from the beginning until now. Lay all this lamentation upon the heart of Jesus the Christ. Heap the guilt of all sinners, guilt on guilt, mountain on mountain, pyramid on pyramid, Ossa on Pelion, and lay it upon the heart and conscience of him who tasted death for every man. Was ever sorrow like unto his sorrow? Now we can understand why nerve and sinew shook and quivered in view of Calvary. Now we are beginning to understand somewhat of the anguish that rang through that bitter cry in the awful night, "*Eloï, Eloï, lama sabachthami?*" He descended into hell for us.

III. One more inquiry: *What compensation was there for all this?*

> "Work without hope draws nectar in a sieve,
> And hope without an object cannot live."

The farmer is encouraged to till the field and scatter the grain because he looks for a harvest. So it is written of Jesus, "For the hope set before him, he endured the cross, despising the shame, and is now set down at the right hand of God."

The promised reward was to be in part a glorious triumph over death and a perpetuation of his influence among men. "When he shall give his soul an offering for sin, he shall prolong his days." The centurion saw the pallor on the dead features of Jesus and said, "He is dead." The Rabbis said, "He will trouble us no more; he is dead." The disciples looked on with unspeakable grief, saying, "We hoped it was he that should deliver Israel; but alas, he is dead." And at that moment all heaven was ringing with the cry, "He that was dead liveth, and is alive forever more, and hath the keys of death and hell!" The angels and archangels knew when the tense and fevered sinews quivered for the last time, that the life of that frail body, like the tenant who closes the door of a forsaken house behind him, went forth to resume the glory which he had with the Father before the world was.

"And he shall see his seed." Here is the promise of posterity. It was written in prophecy, "He shall be cut off in the midst of his days; and who shall declare his generation?" His was to be the deepest sorrow known to an Oriental, that of childlessness. Nay, not so, he was to be the first-born among many brethren, for by the travail of his soul he should bring a great multitude into the glorious liberty of the children of God. He saw some of them already; John, Peter, and the Magdalene; others were coming, Saul of Tarsus, Lydia, the seller of purple, and the chancellor of Queen Candace; more still, three thousand on the Day of Pentecost; multitudes more, for the Church shall be an ever-increasing company from age to age; an army of crusaders, ministers and missionaries of the cross, souls enquiring the way of everlasting life. "Lift up thine eyes round about and see; all that gather themselves together, they come to thee." Listen to the footfall; the dromedaries of Midian and Ephah are drawing near. Hark to the rustle of wings: "Who are these that fly as a cloud, and as doves do fly to their windows?" See yonder the waving of banners: the kings of the earth are bringing their glory and honor unto him.

"And the pleasure of the Lord shall prosper in his hand." What is the pleasure of the Lord? The deliverance of this world from sin. The gathering in of the multitude who have been in bondage under sin. This is the mighty work for which Jehovah made bare his arm. Who are the three mighties of this world? Cæsar, Alexander and Napoleon. They all sought universal empire. Here lies Cæsar, at the foot of Pompey's pillar and none so poor to do him reverence, dead; write on his gravestone, Failure. Here lies Alexander under his table, dead as the result of a drunken revel; write upon his gravestone, Failure. Here lies Napoleon under the dome of the Invalides, with his battle flags around him; write upon his tombstone, Failure.

> "But yesterday their names were as mighty on the earth;
> To-day, 'tis what?"

But there is one name above them all. One who also sought for universal empire, and he won it. Write above the superscription on the cross this word, Success. The pleasure of Jehovah prospers in his hand. He sees of the travail of his soul and is satisfied. On his transcendent throne he sits and looks toward the eastern gates of heaven, and the multitude of the redeemed are thronging in. He looks toward the western gates, and the multitudes are thronging in. He looks toward the southern and northern gates, and multitudes on multitudes are thronging in. And as they cross the threshold of the kingdom, all alike join the universal tribute of praise, "Thou art worthy to receive honor and glory and power and dominion, for thou hast redeemed us out of every nation and kingdom and tribe, and made us to be kings and priests unto God."

One closing word: It is for ourselves to appropriate, by faith, the benefits of this glorious work. So far as our personal salvation is concerned, the redemption wrought by Christ will be of no avail, except as we believe in him. Faith is the hand of the heart stretched forth to receive what Christ would give us. If we are willing, the benefits of the great redemption shall be placed to our credit; if not, the Lord respects our right to reject him and bear the burden for ourselves. When Handel was engaged upon the Oratorio of the Messiah, he was found with his face resting upon the table, his form shaken with sobs.

Before him lay the score open at the place where it is written, "He was despised, he was rejected." Alas! that we should read the story of the passion so lightly. Alas, that he should be despised, and that we, for whom he died, should esteem him not. Let us take heed that we are not among the multitude who stood on Calvary with cold eyes "beholding;" or with those who, as the great burden-bearer passes by, hide their faces from him. Let us receive the proffer of his grace with thankfulness. For if we sing the Golden Passional here, we shall join in the hallelujahs of the kingdom of God.

THE SERE AND YELLOW LEAF.

"We all do fade as a leaf."—Isa. lxiv. 6.

An old proverb says, "The wise man's eyes are in his head, but the fool walketh in darkness." The habit of observation is better than university culture. It was a great day for the world when Galileo saw the swinging chandelier in Pisa Cathedral—saw, pondered, and drew his conclusion. It was another great day when the lad Isaac Newton lay in his mother's orchard, watching the apples that fell from the trees —watching and reasoning. It is such as these—whose eyes are in their heads—that roll the world around, and always further into the light.

It was fortunate for us that Luther knew how to observe. He went down to Rome on a sacred pilgrimage, and all the results of his monastic studies and the convictions of his former life were overturned by what he heard and saw around him. "I would not have taken a hundred thousand florins for the information I picked up." A hundred thousand florins! The information he picked up in the Papal city on that visit gave propulsion to the Reformation; and the world is largely indebted to it for civil and ecclesiastical freedom.

The wise man need not go to the university for information. All things are full of suggestion for him. "There are so many voices, and none of them is without signification." He gathers his science from common things that lie along his path. He finds his theology written all across the starlit skies. For him there are "sermons in stones, tongues in trees, books in the running brooks, and good in everything."

The Greatest of preachers was a close student of nature and common life. He found the themes of his discourse in clouds and flowers, the rising sun, the whistling wind, the fowls of the air, a sower scattering seed. In these he found helpful suggestion as to duty, and the sublime truths that reach forth to the eternal ages.

The autumn is here; "the melancholy days have come, the saddest of the year." But why melancholy? As we go about our tasks the autumn leaves lie in our path and flutter down about us. If we will, each shall be a silent messenger from above, and their word shall bring good cheer and enheartenment to us.

I. The first lesson is in *Beaux Arts*. We are living in a beautiful world adorned by a kind Father for us.

> "This life, sae far's I understand,
> Is a' enchanted fairy land,
> Where pleasure is the magic wand
>   That, wielded right,
> Mak's hours like minutes, hand in hand,
>   Dance by fu' light!"

A few days ago I made a brief journey on the railway. The forests through which we swept were a panorama of indescribable beauty. They were carpeted with velvet and tapestried with Tyrian purple;

decorated with chaplets and garlands, festoons of scarlet vines, hangings of Gobelin with tassels of gold. No artist could paint, no poet could sing it. The heart alone can celebrate such beauty with an uplift of devotion. O the riches of the wisdom and power of God!

Ours is indeed a beautiful world to live in. But there is a better world awaiting us. It was my good fortune once to be at Holyrood Palace when preparations were being made for the coming of the queen. All the rooms in that historic edifice were arrayed in their best; but the throne room—when we came to that, we were allowed only to stand at the threshold and gaze wonderingly on its magnificence. The world in which we are living is beautiful indeed to an appreciative soul, but after all it is only the ante-chamber of the king. What must the throne room be!

II. Our next lesson from the falling leaves is in *Chronology*, or the science of time. *Tempus fugit*, we lightly say; but there is no more impressive truth than this: "Time flies." The man in "As You Like It," who moralized about time is usually called a fool. But there was naught foolish in his moralizing. He drew a dial from his poke, and said:

> " It is ten o'clock:
> Thus may we see," quoth he, " how the world wags:
> 'T is but an hour ago since it was nine;
> And after one hour more 'twill be eleven;
> And so, from hour to hour, we ripe and ripe,
> And then, from hour to hour, we rot and rot;
> And thereby hangs a tale."

The tale that hangs thereby is this: " Whatsoever thy hand findeth to do, do it with thy might; for there is no work, nor device, nor knowledge, nor wisdom, in the grave whither thou goest." If you have prayers to make, pray now. If you have wrongs to undo, old grudges to wipe out, sins to atone for, delay not. If you have work to do for the Master, there is no time to waste; to-day is yours, to-morrow is God's.

Our time here is probationary. We are building character that shall endure forever. We are serving an apprenticeship for eternal usefulness. The deeds done in the body shall confront us in the great day of reckoning. A certain Phœnician, having determined to remove to Rome, thought it wise to send his possessions before him. He chartered a fleet of transports, and one by one he loaded them with grain and precious ore and household wares. On the last vessel that sailed, he was himself a passenger; and on reaching Ostia, the seaport of the Imperial City he found his fleet awaiting him. It is a parable Each day is as a vessel sent forth to the eternal shores. Alas, that so many of our ships should carry naught but ballast! All shall meet us again at Ostia Our life in eternity will be what we now make it.

III. Our next lesson is in *Senescence;* the art of growing old, of growing old gracefully and well. We look upon the aged with compassion; pitying "the sorrows of a poor old man." The poet Holmes was thus minded when he wrote:

> " But now he walks the streets,
> And he looks at all he meets,
>   So forlorn;
> And he shakes his feeble head,
> That it seems as if he said,
>   'They are gone!'

> "And if I should chance to be
> The last leaf upon the tree
> In the Spring,
> Let them smile, as I do now,
> At the old forsaken bough
> Where I cling."

The aged, wearing their "silver crowns as a diadem of praise," should know two things well:

First, *How to hold on.* Our usefulness is not over when life passes its meridian. Cæsar planned his victorious campaigns when he was past fifty years of age. Herschel discovered Uranus after he was fourscore. And John Milton, who had written his early years away in the tripping music of L' Allegro, did not find his holiest mission until, as he tells us, the vapors of youth were past, and the veil of blindness was drawn across his eyes. Then he saw the visions of Paradise Lost, such visions as never came to fleshly sight. His soul rose from the earth like an eagle in its flight, and kindled its eyes at the full midday beam. Gladstone and Bismarck are the greatest names in the world of diplomacy; and both of them wear the silver crown.

Then second, *How to let go.* There is nothing sadder than to see a man clinging to "the old forsaken bough" when the autumn call has come. Why, what is there in this world of pain and labor and weary decrepitude to hold a soul for which the golden city waits? Old Simeon in the temple had lingered long in hope to see the Christ. One day a mother entered the temple with an infant in her arms. The time had come; the gates of glory were on the instant thrown wide open and the old man sang: "Now lettest thou thy servant depart in peace; for mine eyes have seen thy salvation!" That was as it should be. When hope ceases, welcome the life of glad fruition and everlasting youth. So John in Patmos, last of the twelve, vainly longing to mingle in the busy life of those who, beyond the waters that washed the desert island, were facing persecutions for the Lord's sake, heard the call, "Behold, I come!" and, lifting up his withered hands, answered, "Amen. Even so come, Lord Jesus," and went to his rest with a benediction on his lips, "The grace of our Lord Jesus Christ be with you all."

IV. Our next lesson has to do with *Mortality*. And why should we shudder at mention of death? Of all God's angels there is none more gracious. He has light in his eyes, warmth in his heart, and he speaks the promise of endless life.

We think of death as the great mystery. But two things are certain respecting it: First, *It is sure*. We have a proverb "as sure as death." The actuaries of our life insurance companies can approximate, with some degree of certainty, as to relative chances. They will tell you that the farmer is a "good risk," as he ought to be, living in the clear air and sunlight and earning his bread by honest toil. They will tell you the probabilities at various periods of life. All this, however, is guess-work. One thing only is sure; the black camel kneels at every gate. So it is written in the genealogies: "And Adam lived an hundred and thirty years, and he died. And Mahalaleel lived eight hundred thirty and five years, and he died. And Methuselah"—that long lived ne'er-do-weel who has no biography but this—"he lived nine hundred and sixty and nine years; *and he died*."

"Life! I know not what thou art,
But I know that thou and I must part;
And when, or how, or where we met,
I own to me's a secret yet.

"Life! we have been long together
Through pleasant and through cloudy weather,
'Tis hard to part when friends are dear—
Perhaps 'twill cost a sigh, a tear—
Then steal away, give little warning,
Choose thine own time;
Say not good night—but in some brighter clime
Bid me good morning."

The second certainty as to death is that *it comes on time*. There is no accident here. It is a mistake to suppose that the leaves fall because they are frost-bitten. They fall because they are ready and ripe to fall. So death is no accident; it is but an episode in life. There is a truth in what the Moslems say, that every man has his time written on his forehead. It is never too soon, never too late. No life is incomplete, however it may seem to us. When the summons comes, it is high time to go.

V. Our next lesson from the falling leaf is with respect to *Immortality*. The leaf is not without its memorial. It leaves a record behind it. You may note upon the tree a scar—the eloquent epitaph of the departed. So the life is followed by influence. Our names may be forgotten, but the good or evil we have done will live after us.

As Coleridge passed along the country road in the twilight, he heard a reaper singing as he returned from the field; and the poet wrote,

> "I listened till I had my fill,
> And as I mounted up the hill,
> The music in my heart I bore
> Long after it was heard no more."

Our words, though they seem of little moment, are spoken into a phonograph which will reproduce them forever. Our deeds are perpetuated in the character of those who remain after us. The singer goes his way, but the song lives on.

There is, however, a more real and personal immortality than this. We are destined to live forever in another clime. That which we call the falling leaf, is indeed not the leaf at all. Its chlorophyl, or real substance, its life principle, has withdrawn into the tree itself, and only the husk falls. The body returns to earth as it was, and the spirit to God who gave it. That was a glorious truth which was uttered by the Lord Christ as he stood beside an open grave : ' I am the resurrection and the life ; he that believeth in me though he were dead, yet shall he live ; and whosoever liveth and believeth in me shall never die."

VI. Our last lesson is in *Practical Religion.* The leaf lives from above. It is a mistake to say that it gets its nutriment from the earth. The soil furnishes only the silica for its framework; all else comes from the air and sunlight. So is our life, our real spiritual life ; " Verily, verily, I say unto you, except a man be born," *ánothen*—from above—" he shall not see the kingdom of God."

We have not entered upon the true life, unless we have entered into vital union with him who is the life of all. He who dwells amid the sordid cares of this lower world, serving self in pursuing the things that perish with the using, may have a name to live but he is dead. And dead he will continue to be, until he shall find the life which is hid with Christ in God. Then self is more and more forgotten as heaven dawns upon him. "I no longer live," said Paul, "but Christ liveth in me." And living thus, no chill of autumn winds can reach his soul. Death shall be but the King's herald summoning him to a continuance of life in nobler tasks and duties. A glad welcome awaits him in the land of eternal sunshine and beauty; "My beloved spake, and said unto me, Rise up, my love, my fair one, and come away. For, lo, the winter is past, the rain is over and gone; the flowers appear on the earth; the time of the singing of birds is come, and the voice of the turtle is heard in the land ; the fig tree putteth forth her green figs, and the vines with the tender grape give a good smell. Arise, my love, my fair one, and come away."

"YE SERVE THE LORD CHRIST."

"For ye serve the Lord Christ."—Col. iii. 24.

The occasion of this letter to the members of the Colossian Church was what has been called "The Colossian Heresy." It was a commingling of Oriental Mysticism with Jewish Essenism, *plus* a modicum of the Gospel of Christ. There are people in these days, also, who incline to a meditative religion. Dreams are more to them than duties; and transcendentalism more than the power of an earnest life.

> My willing soul would stay
> In such a frame as this,
> And sit and sing herself away
> To everlasting bliss.

It was scarcely to be supposed that Paul would countenance anything of that sort; he was so eminently practical in his religious views. He would have the Christians of Colosse know that the true Christian life was not in sitting at Jesus' feet, but rather standing beside him in the great harvest, sickle in hand. "Ye are not called," he says to them, "to be dreamers among the shadows, but to deny self take up the cross and follow him; for ye serve the Lord Christ."

The motto of the Prince of Wales is *Ich dien*. It

is a truism. Of course he serves. Everybody serves. The basest serve themselves. This is what the multitudes are doing who throng our thoroughfares with restless eyes and furrowed brows. They are spending their energies in pursuit of wealth or pleasure; lust of the flesh, lust of the eye, pride of life.

It is a higher form of self-seeking which we observe in those who agonize for a personal deliverance from sin. This should be, indeed, the first business, logically and chronologically, of every earnest man. But having met the necessary conditions of salvation in Christ, we should linger no longer at that point, but, taking God at his word, "leave the rudiments and pass on unto perfection."

We note another phase of self-service in much of what is felt and written concerning "The Higher Life." By this is usually meant a passive opening of the soul to the influences of the Spirit of God. In other quarters it is called, "self-culture"; that is, the adding of one grace to another in the building of character. This also is good as far as it goes, but it does not go far enough. The cultivation of the passive graces of character may constitute "The Higher Life," but the highest life lies further on.

A better sort of service is that which seeks the welfare of others. One of the significant signs of the times is the general interest in sociology. A new name has been invented: "altruism" or otherism. The thing which it signifies, however, is as old-fashioned as the Christian religion. It is simply philanthropy; the love of our fellowmen. It matters little, however, what we call it; otherism in any form or under any name, is better than egotism. Let us be thankful that so many are disposed to serve society rather than themselves, and strive to make the town, the commonwealth, the world, a better place to live in.

But this is not the highest. There is only one ultimate fact; to wit, God. No purpose is supremely or absolutely right unless it terminates upon him. We know God, however, only as he has manifested himself in Jesus Christ; he is set forth as the fulness of the Godhead bodily, dwelling among us. He is Alpha and Omega; the beginning of all noble aspirations and the objective point of all holy life. So then the Apostle spoke of The Highest Life when he put the Colossians in remembrance, saying, "Ye serve the Lord Christ." It was but another way of saying, "The chief end of man is to glorify God."

I. *But who is this Lord Christ?* He lays claim to our service, saying, "Ye call me Lord and Master and ye say well, for so I am." If I am to serve him reasonably, I must know that he is highest and worthiest of all.

In the Cologne Cathedral there is a rude image of oak bearing the marks of extreme age, representing a giant with a child upon his shoulder. "Who is this?" I asked of the sacristan; and he answered, "This is Offero, the man in search of a master." Then he related the story: Offero would serve only the mightiest. He offered himself to the greatest of earthly kings, and served him well, until, on a certain occasion in the banquet hall, the name Satan was mentioned; whereat the king turned pale and trembled. "Why art thou frightened, O King?" he asked. "Because this is the prince of darkness and he is mightier than I." Then Offero went in search of the prince of darkness and found him without difficulty. He entered his service, and all went well until, as they were journeying on the highway, they came to the cross-roads, where stood a crucifix. There Satan fell a-trembling and refused to pass on. "Why art thou afraid?" asked Offero. "Because this is the Christ, who rules in heaven and suffered on the cross for men, and he is mightier than I." Then Offero went seeking for the Christ. A barefoot friar said to him, "If thou wilt do good as thou hast opportunity, he will present himself to thee." The giant built himself a hut at the ford of a river, and devoted himself to helpful deeds. One dark night he heard a voice without calling, "Offero, come and carry me over!" He found a child awaiting him, lifted it upon his shoulders and, staff in hand, he entered the ford. As he proceeded the winds blew fiercely and the waters rose about him; the burden on his shoulders grew heavier and heavier until it seemed to crush him. At length he reached the other shore, set down his burden, and lo! the Lord Christ stood before him, saying, "Inasmuch as thou hast done it unto one of these least, thou hast done it unto me." He had found the Mightiest, and thenceforth devoted his life to him.

The men who write history are at odds respecting the historic method, but all are agreed as to one divisional line; all pay tribute to the cabalistic letters, A.D. The advent of Jesus Christ marks the zenith of history; up to that time events were all prophetic and all prophecies pointed toward Christ, as all brooks and rivers run into the sea. Since then the path of history has been a highway for the King; its records are but the story of his triumphal march. The progress of civilization is the manifestation of the power of his name. Christendom is the world under the luminous shadow of his cross. The hope of all nations is the coming of his millenial glory. Earth answers back to heaven more and more along the passing years: "Worthy art thou to receive honor and glory and power and dominion forever and ever. Amen."

You have seen, perhaps, a remarkable picture called, "The Conquerors." Here they come, Cæsar, Alexander, Napoleon, Attila the Scourge, Boadicea, Timour the Tartar, Cleopatra—on battle steeds and in war chariots, with waving trumpets and flaring banners, leading on a militant host. On either side of them, far as the eye can reach, are naked bodies of the slain in attitudes of anguish, headless, dismembered. Such is the story of the advance of the mighty toward the conquest of the world. Not such has been the progress of the Prince of Peace. He has come down through the centuries a beneficent Presence with hands stretched out in blessing. The eyes of the blind are opened, the ears of the deaf are unstopped, the lame man leapeth as an hart, the wilderness and the solitary places are glad because of him, the trees of the field clap their hands. O Lord Christ, thou art worthiest of all!

II. *But how shall we serve him?* The rules of the service are in two brief words, "Come" and "Go."

We come to him to receive our qualification and commission for service. Do the first things first. There is no serving Christ until we have passed under his yoke. If any man will come after him let him deny himself, take up his cross, and follow him.

We come to the Lord Christ for our creed. He tells

us what to believe respecting the great verities of the endless life. He instructs us as to God, as to life and immortality, as to final judgment. And his word is our oracle. Let there be no murmuring; if we serve him, it is sufficient that the Lord has said it.

And we come to him for character. Our self-culture is the imitation of Christ. It is for us to copy his hatred of sin and love of holiness; his meekness on the one hand, his courage on the other; his transparent honesty, his submission to the divine will.

> My dear Redeemer and my Lord,
> I read my duty in Thy Word;
> But in Thy life the law appears
> Drawn out in living characters.
> Such was Thy truth and such Thy zeal,
> Such deference to Thy Father's will,
> Such love and meekness so divine;
> I would transcribe and make them mine.

Then, "Go." "*Go down to thine own house,*" he said to the Gadarene, "and show what great things the Lord hath done for thee." Home is the innermost circle of our influence. Let us show our religion there. Many a man is popular among his fellows, well-liked in business, genial in all other associations, who becomes a wretched kill-joy, cross-grained, dictatorial and churlish, the moment he crosses his own threshold. No man has found the true religion who does not make wife and children the happier for it.

"*Go to the temple,*" said Jesus to the ten lepers, "and show yourselves unto the priest." The Lord Christ honored the sanctuary as a divine institution. The Church was his bride, and no man can love the bridegroom and cast reproach upon his spouse. The

Church affords a sphere for the activities of all true followers of Christ. The Church is the organism through which he is working for the setting up of his kingdom on earth. Find your place there, O servant of the Lord Christ, and busy yourself over against your own place in the building of the wall.

Go out into the community and show forth your religion among all. The circle widens. Neighbors and friends make their demands upon you. Ye are as salt; but if the salt have lost its savor, it is thenceforth good for nothing but to be cast out and trodden under the foot of men. Ye are as light; let your light so shine before men that they may see your good works and glorify God.

"*Go ye into all the world*" and tell the good news. Charity begins at home, but it journeys to the uttermost parts of the earth. The glory of Christianity is that it enlarges the heart. The man who has caught the spirit of Christ is in cordial sympathy with every home missionary who rides his Indian pony across the plains, and with every foreign missionary who preaches the Gospel to those who lie in darkness and the shadow of death. A Christian is a cosmopolitan.

There is only one thing the servant of the Lord Christ cannot do; he cannot *stay;* he cannot linger, forever looking up into the Master's face. The world calls him. The word of the Master rings out like a clarion, "Go ye!" The true servant of the Master feels that word thrilling through heart, and conscience, and soul: Go ye! beginning at the innermost point of influence and reaching to the uttermost.

On the mount of Transfiguration, the disciples,

witnessing the transfigured glory of their Master, were filled with a transport of peace. And Peter said, "It is good for us to be here. Let us build three tabernacles; one for thee, one for Moses, and one for Elias." He would have lingered in that luminous cloud and amid the transcendent visions of that hour; but he wist not what he said. At the foot of that mountain was a demoniac boy, foaming at the lips, waiting to be dispossessed. And there were numberless others needing help and dumbly appealing to the followers of Christ. Go ye, and relieve the sufferings of your fellowmen. Go to those who bear the burden of sin and tell them that Jesus is mighty to save. Go to those who are bound with the chains of habit and tell them in earnest words and in your own walk and conversation, that Jesus calls them to the glorious liberty of the children of God.

III. *But why shall we serve the Lord Christ? What are the motives?*

First, *Duety*. If the word seems quaintly spelled with an "e," let us remember that obligation is the very heart of it. Duty is that which is owed to God. The service which you pay to the Lord Christ is in recognition of the service which he has rendered to you. "Ye are not your own, ye are bought with a price, not with silver or gold, but with the precious blood of Jesus as of a lamb without blemish and without spot.' Nothing that we can render is too good for him.

Second, *Because of the joy of service*. The happiest man in the world was Jesus; the next happiest is he who most nearly follows Jesus in doing good unto all. A clerk searching among the accounts of Edward II. found this strange entry, "A crown for making the king laugh." Poor, melancholy Edward. It was a gracious thing to make him laugh and the jester well deserved his crown. But after all the crown was the smallest part of his requital, for it is safe to say that when Edward laughed, the jester laughed too. Joy is infectious. The heart burns in loving service. There is no pleasure like "the generous pleasure of a kindly deed."

> The quality of mercy is not strain'd;
> It droppeth, as the gentle rain from heaven
> Upon the place beneath: it is twice bless'd;
> It blesseth him that gives, and him that takes.

Third, *The perpetuity of influence.* We shall presently go our way and our names will be forgotten; all that will remain will be the influence of our lives.

The artist Wilkie visited the Escurial to see Titian's picture of the Last Supper. An old Jeronomite stood by and said, " I have sat in sight of that picture nearly three-score years. The visitors have come and looked and wondered and gone their way. My companions have dropped off one by one. But these remain; these painted men. They are the true realities; we are but shadows." This is the solemn truth. Titian dies, but his work remains. Influence is immortal. We are but shadows, the sun sets and we are gone; but our works do follow us.

Fourth, *Because of the penny at evening.* The Lord has a great reward awaiting those who faithfully follow him. He meets them at the threshold, saying, "Well done, good servant, enter thou into the joy of thy Lord." And then, promotion. I was speaking but yesterday with a friend, of the faithful life of John Graham, who has recently been called home. He said, "Is it not strange that a man so useful as he should be arrested in the midst of his work?" Arrested in his work! There is no arrest of Christian work. Death is promotion. All our preparation here will surely be called into requisition for the discharge of higher tasks in that blessed country of which it is written, "His servants do serve him."

O friends, there is no sweeter word than this, "My Master." It was the word of Mary Magdalene when she stood by the open sepulchre. He who had been borne to that sepulchre was her dearest friend, who had saved her from the shame of a mislived life and pardoned her sin. But he was gone, and her tears flowed fast. "Why weepest thou?" said a voice beside her. She saw but dimly through her tears, and supposing it to be the gardener, said, "O sir, if thou hast borne him hence, tell me where thou hast laid him." "Mary!" She knew his voice and, casting herself at his feet, cried, "Rabboni!" which is to say, "My Master." The sorrow of her heart was lost in the joy of a new devotion. Her word gave inspiration to quaint George Herbert to write:

> How sweetly doth "My Master" sound!
> My Master!
> As ambergris leaves a rich scent
> Unto the taster:
> So do these words a sweet content,
> And oriental fragrancie,
> My Master!

PROGRESS IN OLD PATHS.

"Beloved it was needful for me to write unto you and exhort you that ye should earnestly contend for the faith which was once delivered unto the saints."—JUDE iii.

The writer of this epistle, Judas, was handicapped by his name. He is never mentioned, however, in the gospels, without the qualifying phrase, "not Iscariot." Indeed he was a very different sort of man. He was a kinsman of Christ after the flesh and called to be an apostle, but his chiefest joy was that he was a servant of Jesus Christ; that was honor enough for him.

This epistle is called "general" or "catholic," because it is addressed, not to any particular church or individual, but "to them that are sanctified by God the Father, and preserved in Jesus Christ, and called." To all such the world over and through the ages he addresses his benediction, "Mercy unto you and peace and love."

The occasion of this epistle is given in these words, "It is needful for me to write and exhort you that ye should earnestly contend for the faith which was once delivered unto the saints. *For* there are certain men crept in unawares, ungodly men, turning the grace of God into lasciviousness (that is, lawless freedom of thought and conscience), and denying the only Lord God and our Lord Jesus Christ." This was Anno

Domini 66. A generation had passed away since the ascension of Christ. The early flush of enthusiasm was gone, and the world was getting a firm grip on some of the disciples. Now came false teachers, "creeping in unawares," like the serpents of Tenedos under the altar. They had new philosophies to suggest for the toning down of the asperities of the Gospel and the removal, or the modification, of the offence of the cross.

There is no uncertain sound in Jude's characterization of these errorists. He says, "These are spots in your feasts of charity;" rather, lepers. It is scarcely possible to conceive of a greater kill-joy at a feast than a seat-mate with his fingers dropping from the joints. And again, "They are clouds without water, carried about of winds." In time of drought you look to them in vain for relief; they are beautiful, but barren; so are false teachers, abounding in fine phrases, but not satisfying the soul. And again, they are "trees whose fruit withereth, without fruit, twice dead, plucked up by the roots." Twice dead! Once is usually enough. But these men are like trees so dead that they have no fruit for the hungry nor shadow for the weary, and are hardly fit for firewood. And again, "They are raging waves of the sea, foaming out their own shame." The storm is over and the damage done. The billows roll in bearing flotsam and bodies of the dead, and roll back again triumphant, in masses of foam. So do false teachers lure away the thoughtless from truth and righteousness, and glory in it. And again, they are "wandering stars, to whom is reserved the blackness of darkness forever." They are not like those orderly planets that revolve in their orbits under wise law;

but, whizzing forth into space on their own account, with much noise and spectacular display, they lose themselves in endless night.

A stern denunciation this, but not enough. The apostle says furthermore, "Woe unto them! for they have gone in the way of Cain." And what did Cain do? He set up his own reason against divine authority, and brought to the altar the first fruits of the field in which there was no blood; and the Lord rejected his offering. And they have "run greedily after the error of Balaam for reward." What was the error of Balaam? He denied divine authority in insisting that one religion was as good as another; as between Baal and Jehovah it mattered little, if the worship were only sincere. And they have "perished in the gainsaying of Core." Who was Core? A man who set himself up against the Mosaic claim of divine authority, who called in question the oracles, saying, "I will do as seemeth right unto me"; and the earth yawned and swallowed him up.

No uninspired preacher would dare to use such impassioned invective in these days. Let it be remembered, however, that Jude wrote as he was moved by the Spirit of God, and gave as a reason for his severity, "because they have turned the grace of God into lawless liberty and have denied the Lord Christ." We find the same class of errorists to-day. And for that matter there is no new heresy. The wind whirleth about continually and returneth again according to its circuits; the thing that hath been, is that which shall be. We hear much of a theological renaissance, a new theology, a new Christ! "Our religious thought must be brought up abreast of the age." In this connection there are certain considerations which may profitably engage our thought:

I. *The world moves.* There can be no doubt about that. Civilization is a fact. Evangelization is a fact. The ever-enlarging boundaries of Christendom are a glorious fact. There can be no pessimists but blind men. Truth and goodness are making headway every day. The Pope required Galileo to kneel down and recant his statement that the world moved around the sun, under pain of anathema, but as he arose from his knees he muttered between his teeth, "Nevertheless it does move." It does move and no conservative denial can stop it.

II. *The Church must move with it.* If Solomon were to undertake the building of the temple to-day, would he float his cedar logs along the western coast of Palestine and laboriously drag them over the mountains to the Holy City? Nay, in recognition of the progress of the centuries he would employ a steam tug to push his rafts from Tyre to Joppa and a locomotive with flat cars to carry the great timbers to the station at Jerusalem. If he pursued any other course, the world would make sport of him.

There is a single branch of the Christian Church which glories in being *semper idem.* In the village of Minstead in England, you may read this sign: "John Purkes, charcoal burner." It was away back in the year 1100 that a man named John Purkes, driving his charcoal wagon through the forest, picked up the body of King William Rufus with three arrows in the breast. And here, eight hundred years later, is his remote descendant bearing the same name, driving the horse and cart, and doing the old business at the old stand. God's people cannot afford to be conservative in that way. The world moves and the Church must move with it.

III. *There are, however, some things which remain forever the same.* They are unchangeable in the nature of the case. Such are the four elements, as the old scientists named them: Air, earth, water and fire. These are constant factors in physics. It would be preposterously foolish to attempt to improve upon them or to change them in any way. In like manner there are certain constant factors in theology, known as "Credenda." They are elemental, eternal facts.

(1) *God.* He is the same yesterday, to-day and forever. There is inexpressible satisfaction in feeling that whatever else may come or go, with him is neither variableness nor shadow of turning. The sailor always knows where to find the North Star. Quadrants, compasses, chronometers and "dead reckonings" may fail, but yonder in heaven shines the mariner's guide. So sings the Psalmist, "Lord thou hast been our dwelling place in all generations; before the mountains were brought forth, or ever thou hadst formed the earth and the world, even from everlasting to everlasting thou art God."

(2) *Man.* The conditions of life may be improved and the level of character may be raised, but there is no change in the constitution of the race. Our hopes, griefs, aspirations, are the same that our fathers have had before us. *Sin* is just what it was when Cain, looking at his red hands, in horror cried, "My burden is greater than I can bear." All self-culture and moral cosmetics cannot affect the awful, abhorrent fact. And *responsibility* is what it

has always been; all the duties of this present life thrown into bloody, startling relief in the lurid glow of the judgment day. And *spiritual death* is what it has always been; the hearts of men are moved as ever with a certain fearful looking-for of judgment, and the law rings out as it has ever done, "The soul that sinneth, it shall die." And our *helplessness* is as absolute as ever, forcing from us the cry, "What shall I do to be saved?"

(3) *The Cross.* No new theories can affect it. The Jews require a sign and the Greeks seek after wisdom, but we preach Christ crucified, because there is none other name under heaven given among men whereby we must be saved.

> This is the way the prophets went,
> The way that leads from banishment,
> The King's highway of holiness.

We hear much in these times of the "moral influence theory" of the atonement; that is to say, the sacrifice of the cross was "not penal, but didactic." It was intended to teach the race, in an overwhelming manner, the lesson of divine love. And that was all.

There is an outcry against vivisection as practiced in our medical schools. We think with horror of a circle of students gathered about a dumb creature, kept under torture that they may learn how the blood circulates or how the nerves tingle under pain. But what shall be said of this awful vivisection on Calvary; the Father giving his only-begotten and well-beloved Son to be nailed upon the cross for no other purpose than to teach us sinners that he loves us? The hypothesis is inadequate. One of the Greek dramatists was wont to say, "A god should never be introduced into a tragedy unless there is a needs-be." Judged by that pagan standard, the moral influence theory of the atonement has no right to be. Let the Scriptural statement of the fact be sufficient: He took our place as a divine substitute before the offended law, assumed the burden of our sins until his heart broke under it; he was wounded for our transgressions, and bruised for our iniquities, and by his stripes we are healed.

(4) *The Bible.* It was divinely constructed once for all to meet the necessities of men. It was intended to be true, trustworthy and complete. Its last word was Finis. The text-books which are used in our common schools must be changed from time to time in order to keep pace with progress. But the Scriptures were in the beginning adjusted to all possible changes and developments in human life. There are no errata; there is no addendum or supplement. The Book remains just what it was when Jesus said: "Search the Scriptures, for in them ye think ye have eternal life and these are they which testify of me."

These are postulates called "Credenda," because they must be accepted in order to spiritual progress. The athlete who runs in the stadium must have his feet planted on *terra firma:* then let him run so as to win. These fundamental truths are the *terra firma* of Christian progress. We can no more improve upon them than a scientist can improve on air, earth, fire and water.

IV. *But some things admit of betterment.* If the Credenda constitute the substantial body of truth, there are Docenda which are liable to constant change and improvement. Here is the field of progress. We may not affect the elemental forces which furnish the motive power of the spiritual world, but there is illimitable room for new methods, adjustments, applications and combinations of those forces. At this point we raise the song, "Ring out the old! Ring in the new!"

(1) It behooves us to strive continually after *a larger faith in God.* We speak of him as the great Mystery. But there is a real sense in which God is no mystery at all. The best the Greek philosophers could do, was to rear an altar inscribed, "To the Unknown God." No such agnosticism is excusable in us, for God has revealed himself in both his written and his incarnate Word. "Say not, Who shall ascend into heaven, to bring him down? or, Who shall descend into the depths, to bring him up? for lo, he is nigh thee, even in thy heart and in thy mouth." He is an immanent God. He is our Father. He is nearer to us each moment than our closest friend. If we could but realize this fact and bear it with us into the discharge of our common tasks and responsibilities, what manner of persons we should be! Let us seek to make him ever more and more a Real Presence, dominating our lives until every thought and purpose is brought into subjection to him.

(2) *A larger conception of the dignity and possibilities of manhood.* The daily prayer of a humble weaver in England was, "Lord, give me a better opinion of myself." And why not? Were we not created in the divine likeness, and but little lower than the angels? Do we not stand erect, with power to face the great problems and apprehend the sublime truths of the

eternal life? Is it not our privilege to co-operate with God himself in the building up of his kingdom of truth and righteousness on earth? And, despite our sin, are we not moved by the great hope of returning to our original estate by the imitation of Christ the ideal Man? "Now are we sons of God, and it doth not yet appear what we shall be; but we know that when he shall appear we shall be like him, for we shall see him as he is."

(3) *A higher, deeper apprehension of the truth and power of the cross.* We are too prone to regard the cross as an objective fact, the symbol of a sublime tragedy that was enacted 1800 years ago. But this is an eternal tragedy. Christ is the Lamb slain from the foundation of the world. Christ is crucified before our very eyes. Let us gaze upon him affixed to the cross, until the eye shall affect the heart and the heart affect the life. Let us gaze upon him until all else shall vanish; the mocking scribes and Pharisees, the soldiers, Calvary itself, the skies above with the clouds enshrouding them, and naught remains but Christ and him crucified.

(4) *New light on the Scriptures.* This was the word of John Robinson to the Pilgrims as they were embarking at Delft Haven for the new world : " I charge you before God and the angels that ye follow me no further than I have followed Christ, and remember that new light will ever burst forth from the word of God." We are accustomed to say that we are living in an age of Bible study. Not so; we are living in an age of study about the Bible. But the time has come when we should busy ourselves less in the problems that concern the exterior of the Book, and open

it wide to find what God therein says to us. It is the *entrance* of his Word that giveth light.

And finally, there is room for *vastly greater zeal in the service of God*. There is indeed no end to the possibilities of progress at this point. Why shall the Church stand with folded hands in the market-place, while there are multitudes of souls still abiding in darkness and the shadow of death? Why engage in frivolous controversies, while the word of the Master rings out from the Mount of Ascension, "Go ye into all the world and tell the good news"?

But the Church is what we individually make it. O for more of personal zeal in the service of our Lord! We are tarrying too long in Jerusalem awaiting the baptismal power. I have been reading of George Whitefield; how he preached thirty-four years, delivering more than eighteen thousand sermons. He traversed England, Ireland and Wales, and then crossed the sea and passed through the Colonies from Maine to Georgia. He wore himself out most gladly in his Master's service. When the end drew near, he essayed to speak to a multitude who were gathered at evening in the street below. His strength failed him, and he said, "Brother, you must preach, I cannot say a word." Candle in hand, he started for his bed; then he came back, and standing on the stairs he preached the old gospel until the candle burned to its socket, flickered and went out. Then he staggered back to his bed and awoke in heaven. What a glorious life, what a glorious death was that! Is there anything better possible to us than to grow weary and be worn out for the Lord Christ?

O no, beloved! it is not a new theology that we want, but a new life. Not a new Bible, but new eyes wherewith to read it. Not a new theory of redemption, but a new voice to sing the praises of redeeming grace. Not a new Christ, but a new, more absolute, all-consuming devotion to him. Make us willing, O Lord, in the day of thy power, in the beauties of holiness, from the womb of the morning, willing to live, to labor, to suffer for the glory of the Name which is above every other that is named in heaven or on earth!

THE MISSION OF AMERICA TO THE WORLD.

"It is a light thing that thou shouldst be my servant to raise up the tribes of Jacob, and to restore the preserved of Israel; I will also give thee for a light to the Gentiles, that thou mayest be my salvation unto the end of the earth."—ISA. xlix. 6.

God is ever at work. His is a great parish. He ministers to the universe. His thought is given to myriads on myriads of worlds. "Look how the floor of heaven is thick inlaid with patens of fine gold!" If we walk through his vast field of labor, we shall find worlds springing up like daisies and buttercups along the way; and space, stretching infinitely far, is filled with worlds as motes swarming in the air about us. Or let us, if the Master of this great parish will invite us into his chariot, ride along that royal thoroughfare called the "Milky Way," and note how the dust rises about our chariot wheels as we whirl onward; thick clouds of rising dust, and every atom a world.

With our unaided eyes we behold an innumerable host; myriads on myriads, firmaments and systems. But if we summon to our help the telescope we shall see new systems and firmaments come wheeling into view, like an infinite armada on a boundless sea. Eyes are dazzled and brain bewildered by the view.

Mare magnum! Fleets, armies, archipelagoes of worlds! See yonder nebulæ, dull patches of light; every tremulous spark in each of them is a world—a world, for aught we know, populous with immortal beings. There is the "Stratified Nebula," layer on layer of worlds. Yonder the "Spiral Nebula," a multitudinous twist or vortex, a winding staircase of worlds. On this side, the "Perforated Nebula," as if another firmament had whizzed through it and carried away to black chaos some millions or trillions of worlds.

And all this bewildering, incalculable, unthinkable array of systems revolves around a centre, somewhere. Is it Alcyone of the Pleiades, as the fathers of astronomy thought? Or is it yonder fixed star in the remotest distance, so far away that if we travelled on the Empire State Express we should not reach it in four thousand years? Or is this visible universe, after all, but the outer fringe of an inconceivably vaster universe filling all the infinitude of space? Is there no limit? Are there no boundaries? Is the universe a parish vast as its great Minister, from everlasting to everlasting?

Wherever its centre is, the throne of the Eternal is there. He created these worlds by his fiat. "By his spirit he has garnished the heavens." He telleth the number of the stars; he calleth them by name. What a stupendous figure have we here: God calling the roll of the worlds. "O sun, come forth!" and at his word the sun comes forth out of his chamber as a bridegroom, and rejoiceth as a strong man to run a race. "O moon, come forth!" and like Ophelia with wide eyes and disheveled locks, she pursues her way along the night. "O Mazzaroth, Orion, Arcturus with thy sons, and thou, O Star of Bethlehem, come forth!" And each at his summons answers, "Here am I." Thus day after day, night after night, century after century, æon after æon, the great Minister, never slumbering, never sleeping, rules his parish. This is the work of God.

Is this in the realm of speculation? Then let us descend to matter of fact. One thing we know; one world we are familiar with; namely, the world we live in. It is but an infinitesimal part of the great parish, but it requires his constant care. It is, so far as we know, his one lost world. If the other worlds in his universe are peopled, it may be that yonder the fathers point out to their children a twinkling star in the distance, and say, "That is the world that wandered into sin." To bring this wayward sphere to its orbit again, the great Ruler must needs make bare his arm. He did make bare his arm and laid his hand, a piercéd hand, upon our world at Calvary to reclaim it. It is an easy matter for God to manage those nebulæ, for nothing is too hard for him. But the most difficult task to which he addresses his omnipotence is the deliverance of this fair, twinkling orb that swung from its orbit into sin. It is written, "He left the ninety and nine and went out after the one sheep that was lost." O supreme manifestation of divine wisdom and power! He will never cease his exertion in this world's behalf until the last sinner is reclaimed by his grace. This is the great enterprise to which Jesus referred when he said, "My Father worketh hitherto and I work." And again, "As the Father hath sent me into the world, so send I you."

Here is the clew of history. All events are to be weighed and measured by their bearing on this divine work. Dr. Roswell Hitchcock said, "The man who in his reading has learned to ask concerning any event, What did God mean by this? has begun to get at the philosophy of history." Let us go further and say, The man who has learned to measure all events by their relation to the great work of redemption, has fully grasped the philosophy of history. The call of Abraham, the roll of the trumpet waxing louder and louder at Sinai, the rushing wind and lambent flame at Pentecost; Rome, Babylon, Medo-Persia; Cyrus, Alexander, Cæsar, Napoleon; Marathon, Waterloo, Marston Moor, Bunker Hill; Runnymede, the Spanish Fury, the ringing of the bell on Independence Hall—all these are but episodes in the progress of God's great enterprise. They mean much or little, just as they are measured by their influence on the deliverance of this world from sin.

We come now to the one episode which engages our immediate thought, the *Discovery of America*. Let us measure this by the rule of historic importance.

Why was this continent, lying in the "Zone of Power," so rich in possibilities, suffered to lie unknown so long? It was *terra incognita*, a shining nugget at the feet of the nations, unheeded for five hundred years.

What was it waiting for? The science of navigation? Aye. The man who suspended a magnet to a cork and watched it float in a basin pointing ever the same way, wrought better than he knew; for his discovery was to make the pathway through the seas.

What else was the unknown continent waiting for? The art of printing? Aye. When Laurence Coster, sauntering through the wood with his little lad, cut the initials on the bark of an elm tree, saying, "And why not movable type?" he also wrought better than he knew; for this, in multiplying the Scriptures, would furnish a reason for the pathway through the seas.

But the unknown land was awaiting something else: the plethora of the Nations. The fulness of time for its discovery and settlement had not come until the Old World was groaning with its surplus populations. In Holland, the little hollow land, the thrifty masses swarmed like bees. They jostled one another to discomfort in the eager pursuits of life. In France the Huguenots toiling at their looms longed for a larger sphere of labor. In England the Puritans, "cabin'd, cribbed, confined," cried out for room, more room.

So the hour struck. The New World lay open to adventurous and ambitious souls. The Sea-Mew sailed from Holland with her cargo of honest Dutchmen bound for the shores of New Netherland. The Mayflower bore her precious crew of Pilgrims to the shores of New England. And eager bands of Huguenots set sail for our southern ports. It is thus manifest that the concealment of the western world through so many centuries was not beyond the purposes of Providence, and that its discovery was in the precise fulness of time.

I. We are therefore led to observe that America was designed to be logically and chronologically a *refuge for the oppressed of all nations.*

We are distinctly and singularly an immigrant people. The French are the descendants of the original Gauls. The Germans are children of those Germanic tribes of whom Tacitus wrote before the beginning of the Christian era. The English have in their veins the blood of the Angles, the Saxons, the Normans, the Romans, and the Druid worshippers of long centuries ago. But we Americans—what are we? A heterogeneous people. We are made up of the commingled bloods of all nations with one solitary exception: we are in no wise related with the native American race. There is no difference, therefore; we are all alike immigrants at a less or greater remove.

Why are we here? What brought our fathers to these shores? Some came to improve their worldly estate; to better their hope of an honest livelihood. Such were our Dutch forefathers. They did not flee from tyranny. Holland was the only nation on earth which had fought to a finish the conflict of civil and ecclesiastical freedom. But these thrifty men were not content with the industrial opportunities of the mother land. They, and multitudes of others, came to America, as Jason and the Argonauts set forth, in quest of the golden fleece.

Others came hither for a chance to rise. The system of caste prevailed in one form or another in all the nations of the Old World. The scavengers and water-carriers of Bombay to-day are the children of those who were water-carriers and scavengers in Bombay five hundred years ago. The barriers of caste in India are such that they have been unable to rise above their traditional estate. The difficulties in other and more civilized lands are not so serious; nevertheless the gentry, the nobility, the titled and privileged classes, in France, Germany and England, are but other names for high caste. There never have been any such hindrances to ambition in the New World. We hear of the masses and the classes, but this is a wholly artificial distinction. We have no class except such as rises from the mass. There is a continual process of leveling up. The possibilities of social improvement know no bounds. An Italian laborer at work on our streets thinks himself in a sort of heaven because he has the opportunity to earn a dollar a day. He may be satisfied with that for himself, but not for his children. He has a boy in our public schools whom he is educating in the distinct hope that the lad shall presently be able to make more than a dollar a day. And his dream is quite sure to be realized; for wealth, honor, influence, to the very utmost, are possible to the least and poorest. This was the message rung out from Independence Hall. "All men are created free and equal and with certain inalienable rights; among which are life, liberty and the pursuit of happiness."

Others still came to the New World for freedom of conscience. Such were the Pilgrim Fathers. "They sought a faith's pure shrine." To all such refugees our free country has ever extended a most cordial welcome.

A shipload of Armenians has recently landed at Ellis Island. There are some hundreds of these refugees who are detained there awaiting permission to enter. I say, in the name of our national traditions and in the interest of humanity, let them come. Are they poor? Are we not all the children of "poor but honest parents"? I have looked into their faces; brave, honest, stalwart, clear-eyed men and women; these are the very stuff that Americans are made of. They have fled from the foulest and cruelest persecution ever known. Shall that bar their entrance to our free republic? Nay; the same rule would have prevented the landing at Plymouth Rock. Let them come in! If they are poor, they will the more eagerly improve the opportunity afforded here to make an honest living. If their backs are scarred with the scourge of ecclesiastical tyranny, they will the better appreciate our privileges of civil and religious freedom. We are a Christian nation. These men have suffered persecution solely because of their Christian faith. The strife in their fatherland is between the Crescent and the Cross. The Church of Christ is one the whole world over. The "Body of Christ," do we call it? My body is so unified by its nervous system that if you tread upon my foot the thrill of pain is carried, as by electric wires, until it flies tingling to my finger tips. They have trodden upon our brethren in Armenia; let every drop of Christian blood that is in our American veins thrill with sympathy. Welcome to our brethren from afar, fugitives from scourge and fagot. In the name of the God who has kept and preserved us as a nation, let them come in!

II. We observe also that our country in the manifest providence of God is intended to be a *centre of influence for the betterment of all nations.* If it be true that no man liveth unto himself, it is truer still of a nation. The God who led Israel to the little land of Palestine, that from that focal point his chosen people might send forth streams of beneficence to the uttermost parts of the earth, has appointed a like destiny for us. He has somewhat for us to do as a nation in his great work of delivering the world from sin.

It is ours to *propagate the rights of man.* At this moment we are all moaning for poor Armenia. It is indeed an oft-told tale, yet we cannot be silent when the submarine cables are laden from day to day with the message that the war of extermination goes merrily on. A hundred thousand slain in the nineteenth century of the Christian era! Their blood crieth from the ground to God. To God alone? Nay, to God's people also. But what can America do? The seas roll between us. The Great Powers on the other side of the Atlantic are bound hand and foot by their treaties and alliances. France cannot move; Russia cannot move; Germany cannot move; and, alas, England cannot move; and these are Christian nations! They would, but dare not. From Armenia there comes this cry: "In America is our last hope." We have sent our messages of protest and sympathy; can we do more? The Christian nations of Europe tell us over and over again that they would deliver Armenia if it were possible. Can we not test their sincerity? O that by one supreme and glorious impulse we, as the youngest of the Christian nations, untrammeled by alliances, might ask the privilege of interference! O that we might be moved to say to these sister nations of Christendom, "Permit us to send our White Squadron through the Dardanelles. Permit us to champion the rights of these persecuted brethren. Keep your hands off from each other and off from us. Let us have but a fair field and no favor; and with all the power of this Christian republic we will administer the *coup de grace* to the sick man and give him decent burial." I know there are constitutional difficulties in the way, but we have overcome constitutional difficulties when smaller issues were at stake. Would not this be something for our children to tell of? Did not all the Christian nations of Europe rise at the cry

"*Deus Vult*" to deliver a few score prisoners from Moslem jails, and can we not give power to that same cry, "God wills"? And would not this be a crusade worthy of the name? Ah, if it were possible—and nothing is impossible to the magnanimous soul of a Christian nation—we would make for America a golden chapter in the history of the ages.

But the supreme purpose of America in relation to God's great work is *the propagation of the Gospel.* Gladstone says, "You have in America a natural basis for the greatest continuous empire that ever was instituted by men." But that is not the point. Continuous empire is little or nothing in itself. A man does not care for the life of Methuselah so much as to make his life, long or short, tell splendidly for truth and goodness. What we want, is to give to our national life a splendid significance in the great purpose of God.

At the beginning of the Christian era the centre of ecclesiastical life was Jerusalem, but following the enlarged purpose of evangelization it soon shifted to Antioch, the Gentile capital. As time passed, it became evident that Asia was too straitened for the great purpose, and the centre shifted to Rome. But the atmosphere of ecclesiastical narrowness closed in about the Imperial City, and the centre shifted toward the west; England became the coigne of vantage for the Christian Church, and from that time the great enterprises of the Kingdom of Christ have found their propulsion in the Anglo-Saxon race. "To-day," as Dr. Strong says, " all the German missionary societies together do not equal in number of workers and amount of contributions, the smallest of the three great English societies." The gifts of the German

Established Church are about three-fourths of a cent per capita; while in several of our Anglo-Saxon denominations the average is about one dollar per capita. This shows that the Anglo-Saxon race has been and is doing the work of world-wide evangelization. But the centre of Anglo-Saxon power is shifting still. In 1700 there were less than six millions of Anglo-Saxons on earth; in 1800 there were about twenty millions; and now, toward the close of the nineteenth century, there are about one hundred millions; more than one half of these, sixty millions, are in America. Adam Smith in his "Wealth of Nations" prophesied the transfer of empire from Europe to America. Edwin Arnold said, "America holds the future." This is not to boast of pre-eminence, but rather to emphasize responsibility. Westward the star of empire has taken its way.

So at length we have measured the discovery of America along the line of God's great work; his purpose to deliver this world from its bondage of sin.

Two words in conclusion. First, the duty of Home Missions presses itself upon us. Only as we strengthen the boundaries and enlarge the resources of our American Christianity, do we discharge our obligations to the world.

And second, Foreign Missions. God pity the man in this splendid age of Christian progress who says, "I do not believe in Foreign Missions." So Peter reasoned in himself on the house-top at Joppa; and God let down the sheet from heaven with all manner of living creatures; once, twice, thrice, saying, "What God has cleansed, that call not thou uncommon or unclean." Then came the knock at his door and, lo, the centurion was there, calling Peter to let go his Jewish prejudice and set forth to the conquest of the Gentile world. So comes the knocking at our doors to-day. Who knocks? Asia, calling for the gospel of Christ. Africa. Aye, Ethiopia stretcheth out her hands unto God. And the islands of the sea, crying, Come over and help us!

In one of the bold visions of the Apocalypse there appeared a woman, clothed with the sun, having the moon under her feet, and upon her head a crown of twelve stars. She, with her child—the Church uplifting the Christ-child—is pursued by a red dragon having seven heads and ten horns and drawing after him one-third of the stars of heaven to hurl them down. And the woman flees "into a wilderness where she has a place prepared of God." The Church of Jesus Christ has found a place for herself in the New World from which, if faithful to her trust, she may exalt before the nations the glory of the Christ.

I see from time to time Bartholdi's statue of Liberty in our harbor, and always with an increasing interest. It is indeed a magnificent conception of human genius; Liberty upholding her torch, enlightening the world. But let us close our eyes and look again. Here is a still more magnificent conception. A woman fairer than Freedom, the comely figure of the Bride of God. With one hand she lifts the veil of slumber from her eyes, and with the other upholds the Cross, from which radiates a brighter and more glorious light than ever shone on land or sea. Liberty enlightening the world? Nay, the Church of the Lord Christ enlightening the world, and giving to all men the only true liberty, the liberty of the sons of God, whom the truth makes free indeed. This, I believe, is God's great purpose concerning our republic. This is the mission of America to the world.

SEARCH THE SCRIPTURES.

"Search the Scriptures; for in them ye think ye have eternal life: and they are they which testify of me. And ye will not come to me, that ye might have life."—JOHN v. 39, 40.

The word is *Ereunate*. And the question is, whether it shall be rendered "Search" or "Ye do search." Either is true to the original, because the indicative and imperative are in form identical. For the present rendering stand Augustine, Chrysostom, Calvin, Martin Luther, the Greek Fathers generally, and the King James' Version. On the other side are Beza, Bengel, Erasmus and the Revised Version. But why shall we have a battle royal about a word? Indicative or imperative, the meaning is the same in the end. Our Lord was speaking to the Jewish savants, who caviled at his divinity. He called the Scriptures to witness that he was the very Son of God. "Search them," he said, "and see." Search them indeed! That was distinctively the business of these men. They were Bibliolaters. They scrutinized with the utmost care the letter of holy writ; they counted its syllables; they weighed the relative merit of its precepts; they analyzed and classified it; they treated it as a fetich, declining to touch it with unwashed hands. "Search it indeed! We are the Biblical inquisitors." "Aye," said the Master, "ye do search it, but in your devotion to its letter ye lose the spirit of it. Ye do search the Scriptures, for in them ye think ye have eternal life. And, behold, these are they which testify of me. Yet, strange to tell, ye will not come unto me for the eternal life ye seek. Thus ye miss the deep meaning and the glory of this revealed word of God."

There is the Book—the Book of our fathers. How reverently they touched it; how profoundly they loved it; how sincerely they sought to obey it! It is the Book of all ages. Its place is unique in history; wherever it has gone, humanity has gone; wherever it has gone, freedom, enlightenment, civilization have gone. It is the fireproof Book. Its enemies have piled up the parchments and consumed them in great bonfires all in vain. There are to-day more Bibles than ever. It is published in three hundred languages and dialects. Its leaves flutter from the press like leaves from the tree of life for the healing of the nations. It is the Book of the centuries, and the Book of the times we are living in. Nothing can take its place The Bishop of Winchester was offended by the new portrait of Henry VIII, because he was represented with a book in his right hand which bore the words *Verbum Dei*. "Paint it out," said the Bishop; and in that portrait, as you may see it in the royal gallery to-day, the king holds in his right hand a pair of gloves. So would they substitute for *Verbum Dei* all sorts of vain philosophies, but nothing can take its place in the conscience and convictions of the people. No mode of self-culture, no moral cosmetics, no inner consciousness of truth, can be substituted for it.

There is the Book. What shall be done with it? "Search it," the Master says. But first a preliminary inquiry: Before we search the Scriptures, we must know whether they are worth searching or not. They claim to be inspired with an inspiration which gives them a unique place in the literature of the world. The word is *theo-pneustos*, God-breathed. All Scripture is given by inspiration—is divinely breathed. "Holy men of God spake as they were moved by the Holy Ghost." Is this true? That must be determined before we can go further. Here is a book that makes a tremendous claim: it predicates its truth on its divine authorship. Let us determine at the outset the validity of this claim. Turn on the lights, pour on the acids. Call in your Higher Criticism. Let the severest tests of hostile as well as friendly scholarship be applied. Inquire if its doctrines are true, if its ethics are right. Test its science, test its philosophy, test its accuracy at every point. We should not take for our infallible rule of faith and practice a book that tells us fables with a "Thus saith the Lord."

Not long ago I was informed that one of Rubens' pictures was for sale in a gallery nearby. On my way to the gallery I met a man expert in art matters, who said: "A Rubens, forsooth! It is counterfeit; there is not a line of Rubens in it." And I turned back. What did I care for a Rubens that Rubens never saw? Everything depends upon the authenticity of the signature. Anybody can write a check and sign it "Rothschild"; but the trouble is, no banker would cash it. Is the Bible what it purports to be? Is it a genuine autograph, bearing the true sign-manual of the living God? Let us have the pros and cons, and let us weigh them all. We can only come to one of two conclusions: it is divinely given, or it is not. If it came from God, it can be absolutely depended on; if not, my interest in the book ends here and now. It is no more to me henceforth than any other of the important works of literature. If, however, it is God-breathed, and therefore true and trustworthy, I am ready to take it as my "infallible rule of faith and practice." I will henceforth take its statement as the last word respecting creed and conduct. And what then?

I. *Search it.* Thank God that we can! An open Bible is the greatest privilege of these days. It is accessible to all. It is no longer under the ban; it is no longer in the *Index Expurgatorius.* It is no longer chained to the altar, as I have seen it in the Cologne Cathedral, closed with golden clasps and locked. All praise to the noble men of Reformation times, who gave their lives to secure this great privilege for us. Dark days were those in which the sacred parchments were in charge of monks who spent their days in illuminating missals and breviaries, while the people under the shadow of the monasteries were dying in hunger of the Word. "There is no hope," said Tyndale, "for the unshod except as they shall have access to God's Holy Word." And again he said, "If God spare my life, I will, ere many years, cause that a boy who driveth the plough shall know more of the Scriptures than many a learned ecclesiastic knoweth in these days." The prophecy has come to pass. The Bible is an open book for lofty and lowly, for the learned and unlearned, for all sorts and conditions of men.

II. *But why should we search it?* Because it holds the mystery of life. Search the Scriptures, for in them ye think, and rightly think, ye have eternal life.

The deep longing of every earnest soul is for eternal life. The young ruler who threw himself before the Master's feet intensely desired this: "Good Master, what shall I do that I may inherit eternal life?" The man who, in the allegory, fled from the City of Destruction, thrust his fingers into his ears, lest he should be turned aside by the appeals of friends and kinsfolk, and ran, crying, "Life! Life! Eternal Life!" We were made in the likeness of God. There is something beyond and beneath the surface of things. Our spiritual nature craves something better than the world can give. The Bible holds the clew of the maze, and the earnestness of our search of the Scriptures will be measured by the sincerity of our longing for life.

In one of Æsop's fables he tells of a hound which was pursuing a hare, falling behind, and at length abandoning the chase. A goatherd who was passing by, jeered at the hound, saying, "Shame that a hare should get the better of thee." "But you forget," the hound replied, "that it is one thing to be running for your dinner, and another to be running for your life." The life that our spiritual nature longs for, begins here and now. The Greeks accounted for the strength of Hercules by the fact that the centaur, Chiron, fed him in his infancy on the marrow of lions. There is no diet like truth. "Sanctify them by the truth," the Master prays for his disciples, adding, "Thy Word is truth." Truth knits the muscles, calms the nerves, warms the blood. Truth cultivates energy, influence, character. Truth makes men.

And the life that we long for, reaches on forever. It is eternal life, and this eternal life is found only in

Christ. He said, "I am the life." The supreme power of the Scriptures lies in the fact that they set forth Christ as the life-giver. His face shines forth in all the pages of the Book.

Turn to the Old Testament for prophecy: "A virgin shall conceive and bear a son, and call his name Immanuel; which is, being interpreted, God with us." Turn to the New Testament for the fulfillment of that prophecy: "And they found the babe wrapped in swaddling clothes, lying in the manger"; "great is the mystery of godliness, God manifested in the flesh."

Turn again to the Old Testament for prophecy: He is "a man of sorrows, and acquainted with grief; he was wounded for our transgressions, and by his stripes we are healed." Turn to the New Testament for the fulfillment: "And they led him out to Calvary, and there they crucified him"; "he bare our sins in his own body on the tree"; "his blood cleanseth from all sin."

Turn once more to the Old Testament for prophecy: "He will not leave my soul in hell, neither will he suffer his holy one to see corruption." And turn again to the New Testament for fulfillment: "Now is Christ risen from the dead, and become the first fruits of them that slept." So is come to pass the saying that is written: "Death is swallowed up in victory. O death, where is thy sting? O grave, where is thy victory? The sting of death is sin; and the strength of sin is the law. But thanks be to God which giveth us the victory through our Lord Jesus Christ."

Thus we have, in prophecy and fulfillment, in the Old Testament and the New, Christ assuming our flesh, dwelling among us, suffering for us, enduring our shame and bondage on the cross, risen from the dead, and ever living to make intercession for us.

Here is the quickening truth which we seek in Holy Writ; but, alas, that too often, in pursuing our quest, we should fall short of the vital truth! Ye do search the Scriptures, for in them ye rightly think ye have eternal life, and they are they which testify of me. Yet, alas, ye will not come unto me that ye might have eternal life!

III. *How shall we search?* The word itself is significant; it is used of those who search for gold or for hid treasure. The truth, indeed, cannot be valued with the gold of Ophir. Search the Scriptures as realizing that truth is above all.

(1) *Search frankly.* Put prejudice aside. Do not allow your self-formed opinions to give color to these inspired words. Do not come hither to confirm your previous views. It is said that Sir Isaac Newton was an absent-minded man, and that he tried repeatedly to light a candle when there was an extinguisher upon it. We are convicted of like folly when we bring our prejudices with us into the investigation of truth. If you are a premillenarian or a postmillenarian do not seek to enlist the Scriptures in behalf of your partisanship, but ask at the threshold of the oracles that the truth may be revealed to you. Or if you are pursuing a questionable habit, do not come to confirm yourself in your indulgence by reading an apology into the Scriptures, but to find out with all candor what God has to say about it.

(2) *Search carefully.* Read the Scriptures with pious regularity. Search them in the morning for the strength needed to face the tasks and obligations of

the busy day. Read them at night for the comfort you need on entering the unknown country of sleep and for the joy that shall come in the night watches as you reflect upon the sweetness of God's word. We are told by physicians that our health is largely determined by the regularity of our habits; and this is true of our spiritual as well as of our bodily health.

And bring all your industry to bear upon this sacred quest. Prospectors do not race over the fields and through the cañons; they stop and scrutinize and analyze; they are searching for gold. You are searching for life, and you cannot search too earnestly. There is an island off the Long Island coast where tradition says Captain Kidd buried his treasure. Its soil has been turned over and over, with unsparing toil. Let us bring a like industry to our study of the Scriptures.

It is important also that we should use proper tools. I have little sympathy with the man who, in his over-zealous reverence, says, "I want nothing but the Bible." He is like the Egyptian farmer who uses only a crooked stick in turning the soil. He is a foolish student of the Scriptures, who will not take advantage of all wise labor-saving devices. Three books are necessary : First, a good copy of the Bible itself; clear type, good paper, broad margin. Second, a copy of Cruden's Concordance; a wonderfully helpful and, I had almost said, indispensable book. And third, a good commentary. At the risk of seeming quite behind the times, let me commend old Matthew Henry; but any other commentary will answer, so long as you are quite sure that the editor was not an irreverent and destructive critic, but a sincere lover of the word of God.

(3) *Search systematically.* Let the Scriptures be read consecutively. Not all portions are for public reading, not all are even appropriate for the uses of the family altar; but all Scripture is profitable for personal use, for doctrine, for reproof, for correction, for instruction in righteousness. George Mueller of Bristol Orphanage read the Bible through one hundred times in forty-seven years. Many others pursue a similar plan. It is not wise to confine our attention too much to favorite chapters, but to secure a large grasp of the teaching of the entire word.

But in connection with this consecutive reading of the Scriptures, we should study them topically above all. Take for example the subject of " Prayer," and turn to Cruden's Concordance. Here are four hundred and thirty-one references; look them up in your Bible, compare and classify, and you will have formed a comprehensive statement of the truth respecting prayer. So of other themes such as faith, charity, redemption and the like. This is profitable work. It is like mining; it is digging out gold.

(4) *Search prayerfully.* We shall make little progress in our quest unless God shall illuminate the pages of the book and then open our eyes to behold it. It is one function of the Holy Spirit to guide us into the truth. The boy Aladdin would have found little treasure had he entered the cave without his magic lamp; but with that in his hand, lo, the darkness was all asparkle with gold and silver and precious gems. Prayer is our Aladdin's lamp. Rise from your knees to open the book and then behold how the entrance of God's word giveth light.

(5) *Search experimentally;* that is, with the purpose of applying the truth and testing its quality in the conduct of your daily life. The only science worth acquiring is applied science. We have been told during the recent political campaign that there was great lack of currency in this country. But no sooner had the campaign closed than currency in vast quantities came out of hiding, and lo! there is abundance of it. There was gold hid away in strong boxes, in hollow trees, and under the hearthstone. What we have needed was not more currency, but to have our currency put into circulation, passing from hand to hand. So it is with truth. The Bible is full of truth, but, after all, your search will be unprofitable unless the truth you acquire shall be used in your walk and conversation; used for your personal upbuilding and character, and for the betterment of the world about you. The man who thus delights in the law of the Lord, meditates in it day and night, and uses it constantly, is said by the Psalmist to be "like a tree planted by the rivers of water, that bringeth forth his fruit in his season; his leaf also shall not wither; and whatsoever he doeth shall prosper."

There is the Book—Book of the ages past and of the ages to come. The future of all nations depends upon our proper use of it. The Church is pursuing a campaign of education. We cannot regenerate those who lie in darkness and the shadow of death, but we can carry to them the regenerating word through which the spirit of the living God shall convert them. Go, evangelize. Go, preach the word and live it. Our work will not be finished, nor shall we realize God's purpose in the great propaganda, until we shall have carried the glad tidings of these

Scriptures to the remotest parts of the earth. God himself will do the rest. Here is the promise: "As the rain cometh down and the snow from heaven, and returneth not thither, but watereth the earth, and maketh it to bring forth and bud, that it may give seed to the sower and bread to the eater: so shall my word be that goeth forth out of my mouth; it shall not return unto me void, but it shall accomplish that which I please, and it shall prosper in the thing whereto I sent it."

JOHN THE BAPTIST.

"I am the voice of one crying in the wilderness."—JOHN 1, 23.

The Augustan era marked the flood tide of pagan civilization. Art, science, literature, philosophy, were at their very best. The splendid culture of Greece had lent itself to the decoration of the Imperial City. The schools of Athens had inclined the sturdy Romans to divide their energies between the march of empire and the quest of knowledge. But what mattered it? The Golden Age of culture was overshadowed by the despair of the soul. True, Augustus, "finding a city of brick, transformed it into marble"; but the palaces which he reared were resonant with the orgies of nameless vice and the groans of anguish attendant upon it. Side by side dwelt misery and luxury. Here were ten thousand knights and senators in purple and fine linen, faring sumptuously every day, and here were a million slaves in ergustula, of less worth and esteem than sheep and cattle. There was pride, but no purity. There was culture, but no charity. There were palaces, but no hospitals. It was a world without love. It was the beauty of the upas-tree, that flourishes in death. Marriage was neglected and laughed at. Honest toil was disreputable; Rome was the paradise of paupers. "Bread and games!" was the universal cry. Here was dissoluteness unspeakable. Suicide was the fashion. As for religion, the gods of all nations were in the Pantheon. There was no lack of toleration; all religions were equally true, and all equally false. The priests laughed in each others' faces. The people cried, "Who will show us any good?" The times were out of joint.

The saving factor of this Golden Age was the Jews. They resisted the downward tendency. Though subjugated by Rome, they held to the worship of the one true God. There were three sects: Sadducees, Pharisees, Essenes. The Pharisees were the conservatives, but their very orthodoxy was their ruin. They made a fetich of the outward form; new moons, holy days, fat of rams and fed beasts, fringes and phylacteries, long prayers, and works of supererogation. They worshipped God with their lips, but their heart was far from him. The Sadducees were the liberals of that day. They denied immortality, flouted the supernatural, and patronized, if they did not question, the doctrine of God. The Essenes, affronted by formalism on the one hand and infidelity on the other, betook themselves to the solitudes for communion with God.

It was four hundred years since the torch of Malachi, the last of the prophets, had gone out. Four hundred years of darkness; a deep, Egyptian night, in which no sound was heard but the cry of those who hopelessly searched for truth, and the cursing of those who jostled each other in their reckless way to death. All open vision had ceased; the lights of the golden candlestick in the sanctuary had been extinguished. Far away seemed the voice of Malachi, as he closed the oracles: "*Behold, the day cometh that shall burn as an oven; and all the proud, yea, and all that do wickedly, shall be stubble: and the day that cometh shall burn them up. . . . But unto you that fear my name shall the Sun of righteousness arise, with healing in his wings; and ye shall go forth, and grow up as calves of the stall. . . . Behold, I will send you Elijah the prophet before the coming of the great and dreadful day of the Lord; and he shall turn the heart of the fathers to the children, and the heart of the children to their fathers, lest I come and smite the earth with a curse.*"

And, lo, here is the antitype of Elijah. The parallel is singularly close. The appearing of Elijah, the Tishbite, was as sudden as a meteor. He stood at Ahab's threshold — tall, sinewy, dark-browed, wrapped in a shaggy mantle, unbidden and unheralded—saying, "As Jehovah God of Israel liveth, there shall be no rain except at my word." And before the king could call his guards to seize him, he was gone. Then the three years of famine, during which the Tishbite flitted like a spectre between the king's ivory house and the defiles of the mountains, until at length they met on the heights of Carmel for the Lord's controversy. There is no more terrific scene in history. The king and his courtiers, prophet of Jehovah, and pagan priests, and the long-suffering people were there. "O Baal, hear us! O Baal, hear us!" Then the low prayer, "O Jehovah, let it be known this day that thou art God in Israel!" The panorama moves swiftly on; the fire descending, the bullock blazing, the clouds gathering above, the people shouting, "Jehovah! he is the God! Jehovah! he is the God!"

Enter Elijah's antitype. "Then cometh John

the Baptist out of the wilderness of Judæa"; a thin, cadaverous man; grown lean on a sparse diet of locusts and wild honey; clad in camel's hair, and girt about his loins with a leathern girdle; erect and unbending as his sense of duty. He stands at Bethabara by the Jordan, and all Jerusalem and Judæa are come to hear his message. He is the wonder of the time. The last word is, "Have ye seen the prophet in the wilderness?" Priests, rulers, soldiers, people, gather about him. Many who come to scoff, remain to pray. Let us stand among them. What is the message that he brings us?

I. *The Kingdom.* "The kingdom of heaven is at hand." He announces a new cycle, a new order of things. A belated son of the Old Economy, he does not himself belong to this kingdom of gospel privilege, but holds open the door that multitudes may enter. The Master said, "What went ye out into the wilderness to see? a reed shaken with the wind? But what went ye out for to see? a man clothed in soft raiment? Behold, such are in kings' houses. But what went ye out for to see? a prophet? yea, I say unto you, and more than a prophet. Verily, I say unto you, Among them that are born of women, there hath not risen a greater than John the Baptist: notwithstanding, he that is least in the kingdom of heaven is greater than he."

But what is this "kingdom"? It is variously called "the kingdom of God," "the kingdom of heaven," "the kingdom of Christ." It is important that we should understand the kingdom, for here is the key of the Scriptures, the clew of the mystery. The Gospel of Christ is the Gospel of the Kingdom.

It means the reign of Jehovah, beginning in the individual soul and extending itself into the home-life, the neighborhood and the nation, completing the universal symphony of worship of the living God.

(1) *It has its beginning in the individual soul;* as Jesus said, " The kingdom of heaven is within you." And again, " Verily, verily I say unto you, except a man be born again he cannot see the kingdom of God. And except a man be born of water and the spirit," that is, of purifying and quickening energy, " he cannot enter the kingdom of God."

(2) *It finds its outward manifestation in the visible Church.* The Church indeed is not what it ought to be, for the wheat and tares must grow together until the harvesting and winnowing of the great day. Let this be remembered, however, that the Church, as it exists, is a divine institution, and through this living organism God is working for the deliverance of the world. This is a fact to be remembered by those who hold themselves aloof. Dr. Johnson said of his friend, Dr. John Campbell, a distinguished political writer of that time, " He is a good man ; to be sure he is not in the habit of attending church, but to my knowledge he never passes a sacred edifice without removing his hat." There are multitudes of serious people who assume the same attitude toward the Church. Let them consider that, whatever its faults, it represents the accumulated sum and substance of evangelizing effort on earth ; and if so, all who are in sympathy with its supreme purpose, should be associated with it.

(3) *It finds its ultimate consummation in the millenial glory of Christ.* This is the fifth monarchy of Daniel.

He saw the great image; head of gold, breast of silver, thighs of brass, legs of iron and feet of clay, representing the successive powers of Babylonia, Medo-Persia, Greece and Rome. And then a stone hewn out of the mountain rolled toward it and smote the great image and ground it to powder, which was swept away as chaff is blown from the threshing-floor. And, lo, the stone hewn out of the mountain increased until it became itself a mountain which filled the whole earth. This is the ultimate kingdom. The largest prayer that any Christian can offer is, "Thy kingdom come." The supreme duty of every Christian is set forth in these words, "Seek ye first of all the kingdom." When this prayer shall rise from the earnest hearts of all believers, and this duty shall be universally discharged, the vision of St. John the evangelist will be fulfilled: "I saw the new Jerusalem, coming down from God, out of heaven, prepared as a bride adorned for her husband. And I heard a great voice saying, Behold the tabernacle of God is with men, and he will dwell with them and they shall be his people, and God himself shall be their God."

II. *Repentance.* "Repent ye, for the kingdom of heaven is at hand." What is repentance? The word is *metanoia*, meaning a change of heart, conscience and will. Right about face! The face of rulers and people in the Baptist's time was set toward sin and death. In repentance they were to turn about and look toward truth and righteousness. This is the preparation for the coming of the King. It rests on three important facts:

(1) *Sin.* The preaching of John the Baptist was a plain setting forth of sin. This sort of preaching

is measurably gone out of fashion ; but it is indeed as necessary as ever, and as necessary in the Church as outside it. We who profess the Christian life, are wont to think that sermons on sin are for sinners, and by sinners we mean the impenitent. In point of fact, however, we are all sinners ; some of us sinners in grace, others sinners against grace, but there is no difference, for all have sinned and come short of the glory of God. We need to know better and better the true character of sin, that we may hate and abhor and avoid it. Let the Master come, and with his scourge of small cords purge the temple. Judgment must begin at the house of God.

(2) *Judgment.* " The axe is laid at the root of the tree." It is the gleaming of the cold blade that flashed at the gate of Paradise when the first sinner passed out ; the sword in the hand of the destroying angel that passed over Egypt at midnight. " His fan is in his hand and he shall thoroughly purge his threshing-floor, and the chaff shall he burn with unquenchable fire." It is the same fire that cast its lurid glow on Belshazzar's wall when the spectral hand wrote, " *Mene, Mene, Tekel, Upharsin!* "—the same fire that gleamed on all the hillsides round about Jerusalem, when Titus reduced the Holy City. " Be not deceived ; God is not mocked ; whatsoever a man soweth, that shall he also reap." This was the truth that Peter preached at Pentecost when his congregation was pricked to the heart. This is the truth that Jonathan Edwards preached from the text, " Their feet shall slide in due time," when the people rose and grasped the pillars of the church in terror and cried to God for mercy. This is the truth that Luther

preached in the mighty days of the Reformation and embodied in his hymn :

> Great God, what do I see and hear?
>   The end of things created,
> The Judge of all mankind appear
>   In crowds of glory seated.
> The trumpet sounds, the graves restore
> The dead whom they contained before ;
>   Prepare, my soul, to meet Him.

(3) *Reformation.* "Bring ye forth fruits meet for repentance." To the tax-gatherers the Baptist said, "If ye would prove the sincerity of your repentance, cease from your extortions"; to the soldiers, "desist from your violence"; to the priests and Pharisees, "O generation of vipers, who hath warned you to flee from the wrath to come? bring ye forth fruits meet for repentance."

This was the meaning of John's baptism. It symbolized the putting off of evil deeds in preparation for the kingdom. "I indeed baptize you with water, but there standeth one among you, whose shoe's latchet I am not worthy to unloose ; he shall baptize you with the Holy Ghost and with fire."

III. *Behold the Lamb of God.* This is the conclusion of all Christian discourse. Terrible preaching was that of John the Baptist, except as his hearers followed him to the last word. Did you hear him say, "Repent ye"? Did you hear him say, "The axe is laid at the root of the tree"? Did you hear him say, "The King, when he cometh, shall have a fan in his hand and shall thoroughly purge the floor, and he shall burn up the chaff with unquenchable fire"? Dreadful truths indeed. But did you hear him say, "Behold the Lamb of God"? What is the Law indeed but a schoolmaster to lead us all to Christ? Behold him, therefore! Behold the Lamb of God!

(1) *Behold him as an objective fact.* See him yonder on Calvary, nailed to the accursed tree. The beginning of wisdom is attention. "Look," cried Moses, "on the brazen serpent. Look and live!" Let us gaze upon the cross, therefore, until the great historic fact shall impress itself upon us, until the eye affecteth the heart, and the heart affecteth the life.

(2) *Behold him as a subjective fact;* that is, receive him into your heart and conscience, so that you may say, "My Saviour and my Lord!" Cato, the younger, was asked in his boyhood, "Who is nearest to your heart?" He replied, "My brother." "Who is next?" Again, "My brother." "And who is next?" And still, "My brother." Thus let us receive Christ until every thought is brought under subjection to him. Let us so appropriate him, the merits of his death and the power of his example, that we may say, "Christ first, last, midst, and all in all!"

(3) *Behold him as a universal fact*, the great, living power of the spiritual realm. He is the great magnet, who, being uplifted, shall draw all men unto him. The world is to be saved by the preaching of Christ. I hate the words, "Holy Orders." The pews as well as the pulpit are ordained to the preaching of the glorious gospel. Preaching is telling the glad news. Let all who love our Lord and Saviour, Jesus Christ, preach him by seasonable words, by right living in walk and conversation, always and everywhere. A sermon, whether from the pulpit or the pew, which does not thus exalt Christ, is no sermon at all. Dr.

McCosh, in his early ministry, asked Sir William Hamilton whom he thought to be the greatest living preacher. The answer was, Dr. Guthrie. "Dr. Guthrie! His sermons are without argument; he does not know the power of a syllogism; there is but one step from his premise to his conclusion." "Aye," said Sir William, "but that one step brings us into the presence of God."

This was the preaching of John the Baptist: *The kingdom, repentance, the Lamb of God.* And so he vanishes from sight. Here the parallel ceases. A fiery chariot came down out of heaven for Elijah, the opening clouds received him, while down below the lamentable cry was heard, "O my father! my father! the chariots of Israel and the horsemen thereof!" But how went John the Baptist to his rest and his reward? Out of the lone prison, Machærus by the Dead Sea, he followed his executioner to the block, and his head was carried thence to the palace to satisfy a woman's whim. A gory head on a charger! The flaming light of his great eyes is quenched. The lips that preached of sin, and judgment, and the Lamb, are cold and still. But what matters it? He was but a voice, and the voice lingers still. Being dead, he yet speaketh. Long centuries have passed, and still we hear him: "Repent ye, for the kingdom of heaven is at hand. Bring forth fruits meet for repentance. There cometh one whose shoe's latchet I am not worthy to unloose. Behold the Lamb of God!"

THE OUTSIDE OF THE PLATTER.

"Now do ye make clean the outside of the cup and the platter."—Luke xi. 39.

The reference is to the superficial piety of the Pharisees. They had more regard for the outside of the cup than for the wholesomeness of the draught within it. They were much given to external rites and ceremonies. The most important of the six books of the Mishna is devoted to purifications. The washing of the hands is prescribed with utmost particularity: One and one-half eggshells full of water must be used; the hands must be lifted in a certain position when the water is poured upon them; then the right must rub the left, and the left the right; then they must be held at a downward incline so that the water may drip off. And the towel must be properly held. The schools of Hillel and Shammai were wont to discuss with great earnestness the holding of the towel. Furthermore, there were thirty chapters bearing on the cleansing of cups and platters. The ceremony is called Kelim. At the marriage supper of Cana there were six water pots containing not less than twenty gallons each, ready for this use. And this was but an inconsiderable part of the elaborate ceremonial of orthodox Jewish life. On the 15th of Adar, every year, it was appointed that the people should go out and whitewash the tombs of the departed. In many cases, doubtless, this was not so much out of respect to the dead as to make their grief conspicuous; for these sepulchres were arranged along the public roads.

How the Lord Christ hated all shams! The Pharisees stood before him in their frontlets and phylacteries, as if to say, "Behold how fair!" He tore away the turf and exposed the dismal fraud: "Woe unto you, ye hypocrites! Ye are as whited sepulchres, fair without, but within full of dead men's bones and all uncleanness."

But the Pharisees are dead. We have to do, not with the faults and follies of long centuries ago, but with the superficial piety of to-day. God sees us through and through. It is monstrous trifling to be tithing mint, anise and cummin, while neglecting the weightier matters of law. The form of godliness without the power thereof is but the garniture of death. Man looketh on the outward appearance, but God looketh on the heart.

The fault lies at the very beginning. Well begun is half done. Ill begun means staggering and stumbling all along the way. We speak of being "soundly converted"; in point of fact, however, there is only one sort of conversion, namely, that which turns the whole man right about in a thorough and unreserved consecration to the service of God.

We are hoping and praying for a revival. And, thank God, there are signs of moving in the tops of the mulberry trees. Come, Holy Spirit, and baptize our churches and this community with a baptism of fire and power! But there is danger. The best infection in the world is that of religious fervor; but there are always some who go with the multitude through sympathy and in a little while fall out along the way.

Our Lord, in the parable of the sower, spoke of stony ground where there was not much earth, and the seed which fell upon it forthwith sprang up, only to be scorched and withered when the sun rose upon it. His disciples asked him for an explanation. And he said, "These are they which hear the word and anon with joy receive it; yet have they no root in themselves, but dure for a while; for when tribulation and persecution ariseth, by and by they are offended." Have you never known such? I recently met a friend who, as far back as I remember, was wont to profess conversion in the winter with a reasonable certainty of falling from grace before the spring had fully come. Let it be understood that there is a vital difference between faith and feeling; the latter is to the former as a burst of the Marseillaise on a fete day is to the battle of Waterloo. Religion is founded on principle, and, feeling or no feeling, it proceeds with its tasks. If the stars go out, it finds its way, like a skilful mariner, by a "dead reckoning."

In times of general religious interest it is well to remember two things: First, *Act*. Do not be afraid to act on impulse. If it were done, when 'tis done, then 'twere well it were done quickly. The issues at stake are so momentous that there should be no delay. Second, *Act advisedly*—count the cost. Third, *Act immediately*—deliberation does not mean delay. The gunner in the thick of conflict must not fire at random, but must fire at once.

Our Lord on one occasion declined the service of three men who desired to follow him. One said, without having fully thought the matter over, "Lord,

I will follow thee." He answered, "The foxes have holes and the birds of air have nests; but the Son of Man hath not where to lay his head." The second said, "Lord, I will follow thee; but suffer me first to bury my father." He answered, "Let the dead bury their own dead; but go thou and declare the kingdom of God." The third said, "Lord, I will follow thee, but let me first bid farewell to the loved ones at home." He answered, "He that putteth his hand to the plough, and looketh back, is not worthy the kingdom of God."

It is for want of a wise consideration of the true significance of the Christian life that so many, beginning wrong, fail to hold out. In fact, their religion is merely superficial. It is not always insincere, but it is always inadequate to meet the demands of their souls or to please God.

I. *The Religion of Form;* tithes and fastings, fringes and phylacteries.

I know of a church not a thousand miles away, where young ladies of a sentimental age, particularly, are wont to resort for the worship of God. It is a Protestant church with Romanist leanings. It has not the courage to go nor the honesty to stay. The preaching is a ten minute affair, and below mediocrity. But the rites and ceremonies; the boy choir, the imposing processionals and recessionals, the bowings and genuflections, the swinging of censers, the lifting of the mass, the holy millinery, the dim religious light! It is enough to make an angel—weep, or laugh? The effect of such a performance is wholly sensuous.

It was the opinion of Professor Tyndall that devotion is purely a mechanical effect. He says, "I have watched with deep interest and sympathy the countenances of some worshippers. I have seen a penitent kneeling at a distance from the shrine of the Virgin, as if afraid to come nearer. Suddenly, a glow has overspread her countenance, strengthening its radiance, until her very soul seemed shining through her features; sure of her acceptance, she has confidently advanced, fallen prostrate, immediately in front of the image, and remained there for a time in silent ecstacy. I have watched the ebbing of the spiritual tide, and remarked the felicitous repose which it left behind." He makes use of this to illustrate his theory of heat as a mode of motion! If this were the only form of religion, we should be slow to blame such scientists for refusing to accept it.

II. *The Religion of Rhapsody.* An impression seems to prevail in some quarters that piety consists alone in affection for Christ. This is indeed necessary, but not the whole of it. A man may cry, "Christ! Christ!" with no more piety than other people. The craze for Paderewski does not prove that all his enthusiastic admirers are musical experts. No man has paid more glowing tributes to Jesus of Nazareth than Ernest Renan. It was he who said, "Whatever may be the surprises of the future, Jesus will never be surpassed." It was he who said, "All ages will proclaim that among the sons of men there is none born greater than Jesus." Yet Renan did not profess to be a Christian; indeed he was an open and avowed antagonist of the truths and precepts which Jesus taught.

A play is being enacted at one of our theatres just now, which some Christian people are patronizing because it bears a religious title. It is highly commended by a distinguished ecclesiastic who calls it "a commentary upon the power of the cross and the sustentation of redeeming love." If journalistic descriptions of it be correct, one of its scenes is so realistic in gross suggestion that it is inconceivable how a pure man or woman can sit through it. Behold the hypocrisy of vice. Judas Iscariot who sold his Lord for thirty pieces of silver is outdone. A seduction scene on Calvary! Can blasphemy farther go? If we must choose between the stench of vaudeville and the brimstone flavor of simony affecting the rôle of Christian devotion, let us by all means have the genuine thing. The world hates a lie. The woman whose feet take hold on hell is bad enough as she stands in her doorway flaunting her shame, and beckoning to the passer-by; but worse, a thousandfold worse, is the painted thing that wears a lily on her breast, holds a crucifix in her hand and throws her vile garments over the effigy of Christ upon his Cross. Yet there are people who, because the name of the Redeemer is associated with this play, will think themselves pious in patronizing it.

III. *The Religion of Philosophy.* This a mere affectation. We preachers are greatly given to it. We treat religion as if it were a system of profound truths, when in point of fact—whatever may be said about theology—religion is simplicity itself. Here is an extract from a sermon quoted by Paxton Hood: "The incomprehensibility of the apparatus developed in the machinery of the universe, may be considered a supereminent manifestation of stupendous majesties, whether a man stands upon the platform of his own mind and ponders scrutinizingly on its undecipherable characters, or whether he looks abroad over the magnificent equipments and regalities of nature, surveying its amplitudes in all their scope, and its unfathomabilities in all their profundities." What in the world is this man trying to say? This: "When I consider the heavens the work of thy fingers, the moon and the stars which thou hast ordained; what is man that thou art mindful of him and the son of man that thou regardest him?" Then why did he not say it? Is not this indeed monstrous trifling? The people are not deceived by this affectation of superior wisdom on sesquipedalian phrases.

In the House of Representatives, a member sat as if lost in meditation, with his index finger upon his brow. "What is he doing?" asked one; "is he thinking?" "Well," was the reply, "he is thinking that he is thinking." There is little or no room for this sort of thing in connection with a religion in which all its saving power is transparent as the light. "I thank thee, Father," said Jesus, "that thou hast hidden these things from the wise and prudent and hast revealed them unto babes." And again, "Except ye become as little children, ye shall in no wise see the kingdom of God."

IV. *The Religion of Self-culture.* I believe in the Higher Life; but I do not believe that the business of a Christian is to seek it in an introspective way. I believe in spirituality. But what is spirituality save the influence of God's Spirit upon the whole nature of man?

The objection to much that is said about self-culture in these times is two-fold: First, *It is not always modest.* In this it takes issue with the Spirit himself. The modesty of the Holy Ghost is one of his splendid attributes; "He shall not speak of himself." If you feel, my friend, that you are growing in holiness, then by all means thank God and keep quiet about it.

And second, *It is purely selfish,* as its name self-culture suggests. There is a malady, largely confined to higher social circles, known as nervous debility. One way of successfully treating it is by massage. The whole body is stimulated by rubbing. As a rule, however, the same result would probably be gained by sawing wood or attending to household tasks. Much of our Christian debility—and God knows we are not what we ought to be—is due to overmuch introspection and concern about ourselves. The best prescription for us is that of Dr. Abernethy, "Do something for somebody." If we busy ourselves in looking after others, it is immensely probable that God will look after us. The captain of an Atlantic liner must not be over-nervous about his own life-preserver; his main business is to get his passengers safe over the sea.

V. *The Religion of Altruism.* This is extremely popular just now. A convention of Altruists, after holding its sessions continuously for some days and discussing a variety of sociological problems, has just adjourned. We shall await with interest the practical altruism of these people in the interim. The fact is that almost all the humanitarian enterprises on earth are carried on by the Church of Jesus Christ. Secular reformers meet and adjourn; but the church has been in session ever since the day of pentecost.

It should be remembered that pity, kindness, benevolence, is not the highest element of humanity. We share it with the lower orders of life. In Doré's picture of the Deluge a mother is represented clinging to the rock with one hand and with the other reaching out into the surging flood to save her drowning child. Magnificent! But look, yonder on the summit of the rock is a tigress who has climbed thither for safety, and on her back is her cub.

Let it be remembered, also, that much of boastful altruism is mere sentiment. A mother desiring to adopt a child, is very particular at the foundling's home to ask for a blue-eyed baby. The most successful beggars along the street are "interesting ones"; blind paupers with sweet faces, charming unfortunates. But who shall care for the repulsive; those whose faces are eaten away with cancer, the lepers and the pariahs? Sentimentalists will pass them by; only those who are moved by principle will assist them. True benevolence is more than an emotion; it rests upon the fact that all these who suffer are our kinsfolk, because there is one God and Father of us all; and because he who, being our elder brother, would bring us back to the All-Father, has suffered and died for all. Thus he said, "Whosoever shall give a cup of cold water to one of these for my sake, shall not fail of his reward." And again, "Inasmuch as ye have done it unto one of the least of these my brethren, ye have done it unto me."

Let us hear then the conclusion of the whole matter. The only religion which can fully meet the divine requirement is that which takes hold of our entire nature. It is not enough that it shall touch us at a single point. It must reach the heart as well as the reason, and the conscience as well as the heart. It must take possession of mind, conscience, heart, and will; eyes and ears; hands and feet. It must so penetrate us through and through, so permeate us, that our whole life and character and being shall be full of light.

Furthermore, the religion which meets the divine requirement, must not only give God possession of the entire mind, but must place the mind in possession of the entire Christ. It is not enough that I shall "come to Jesus"; I must come to the Lord Jesus Christ. He is Jesus, my brother. Aye, and more. He is Messiah the Christ. Aye, and more still. He is Christ Jesus my Lord; my Lord, to protect, command, rule over me.

To accept him is to receive him into my life as Prophet, Priest and King. As Priest, he atones for me; as Prophet, he instructs me, sitting at his feet, in such wise that his word becomes my creed; as King, his command is ultimate law to me, and every thought is brought into subjection to him.

Two words in conclusion: "Pure religion and undefiled before God and the Father is this: To visit the fatherless and widows in their affliction, and to keep one's self unspotted from the world." And again, "If any man will come after me, let him deny himself, take up his cross, and follow me."

"THE KENOSIS."

"Let this mind be in you, which was also in Christ Jesus: Who, being in the form of God, thought it not robbery [a prize, a thing to be jealously cherished] to be equal with God: But made himself of no reputation [literally, emptied himself], and took upon him the form of a servant, and was made in the likeness of men: And being found in fashion as a man, he humbled himself, and became obedient unto death, even the death of the cross. Wherefore God also hath highly exalted him and given him a name which is above every name: That at the name of Jesus every knee should bow, of things in heaven, and things in earth, and things under the earth; and that every tongue should confess that Jesus Christ is Lord, to the glory of God the Father."—PHIL. ii. 5-11.

All right-thinking men are anxious to succeed. But what is the secret of success? There is a wide difference of opinion. William E. Dodge said, "The secret is fair dealing"; General Howard, "Diligence and fearlessness"; John Wanamaker, "Doe ye nexte thynge"; Neal Dow, "*Res non verba*" (which being interpreted is, "Do noble things, not dream them all day long"); Bishop Vincent, "An entire surrender to the demands of duty"; Dr. John M. Ferris, "Do with all your might what God gives you to do"; John Ruskin, "To-day."

Let it be observed, however, that the men who thus express themselves have been successful only in a relative sense. The tomb of the man who has attained to the highest measure of success has over it a broken shaft, symbolical of an unfinished work, a life cut in sunder. Indeed, there never lived but one man who could truthfully say that he had finished the work which God gave him to do. The Lord Jesus Christ came into the world to accomplish a definite purpose, and he fully accomplished it. His last word was, "It is finished!" If we would attain to the highest success, therefore, we must catch his spirit; or, as Paul puts it, "Let this mind be in you that was also in Christ Jesus."

But this mind that was in Christ Jesus, what is it? The matter is made clear in these words, "He, being in the form of God, thought it not a matter of supreme importance to be equal with God; but emptied himself and took upon him the form of a servant, and was made in the likeness of men." This is the doctrine of the Kenosis, or emptying of Christ. Edersheim calls it "His self-exinanition." What is meant by it?

I. Here is a suggestion at the outset of what Pearson calls *the precedent plenitude of Christ.* There must have been a fulness before there could be an emptying. This leads us to consider the antecedent glory of Christ, which is fully set forth by the evangelist thus: "In the beginning was the Word, and the Word was with God, and the Word was God."

(1) *Christ was "in the beginning."* Here is a separating gulf between him and all the children of men. He was the pre-existent One Plato spoke of dreams and memories which were like rustling wings, suggesting a former life. The Buddhists have much to say about the re-incarnation of a soul in various forms. Theosophists also are wont to theorize about pre-existence. In point of fact, however, there is not one jot or tittle of evidence to sustain it. The first chap-

ter of every human life is terrestrial birth. "Our birth is our beginning." Not so with Christ. Our immortality is unto everlasting; his life is sempiternal—that is, from everlasting to everlasting. Our life is without end; the life of the Son of God is without beginning and without end. He is Alpha and Omega; the beginning and the end. He said, "Before Abraham was, I am"; not "I was," but "I am"—thus taking to himself the incommunicable name by which God expresses his self-existence—"I am that I am."

(2) *He was in the beginning "with God."* That is, he had a distinct personality. He was in the company or by the side of God. The same truth is expressed in many ways: The Father is the Sender, Christ is the Sent; the Father is the Giver, Christ is the Gift—the unspeakable Gift.

(3) *He "was God."* Or, as the Nicene creed puts it, "Very God of Very God." Our Lord over and over again made this distinct claim. When Philip said to him, "Show us the Father and it sufficeth us," Jesus replied, "Have I been so long a time with you, and yet hast thou not known me, Philip? he that hath seen me hath seen the Father; and how sayest thou then, Show us the Father? Believest thou not that I am in the Father, and the Father in me?" Here is a great mystery—the three in one. It is not against reason—any more than the fact that light, heat and electricity are combined in a single flame; but it is above reason. It must needs be so, inasmuch as a man cannot hold the ocean in the palm of his hand. God would not be the infinite God, if the finite mind could comprehend him. The doctrine of the Trinity is mysterious, but true.

In the Norse mythology, it is said that Thor on his visit to Jotunheim, was required to show his power by draining a great horn. He drank and drank without effect, for he was trying to drink the ocean dry. So is it with the man who thinks to fathom the thought of God. It is indeed impossible to explain the doctrine of the Trinity; but, let it be observed, it is equally impossible, consistently with sound logic, to disprove or deny it.

II. We now come to *the Kenosis or Self-Emptying of Christ.* What was it that he gave up when he "took upon him the form of a servant and was made in the likeness of men"? His Godhood? No; but the "form" of it. His essential glory? No; but the "form" of it.

It must have been a great day in heaven when the Second Person of the Godhead set out for earth to accomplish his great work. How angels and archangels, who had been wont to veil their faces before the effulgence of his glory, must have sent benedictions after him! He vanished; and when next he appeared, lo! it was as a child wrapped in swaddling bands and lying in a manger. Between the gate of heaven and Bethlehem, something had fallen from him. Not his Godhood; it is unthinkable that he should cease to be God. But he had lost the outward form of deity. There was no halo about the Christ-child. There was no form, nor comeliness, nor any beauty that we should desire him. He had emptied himself of the form of God, and taken upon him the form of a man. He was exclusively neither God nor man; but *Theanthropos*, the God-Man.

He was made in this "fashion" for a three-fold purpose: (1) To enter so into participation of our human nature, that he might become a high priest able to be touched with a feeling of our infirmities; (2) to veil in such wise the divine majesty, upon which no man can look and live, as to adjust it to our fleshly eyes; and (3) to prepare himself for the great sacrifice. As Anselm says, "He must be man that he may suffer, and by the same token he must be God, that he may suffer enough for all the children of men."

Let it be remembered, however, that in emptying himself of the form, he still retained the essential glory of God. Now and then his disciples caught a glimpse of it. On the Mount of Transfiguration in the shadow of the luminous cloud, his garments were white and glistering, and his face as the sun shining in its strength.

In like manner he emptied himself of the outward form and exercise of his divine attributes. In becoming a servant, he held these prerogatives in abeyance. But they were always at his command, standing about him like genii awaiting his nod and beck.

Where was his *omnipresence?* He whom the heaven of heavens could not contain, consented to be enclosed within the narrow bounds of a manger, a carpenter-shop, a judgment-hall. Yet on occasion barred doors and gates could not restrain him. And his consciousness of ubiquity was manifest in his promise, "Lo, I am with you alway."

Where was his *omniscience?* In speaking of the Great Assize, he said, "But of the day and hour knoweth no man, no, not the Son, but the Father only." In other words, he had put away the exercise of his omniscience. Yet on occasion he recalled it;

as when he perceived past and future events, and declared his acquaintance with the secret imaginations of the hearts of men. All things were naked and open before him. There was indeed an obscuration, but in no wise an obliteration, of his power of infinite sight. He was the great mind-reader. He needed no cathode rays to help him.

And where was his *omnipotence?* He who created the worlds, consented to earn his livelihood in a carpenter-shop. He was anhungered and athirst, like other men; he lay asleep on the steersman's cushion of the little boat, wearied with the labors of the day; but mark, when the storm rises, and the sailors bend over him, crying, "Master, carest thou not that we perish?" how he summons his almighty power, lifts his hands above the surging waves, and quiets them by his word, "Be still!" until, like naughty children, the winds and billows sob themselves to sleep.

But in his death this "Self-Emptying" went further still. "He became *obedient unto death.*" The self-existent One, centre and source of life itself, bowed to the king of terrors, yet still remained Prince of Life. When Peter drew the sword in Gethsemane Jesus rebuked him, saying, "Thinkest thou that I cannot now pray to my Father, and he shall presently give me more than twelve legions of angels?" In other words, if he consented to die, it was not because he had not the power to live. "I have power to lay down my life," said he, "and I have power to take it again." So when Pilate said, "Knowest thou not that I have power to crucify thee and power to release thee?" he answered, "Thou couldest have no power at all against me, except it were given thee from above." He was not a struggling victim like Iphigeneia, the daughter of Agamemnon, who was dragged to the altar for the deliverance of the Greeks. He came to Calvary as a volunteer, saying, "Here am I, in the volume of the book it is written of me, I rejoice to do thy will, O my God." He addressed himself to his great purpose in pursuance of an eternal covenant for the salvation of ruined men. In full possession of infinite power, he chose to be feeble like other men.

Nor was this all. He became obedient, not to death alone, but to *the death of the cross;* that is, he emptied himself of the form of innocency, consenting to take the place of a malefactor, that he might die for all malefactors on the accursed tree.

At this point he reached the lowest depth of his humiliation; he, the only Innocent One, "was made a curse for us." Aye, in that supreme moment he emptied himself even of the consciousness of his own integrity, and entered into full identity with guilty men. He in whose heart and upon whose lips was found no guile, made the world's sin his own. The purple cup which he pressed to his lips in the garden of Gethsemane, was filled with the bitter draught of conviction. Little wonder that he cried, "O my Father, if it be possible, let this cup pass from me." But he drank it; that is, he bare for us in his own consciousness the anguish of conviction—the sense of ill-doing and certain fearful looking-for of judgment—which comes sooner or later to every man.

Not only so, but he lifted the burden of the world's sin and bore it to Calvary until his heart broke under it. "He that knew no sin, was made sin for us, that we might be made the righteousness of God in him." He went out into the outer darkness of expiation.

He went down into the lowest depths of penalty. He could not actually surrender his holiness, but he did actually surrender the consciousness of it. The fashion of his innocency was laid aside like a garment, that he might be clothed upon with the shame of human guilt. He became obedient, not only to physical death, but to spiritual death in our behalf; to that death which, under the law, is imposed upon the sinner: "The soul that sinneth, it shall die." Not otherwise can we understand the awful cry that marked the consummation of his anguish on the cross, "Eloï, Eloï, lama sabachthani?" Thus, infinite as he was, made up of all divine excellencies, holy, harmless and undefiled, free from the slightest taint of personal sin, he, changing places with us, became in his own consciousness the great sufferer for sin. He descended into hell for us!

III. Now the sequel. "*Wherefore God hath highly exalted him* and given him a name which is above every name; that at the name of Jesus every knee should bow."

The great work being over, the mighty purpose accomplished, he re-assumed the form, the fashion, the resplendent glory, which had been his from the beginning of the ages. To his disciples he said, "If ye loved me ye would rejoice, because I go unto my Father; for my Father is greater than I"; that is, ye would rejoice because out of my earthly humiliation I go to resume my co-equality with God. In his sacerdotal prayer he said, "Father I will that they whom thou hast given me, be with me where I am, that they may behold my glory, the glory which I had with thee before the world was."

The new name which is given to him by reason of

his accomplished work, is JESUS; they "called his name Jesus because he should save his people from their sins." On March 4th, 1493, Columbus, returning from his voyage of discovery, dropped anchor off Lisbon. He was received and escorted to Barcelona, where in the presence of king and courtiers he told his story of the new world Here were gold and silver and parrots, and nine Indians whom he had brought back with him. He had sailed forth as "Admiral of the Seas," but now a new name was given him, "The Discoverer of the New World." He was made a grandee and permitted to ride in triumph at the king's bridle. A new and magnificent escutcheon was blazoned for him; the Lion of Castile blending with the four anchors of his ancestral crest. So Christ on his return to the celestial kingdom was welcomed as Jesus, the Redeemer of the World; and before that name and the unutterable love and power which it suggests, all knees must bow, "of beings celestial, terrestrial and sub-terrestrial." In heaven the angels and archangels add new ascriptions of praise. On earth some hundreds of millions of redeemed sinners bow in humble gratitude before him. And in the region of departed spirits there are multitudes which no man can number, gathered out of every nation and kindred and people and tribe, who sing, "Worthy art thou to receive honor and glory and power and dominion; for thou hast redeemed us by thy blood and hast made us to be kings and priests unto God."

There is a legend of an ancient hero who, as he fell dying in battle, with one hand grasped his bridle and with the other waved his broken sword, crying, "Go tell the dead, I come!" So too the Lord Jesus ascended from Olivet while the opening clouds received him. Lift up your heads, O ye gates, and the King of Glory shall come in! Who is this king of glory? The Lord mighty in battle. The Lord of Hosts, he is the King of Glory. Lift your heads, O ye gates, and be ye lift up, ye everlasting doors and the King of Glory shall come in!

And what is the conclusion? Let this mind be in you which was also in Christ Jesus. He stooped to conquer. Oh that we might also learn the Kenosis! We are tenacious of our rights: we clamor about our petty prerogatives; we forget that the highest right, the most glorious privilege, the most divine prerogative, is to give up everything for others and the glory of God. "He that saveth his life, shall lose it; and he that loseth his life for my sake and the gospel's, shall find it unto life everlasting." To turn our backs upon the form of glory, is to win glory itself. "Except a corn of wheat fall into the ground and die, it abideth alone; but if it die, it bringeth forth much fruit." There is no better word than that of the Apostle, "I am crucified with Christ, nevertheless I live; yet not I, but Christ liveth in me." Self-denial, self-abnegation, self-forgetfulness, —these lie along the path that leads to that highest manhood which can say, "My life is hid with Christ in God."

He who has learned this truth and is willing to entertain the mind that was in Christ Jesus, shall win for himself, as Jesus won, a new name and shall be partaker of his glory. As it is written, "To him that overcometh, will I give a white stone, with a new name written therein, which no man knoweth save he that receiveth it."

IN NO WISE.

"And him that cometh unto me I will in no wise cast out."—JOHN vi. 37.

Our Lord loved the people. He had come all the way from heaven to save them. He had compassion on them because they were as sheep without a shepherd. He desired above all things to win them to the glory of the endless life.

All day long he had been preaching and working wonders in the plain east of Gennesaret. The blind and withered and halt were healed of their infirmities. The place must have looked like a field hospital with crutches and bandages scattered about. Meanwhile he preached the great truths of the kingdom; for he recognized the fact so frequently overlooked by modern philanthropists, that the greatest need of the average man is a spiritual need after all. As the day wore on, the people being anhungered, he wrought for them the miracle of the loaves. But while he satisfied their physical desires, he still preached; for he knew that a man may endure hunger as well as other aches and pains, but as an immortal being he must know the way of spiritual and eternal life. The day was over, and in the twilight Jesus betook himself to a mountain apart for communion with God. The little boat, manned by his disciples, meanwhile pushed out upon the lake, and in the darkness the storm came upon them. On a sudden he appeared walking upon the waves, and they received him into the ship, and lo, the keel of the little vessel grated upon the sands of Capernaum!

The next morning the people, having come around the end of Gennesaret, were there to meet him. The motives of many were not of the best. Some clamored for a sign, others sought him merely for the loaves and fishes. But no matter how sordid or superstitious they were, he longed for their souls. From the little boat at the landing he preached to them, turning their thought to spiritual things. He spoke of himself as the bread which came down from heaven, and besought them to come to him that they might never hunger. "Come!" "Come!" was the refrain of his discourse. His hands were stretched out in invitation: "Come, come, and him that cometh unto me I will in no wise cast out!"

"In no wise"? Did he mean it? Can we take him at his word? Is this not hyperbole? Does he not mean that he is simply very, very willing? No. There is no word of qualification. "Him that cometh unto me I will in no wise cast out."

"What, Lord, not if *a red handed murderer* come to thee?" No; guilt is no bar to the mercy of the gracious Son of God.

Is there *a promise* that will cover the case? "Come now, let us reason together, saith the Lord; though your sins be as scarlet, they shall be as white as snow; though they be red like crimson, they shall be as wool."

Is there *an example?* Aye. There was David. Was there ever a deeper-dyed sinner than he? It was murder; it was adultery; it was secret sin; it was presumptuous sin; it was wilful, deliberate, daring, persistent sin. Hear him: "Have mercy upon me, O God, according to thy loving kindness; according unto the multitude of thy tender mercies blot out my transgressions. Against thee, thee only, have I sinned, and done this evil in thy sight." Did God answer him? Listen again: "This poor man cried and the Lord heard him and saved him out of all his troubles." "He hath put a new song in my mouth, even praise unto our God." "O that men would praise the Lord for his goodness and for his wonderful works to the children of men!"

"But, Lord, if a man come to thee *from the meanest and most sordid of motives?* If he is not conscious of love and gratitude toward thee; if he has not even felt the heinousness of sin; if he is moved simply and solely by the desire to escape from hell?" Yes, even then the promise holds; "I will in no wise cast him out."

Is there *a promise?* "As I live, saith the Lord, I have no pleasure in the death of the wicked, but that the wicked turn from his way and live: turn ye, turn ye from your evil ways, for why will ye die?" So then fear is a legitimate motive. Our Lord himself speaks of the outer darkness, of the undying worm, of the fire that never shall be quenched, in order that we may be moved to escape from spiritual and eternal death.

Is there *a case in point?* The prodigal son is one; he was brought to his good resolution by two considerations: the thought of his own poverty and of his father's wealth. As he sat in the swine-field, his substance all squandered, in rags and shame and pennilessness, he looked at his thin hands, felt the gnawing of hunger and saw visions of plenty in his father's house. "I will arise," said he, "and go to my father." Was there a welcome for him? "And when he was yet a great way off his father saw him and went out to meet him." Listen. There is music and dancing. Look in at the window. Who is it that sits in the place of honor with a ring on his finger and wearing the best robe? The father rises in his place, and says: "Rejoice with me, my friends, for this my son was dead and is alive again, and was lost and is found."

"Yes, Lord; but if a man has *grown old in impenitence and habitual sin!*" Ah! now the heart runs backward along the years. I am standing again at my mother's knee and hearing the old, old story. I am listening again to the preaching in the village church. I am recalling a season of spiritual quickening, when many of my companions came, but I replied, "Not now, but at a more convenient season." That was twenty, forty, sixty years ago. My heart is hard; my conscience is seared; my ears are dull. Will he receive me?

Is there *a promise?* There are many promises. "He is able to save unto the uttermost all them that come unto God by him." Unto the uttermost! That means to the last year, to the last day, to the last gasp.

Is there *an example* of any who came so late? One, that none may despair; and only one, that none may presume—to wit, the penitent thief. The story runs that he had been a highwayman on the bloody road that led down to Jericho. All warnings and remonstrances were unheeded. He pursued his desperate course until he was haled to judgment, to prison, and to the gallows tree. There he hung *in articulo mortis.*

His brief candle was burned out. Hark! "Lord, remember me when thou comest in thy kingdom." And what was the answer? "To-day thou shalt be with me in paradise."

> Depth of mercy! Can there be
> Mercy still reserved for me?
> Can my God his love forbear?
> Me, the chief of sinners, spare?
>
> There for me the Saviour stands;
> Shows his wounds and spreads his hands,
> God is love! I know, I feel,
> Jesus lives, and loves me still.

"But suppose a man is *burdened with doubt?* What then? I, perhaps, am not certain that Jesus is the Christ; am not sure of immortality; wonder sometimes if there be a God. Is there hope for me?"

Is there *a promise?* "He that doeth the will of my Father shall know the doctrine." If I come with the feeblest faith, the Lord will strengthen it. What, indeed, is belief, but doubt looking to Christ and learning of Christ? The antidote for doubt is not knowledge, but faith. So bring your doubts, my brother, and lay them before his feet.

Was ever a skeptic thus received? Many. There was doubting Thomas. He was not at the prayer-meeting in the upper room when the risen Christ appeared to the disciples. And when he was told, he said: "I will not believe. Nay, not unless I may thrust my fingers into the nail prints and my hand into his side." A little later he was with the disciples, when the Lord appeared, saying, "Peace be unto you." Then straightway he turned to Thomas, and said, "Reach hither thy finger and thrust it into these wounds and thrust thy hand into my side; and be not faithless but believing." And Thomas bowed before him, crying, "My Lord and my God!"

"Yes, Lord; but *a backslider?* Is it not written, 'It is impossible for those who were once enlightened, and made partakers of the Holy Ghost, and have tasted of the good word of God, if they fall away, to renew them again unto repentance, seeing they have crucified the Lord afresh and put him to an open shame'?" But this is an impossible hypothesis. Precisely as if the Lord had said, If a star shall swing out of its orbit, who can replace it? The star does not swing out of its orbit, because the Almighty holds it there. A man once converted is held by the great power of God.

Is there *a promise* for the backslider? "Return unto me and I will have mercy upon you." The word rings all through Scripture: "Return!" "Return!" A man grows cold-hearted, neglects his obvious duty, forgets to pray; and still God's word "Return!" pursues him.

If we would have *an example*, there was Peter. Did ever a man fall further from grace? "Lord, though all forsake thee, yet will not I forsake thee." A few hours later in the judgment-hall, a maid servant pointed her finger at him, and said, "Thou also wast with Jesus." And he blushed and trembled, and cried once, twice, thrice with a ringing oath, "I never knew that man!" If there is hope for Peter, there is hope for all. Here on the shore of the lake he stands before his risen Lord. "Simon son of Jonas lovest thou me?" Once, twice, thrice; and thrice, as in the denial, Peter answers, "Yea, Lord, thou knowest that I love thee." "Feed my sheep."

The past is forgotten and his commission is restored. Let this be remembered, "If any man sin, we have an advocate with the Father, even Jesus Christ the righteous." And he knoweth our frame, he remembereth that we are dust; if we return, he will have mercy upon us.

"But, Lord, if one has *committed the unpardonable sin?*" No, not even then will Christ reject him; that is, if we regard the unpardonable sin as usually understood. What is it? "The sin against the Holy Ghost." And what does the Holy Ghost do? He takes of the things of Jesus and shows them unto us. And how do we sin against the Holy Ghost? By refusing to accept Christ. That, in the nature of the case, is the unpardonable sin, and there is none other. It closes the door of pardon against us; for there is none other name under heaven given among men whereby we must be saved.

Is there *a promise* here? "The blood of Jesus Christ cleanseth us from all sin." Therefore if a man accept Christ as his Saviour no sin whatsoever shall be remembered against him.

Is there *a case in point?* If ever a man committed heinous sin it was Saul of Tarsus; a young zealot full of bigotry and superstition, whose conscience was possessed by the very spirit of cruelty and bitterness. He breathed out slaughter against God's little ones. There were lights to warn, there were voices to admonish him, but through them all he pushed his way on his crusade of persecution. God called a halt; through the great noonday light he spoke to him. Saul answered, "Lord, what wilt thou have me to do?" Then and there the new life began, and he was faithful until the day when he was taken out beyond the walls of Rome and his head fell from the block. "I have fought a good fight, I have finished my course, I have kept the faith; henceforth there is laid up for me a crown of righteousness, which the Lord the righteous judge shall give me at that day."

"But surely, Lord, this promise cannot hold in the case of one who is *dead and gone to hell!*" Yes, even then the promise holds. If the lost could come to Jesus, they would find him waiting to receive them.

Is there *a promise?* The twelve gates of heaven are great promises; on the east, on the west, on the north, on the south the gates stand open. They shall never be shut by day and there is no night there. And there are no sentinels or warders to prevent refugees from entering in.

Is there *an example?* Do we know of a single soul that ever came from the outer darkness and passed through those open gates? No, not one! Alas! not one; for there is "a great gulf fixed." A great impassable gulf. But God has not made it; the lost themselves have rendered their return impossible by sinning away the opportunities of their probationary life. Death fixes character; as it is written, "He that is unjust, let him be unjust still; and he that is righteous, let him be righteous still." The lost are forever wedded to sin and darkness. There is only one place in the universe where they would be more miserable than in their present abode; that is in heaven. They would rather endure their shame and remorse than return to God. The gulf is fixed, but over it the promise still and forever rings forth: "Him that cometh unto me I will in no wise cast out!"

What then is the conclusion? "Now is the accepted time, now is the day of salvation." It is not for me to say that this is the last opportunity of any, but I do know that it may be. The man who sins away a moment of grace like this takes an awful hazard. To-day is ours; to-morrow is God's.

It may be that in the soul of some one who reads these words the struggle is now going on. The Heart says, "I want to be reconciled unto God;" the Reason says, "This is the best and wisest thing to do;" Conscience says, "It is right; do it." But what says the Will? There lies the decision. O that it might say, "I will arise and go to him."

In the year 1821 a young lady whose name, Charlotte Elliot, has become familiar with us through one of her favorite hymns, was under deep conviction of sin. For a twelvemonth she could not sleep, but resisted all the overtures of Christ. Then a clergyman was entertained in her father's house, who on leaving said, "Dear Charlotte, cut the cable; it will take too long to unloose it." That very night she made the great resolution and wrote this hymn:

> Just as I am, without one plea,
> But that thy blood was shed for me,
> And that thou bidd'st me come to thee,
> O Lamb of God, I come! I come!
>
> Just as I am, and waiting not
> To rid my soul of one dark blot,
> To thee, whose blood can cleanse each spot,
> O Lamb of God, I come! I come!
>
> Just as I am:—thou wilt receive,
> Wilt welcome, pardon, cleanse, relieve;
> Because thy promise I believe,
> O Lamb of God, I come! I come!
>
> Just as I am, thy love unknown
> Has broken every barrier down;
> Now to be thine, yea, thine alone,
> O Lamb of God, I come! I come!

LUTHER AND THE REFORMATION.

" And God said, Let there be light: and there was light."—GEN. i. 3.

It used to be a favorite objection to the Mosaic account of the creation, that it made light before the sun. In fact, however, that was precisely the case. The darkness of primitive chaos was broken by glimmerings of electric light produced by atomic friction before there was a luminary in heaven. We note a corresponding fact in history. Luther is called "The Sun of the Reformation"; but there were foregleams of that great movement long before his time. The Wyclif Bible was completed Anno Domini 1383. John Huss, who advocated the ultimate authority of Scripture as against ecclesiastical authority, was burned Anno Domini 1416. The voice of Savonarola, who preached vital piety under Lorenzo the Magnificent, was hushed amid the flames, Anno Domini 1498. But the birth of Luther was as the glory of the full midday beam.

His life reads like a melodrama.

First, we see him as a fagot boy carrying fuel for the smelting furnaces in Mansfeld—a fit apprenticeship for one who was destined to kindle the fires that should melt the heart of the nations and recast the lives and characters of men.

It was a time of darkness. A cartoon of the period sets forth the condition of things on this wise :—A king is saying, "I govern all"; a soldier saying, "I fight for all"; a priest, sleek and portly, saying, "I pray for all"; to which he might have added, "I prey upon all"; and a peasant, lean and threadbare, lamenting, "I pay for all." The shoeless people were ground down in manifold oppression and ignorance. There was no open vision. The lights of the golden candlestick were quenched in the sanctuary. Barefoot friars went about crying, *Misericordia!* A fire was sorely needed to illuminate the world and to arouse the dormant energies of the church.

The fagot boy was moved by dreams of greatness. He entered the university with the intention of preparing himself for the practice of law. There an incident occurred which changed the whole tenor of his life. He was walking in the fields with his bosom friend Alexis, when a storm arose and a bolt of lightning smote them. When Martin awoke from unconsciousness, his friend Alexis lay dead beside him. He fled from the place smitten with an unspeakable terror. He could neither eat nor sleep. He had formed a new conception of divine wrath; a certain fearful looking for of judgment took possession of him; he fled to a monastic cell.

Next a monk is bending over a book,—the book that has buttressed nations in truth and righteousness; the book that has guided multitudinous souls to endless life; a book more significant than the Sibylline leaves as to the destinies of men; it bore the name, *Ta Biblia*. The monk knew it only as a forbidden book, listed in the *Index Expurgatorius*. He read it furtively until he came to the place where it is written,

"Search the Scriptures for in them ye think ye have eternal life; and they are they which testify of me." With this search-warrant he read more boldly—read until he came upon a portrayal of sin. By this he was enabled to interpret his own heartache. He read of the fire that is never quenched, of the worm that never dies. He grew lean and haggard. The friars saluted him, "Good appetite, Brother Martin!" But the refectory had no charms for him. He returned again to his book. He read, "By the deeds of the law shall no flesh living be justified." The very terror of his situation enchained him. And now he came upon the word that is written: "What the law could not do in that it was weak through the flesh, God, sending his own Son in the likeness of sinful flesh, and for sin, condemned sin in the flesh." The light began to break. "He that believeth, shall be saved." It was the dawn of day. The song of the new life was within him. It was as when the bridegroom calls to his bride, "Arise, my love; the winter is past, the rain is over and gone, the time of the singing of birds is come; arise, my love, my fair one and come away!"

Again we observe the monk on his way to Rome. The Pope has summoned him. Not long before, the Elector Frederick had a dream in which he saw a monk with a pen in hand, the feather end of it lost in heaven, the point touching the Pope's tiara and then piercing the ears of a lion that shook its mane and roared. This summons from Rome is the lion's voice. The monk sets out afoot and journeys as a barefoot friar begging his way. He longs to enter the Imperial City. On a southern slope of the Alps, he pauses, leaning on his staff; Italy with its blue skies, green vineyards and silver rivers, lies below him, and far in the distance the domes of the great capital. At the Porto del Popolo he falls upon his knees crying, "Hail, Holy Rome; bathed in the blood of martyrs and sanctified by the memories of the holy past."

Great were his anticipations; a sore disappointment awaited him. He had hoped to see a multitude serving God in vows of poverty and consecration. He found palatial halls, where priests with round persons and rubicund faces gathered around the stores of famous wine cellars. He looked for hair-cloth, and, lo, there were purple and fine linen, wealth, splendor, luxury on every side. Here were churches, marvels of architecture, adorned by the art of Raphael and Titian. He looked for voluntary poverty and simple piety; the air was full of ambition and political intrigue. The holy brothers smiled at him as a simple rustic. As he was saying mass, a neighbor elbowed him: "We could say it seven times, brother, while thou art saying it once." It seemed to him, honest devotee, that they were worshipping God with their lips while their hearts were far from him.

There was at Rome—where you may see it to this day—a marble stairway said to have been trodden by the feet of Jesus as he left the Prætorium on his way to the cross. The monk Martin thought to do penance for his sins like others, by climbing this stairway on his knees. Half way up the Scala Sancta, a voice spoke: "The just shall live by faith." It whispered, spoke louder, rolled like a peal of thunder through his heart and conscience: "The just shall live by faith!" He found himself standing upon his feet.

The revelation had come. Never more could the monk Martin be the same man.

And now it is market-day at Jüterbok. Here are dog-carts and donkey-carts; here are singers and acrobats; all manner of commodities are on sale,— meats and vegetables, live stock, clothing and furniture; and two commodities besides which are not so common on market-days; to-wit, indulgences for sin and deliverances from purgatory. The centre of attraction is a booth yonder under a great crucifix from which are suspended the papal arms. A graduated scale of prices is affixed to this booth. Sins are labeled at their market quotations: polygamy, six ducats; perjury, nine; sacrilege, nine; murder, eight; witchcraft, two; and so on. The theory is that the sacrifice of Christ was of infinite merit; he not only atoned for the race, but left a vast treasury of surplus, to which the saints had added by their works of supererogation. It is now proposed to sell out this accumulated surplus for the furnishing of St. Peter's at Rome. The monk Tetzel, who conducts the sale, is an emissary of the Pope. The drum beats and the sale goes on.

In addition to indulgences he disposes of purgatorial deliverances at graduated prices. On a chest suspended from the crucifix is this inscription:

> "Soon as the coin within the chest doth ring,
> The soul shall straightway into heaven spring."

"Hear ye," cries Tetzel, "O bereaved wives and husbands, and parents of children in purgatorial pains. Why should ye permit them to suffer when they can be delivered by a few paltry pence?" The multitudes are interested and money flows in. But Brother

Martin standing in the company sees another picture —One standing as a vender of wares at the crossing of the streets, and crying, "Ho, every one that thirsteth, come ye to the waters, and he that hath no money! come ye, buy and eat; yea, come, buy wine and milk without money, and without price." His soul is stirred within him. Is there no one to expose this brazen-faced charlatan? "God willing, I will make a hole in Tetzel's drum!"

And next we come to that memorable day, Oct. 31st, 1517. It is All Hallows' Eve; to-morrow will be All Saints' Day. The monk Martin with rapid strides approaches the Castle Church in Wittenberg; he draws from beneath his cloak a parchment and unrolls it. The quiet of the evening is broken by the sound of his hammer as he nails that parchment against the chapel door. The sound of his hammer is destined to shake the pillars of papal Rome and awake a sleeping world. That parchment is the protest from which Protestantism shall spring. It contains Ninety-five Theses, such as these: "The Pope has no power to remit sin"; "The man who preaches indulgences preaches a lie"; "The man who sells indulgences shall be cast into hell." The next morning the townspeople, in their wooden sabots, were reading these Theses and gossiping about them in their doorways. The event makes no unusual stir as yet. When Magna Charta was signed in the valley at Runnymede, flags waved and trumpets blared and loud shoutings sounded forth the victory of the people's rights. Here is a greater manifesto than Magna Charta, and destined to a more magnificent place in history; but the river Elbe flows quietly by as if naught had happened to disturb the current of events. The monk's protest meets no response as yet, save from a still small Voice. But the fire and the tempest and the earthquake will come.

And again we see him at the Diet of Worms. A Papal Bull has been issued against him. He is here to defend his protest. All along the way he had been admonished of dangers awaiting him. "Though they kindle fires," said he, "from Wittenberg to Worms, yet will I pass through by God's grace to face Behemoth and break his teeth." His friends admonished him that he must needs confront the great adversary. "Though there were as many devils at Worms as there are tiles upon the housetops, yet will I pass through in the name of the Lord Christ." He has turned not to the right or left, and here he comes. As he enters the doorway, an old captain, bearing the scars of bloody strife, says to him, "My poor monk, a great battle awaits thee; be just and fear not."

He is under the protection of the Elector's guard. The emissaries of the Pope have burned his books, and they would fain burn him. But first they will make an earnest effort to reclaim him. "Revoco' is the word. Revoco! If he will but say "Revoco," all shall be forgotten. He is warned, admonished, tempted with the offer of fat benefices. All in vain. He rises to speak: "Here I stand; I cannot otherwise; God help me!" Never did human lips utter grander words. The clouds are lifting from before the sun; bells ring in heaven; earth echoes with the sound of breaking chains.

Look well at this man. Here is the noblest sight

in the universe. A man under the dominion of conscience. A man true to his convictions. A man standing for the right in peril of death. A man realizing that he is in covenant with God!

And then the monk Luther is spirited away. No one knows whither he has gone. But on a sudden all Germany seems flooded with tracts and pamphlets. They are dated from "The Air Castle," from "The Island of Patmos," from "The Region of Birds." The monk is hidden away in the Castle of the Wartburg, where the ancient landgraves had dwelt. Here he enjoys the friendship of Melancthon. "Come, Philip, let us sing the Forty-sixth Psalm: 'God is our refuge and our strength; therefore will we not fear, though the earth be removed, and though the mountains be carried into the midst of the sea.'" Here he translates the Bible into the vernacular—his great life-work. It is like the forging of a thunderbolt. These Bibles are burned in the streets. There are bonfires in Rome, in Wittenberg, in Worms, in which, with the crackling of parchment, one can hear the prophetic hissing of flesh. But the Bible cannot be burned. The Book of the People has come to stay, and the protest has come to stay.

And now the monk lies on his death-bed. Alas, that his enemies should have been unwilling to leave him unmolested even here. They say that his death was the result of a drunken debauch! And it was but yesterday that he preached his last sermon, taking for his text, "Come unto me, all ye that labor and are heavy laden, and I will give you rest." A friend bending over him asks, "Dost thou die in the doctrines of the Reformation?" "Aye." "Dost thou die in the faith of Christ crucified?" "Aye." His lips are moving: "Into thy hands, O Christ, I commit my spirit; for thou hast redeemed me." And so the great reformer fell asleep. His body was committed to the dust, his spirit to God who had given it, and his work, as Bacon said of his own, to the coming ages.

The smoke of that long battle of the distant past has cleared away. We are far enough from the time of conflict to pass judgment on the cause and its results. Luther is naught; the Reformation is everything. What did the Reformation mean? The Protestant Church stands on *three fundamental facts:*

1. *A free conscience. Ich bin Ich!* Let every man be his own thinker. In the four decades preceding the Reformation, no less than thirteen hundred persons were burned to death for heresy; that is, for thinking for themselves; that being the meaning of heresy in those days. In point of fact, however, every man must think for himself, as he values his soul and hopes to please God. Alone was I born into the world; alone must I face the duties and responsibilities of life; alone must I pass through the valley of the shadow; alone must I stand before the judgment bar. Let no man, therefore, stand in my light. Let no priest or ecclesiastical body prevent my face-to-face communion with God.

2. *An open Bible.* He broke the chains that bound the Scriptures to the altar. He flung open its golden clasps. Was it a great thing for the world when Columbus forced the Gates of Hercules and pushed his way out upon the open seas in conquest of Eldorado? It was a far greater when Luther threw open the doors of the divine oracles, that whosoever would might enter in.

3. *The doctrine of Justification by Faith,*—"*articulum ecclesiæ stantis aut cadentis.*" This doctrine is the foundation of the church; it is also the foundation of personal life and character; as it is written, "Other foundation can no man lay than that is laid, which is Jesus Christ." It is also the sum and substance of all preaching; for no man preaches who does not point an index finger toward the cross, saying, "Behold the Lamb of God!" On this fact rests the renown of the great reformer. His only glory is a reflected brightness from the face of him of whom it is written: "There is none other name under heaven given among men whereby we must be saved." His word was, "Look to the wounds of Jesus! Look and live."

If the Church of the Reformation still lives, it lives by virtue of the survival of the fittest. It was a great truth that was uttered by Gamaliel: "If this counsel or this work be of men, it will come to nought; but if it be of God, ye cannot overthrow it, lest haply ye be found even to be fighting against God." The three centuries of Protestantism have proven its right to survive. One of the most affecting sights in history is the procession of dying religions and philosophies following one another toward oblivion. Truth only can survive.

> Truth crushed to earth will rise again;
> The eternal years of God are hers;
> But error, wounded, writhes with pain,
> And dies amid her worshippers.

In the market-place of Eisleben stands a statue of Martin Luther, before which Charles the Fifth, Frederick the Great, Peter of Russia, Napoleon, the Kaiser

Wilhelm, all have bowed their heads. Well might they; their names have shaken thrones and dynasties; but Luther, by the simple power of truth, has left an abiding influence on the souls of men. Protestantism lives, because the truths it represents all centre in Christ, of whom it is written: "His kingdom is an everlasting kingdom, and his dominion is for ever and ever. The earth shall be consumed with fervent heat, the heavens shall be rolled together as a scroll; but the word of the Lord endureth forever." The mouth of the Lord hath spoken it!

THE STAR OF BETHLEHEM.

"Now when Jesus was born in Bethlehem of Judea, in the days of Herod the king, behold, there came wise men from the east to Jerusalem, saying, Where is he that is born King of the Jews? for we have seen his star in the east, and are come to worship him."—MATT. ii. 1, 2.

The stars are our old friends. They have stood guard in the heavens since the beginning of time ; and all the generations of the children of men have pondered them. Moses saw them from the fields of Midian; the planets revolving in their courses, and the fixed stars like eyes peering out from the background of infinite space. David watched them from the plains of Bethlehem with his flocks about him, and sang, "When I consider the heavens, the work of thy fingers, what is man that thou art mindful of him?" It was the business of these Magians to know the starry heavens, and from them to cast the horoscopes of men and nations. On this occasion they were amazed to behold a new star, bright and beckoning, which seemed to say, "Follow me." A new star? Why not? If God had been leading up through the centuries by a series of miracles to the Incarnation as a stupendous climacteric, why should he not kindle a torch in heaven to light the pathway of those who sought him ?

Was it a comet—as Milton says, "A comet dangling in the air"? The Chinese astronomical tables make it appear that there was a comet in the year 750 of the building of Rome; that is, at the time of the advent of Christ. "Thus," says a German rationalist, "the star of Bethlehem is displaced from the category of the supernatural and reduced to the level of an ordinary astronomical phenomenon." But this hypothesis was long since abandoned, because a comet does not meet the conditions of the case.

Was it then a conjunction of planets? On October 10, 1604, Kepler saw Jupiter and Saturn coming close together, and then red Mars intruding on their symposium; it was shown that there had been a similar conjunction seven years before the beginning of the Christian Era. This phenomenon was, moreover in the constellation Pisces, set apart by astrologers as having a peculiar significance for Judea. But unfortunately the discrepancy in time was fatal, and besides the constellation must have appeared at such an elevation as to make it impossible that it should lead the wise men.

Was it then a meteor? Possibly. But in any case it was miraculous. The Czar, at his recent coronation, drank from a crystal cup to the prosperity of Russia, and then dashed the cup to fragments on the marble floor. It was not meet that any but his royal lips should ever touch it. So perhaps God kindled a light for the occasion of the Incarnation, which, having served its purpose, was extinguished forever.

I. *It was a royal harbinger.* It betokened the coming of a long-expected king. He was known as the desire of all nations. The Greeks were looking for *ho Dikaios*—the Just Man. The Romans were expecting one who should surpass all the Cæsars in the glory of his dominion and usher in the Golden Age. Virgil sang of him in his Ninth Eclogue. The Jews, also, were expecting one who should restor ethe glory to Israel. It had been written: "For unto us a son is born, unto us a child is given, and the government shall be upon his shoulder, and his name shall be called Wonderful, Counsellor, Mighty God, the Everlasting Father, and the Prince of Peace."

There was a special reason why these Chaldean soothsayers should be expecting him, for it was one of their own craft, the Magian Balaam, who had predicted that a star should be the harbinger of the king. He had stood on the heights of Edom fifteen centuries before, employed by the king of the Moabites to curse the children of Israel. He saw their tents spread out among the acacia groves in the valley below. Seven altars were about him, and seven bullocks blazing upon them. In vain did he endeavor to curse. A trance fell upon him, and the Spirit moved his lips. His eyes were opened; the curtain of the years was lifted. He saw the nations discomfited and Israel triumphant. "How goodly are thy tents, O Jacob; and thy tabernacles, O Israel! They are as gardens by the river's side, and as orchards of lign-aloes. I shall see him, but not now; I shall behold him, but not nigh: there shall come a Star out of Jacob, and a Sceptre shall rise out of Israel, and he shall smite the corners of Moab. Out of this people shall come One whose dominion shall be for ever and ever."

No doubt these Magians were familiar with that ancient prophecy. Wherefore, it is written, "They were obedient unto the star." It went before them like a diamond shining on the index finger of the night, pointing the way. They followed it over the mountains of Chaldea, through the valley of the Euphrates, around by Lebanon, southward through the valley of the Jordan, up the steep ascent to Jerusalem, and down again to Bethlehem. There it paused over the stable. There must be some mistake! No; at the threshold they looked upward, and the star was pausing there and slowly fading from view. Then they heard the infant's wail. They entered, and saw the Christ-child. A moment later they had unpacked their treasures, and laid at his feet myrrh and gold and frankincense—fit offerings for a king.

II. *It was a Day Star,*—an augury of the morning. The night upon which it rose was the darkest night the world ever saw. All prophecy had ceased; there was no open vision; the lights in the tabernacle had gone out. It was time for God to interpose in behalf of his people, to bring in the Golden Age.

If we would know the deep darkness that then prevailed, and the influence of this Day Star in history, let us institute a comparison between the great festival of that period, and the corresponding festival of our time. Let us attend the Saturnalia which were celebrated at Rome during the winter solstice.

The streets of the great metropolis are thronged with people. The temple of Saturn is thrown wide open. The woolen fetters have been taken from the feet of the tutelary god. Here are knights and senators in gay apparel riding through the streets; of these there are two thousand, who represent the proprietorship of the empire. Here are multitudes of slaves branded with their masters' names; of these there are sixty millions in the empire, dwelling in ergastula, or stables, herding like beasts. Here are plebeians also, ashamed to beg, yet unwilling to work because labor is for slaves; living on *congiaria*, that is, regular appropriations of food from the government; ever crying for bread and games.

All are wending their way towards the Circus Maximus in which this " Pompa Diaboli " is to be celebrated. The great amphitheatre is magnificently decorated for the occasion. Festoons of roses are hung from pillar to pillar. Awnings are suspended overhead, from which perfumes are showered upon the people. Nuts and dates and roasted fowls are thrown among them. Yonder in the royal booth sits Cæsar Augustus with his favorite courtiers and his wives and concubines about him. The higher tiers are set apart for the patricians: knights, senators and proprietors. Their wives are with them, wearing rings which, as Seneca says, "mark the number of their divorces." Lower down sit the plebeians; still lower the slaves.

The trumpet gives the signal and the Triumphator enters, followed by a Roman guard; after them a procession of gods on rolling pedestals, which are placed on tripods about the arena. The spectators applaud with cheering and clapping of hands. The trumpet sounds and the athletic sports begin: first the foot-races and the boxing contests; at the conclusion of which the victors pass under the royal booth to receive their garlands.

The trumpet sounds again—this time for the chariot races. The assembled populace, divided into parties marked by the colors of the chariots, are moved to wild excitement. Ribbons, garlands, favors of every sort are thrown down upon the contestants. Here and there soothsayers are selling tips for wagers, and along the higher tiers estates are changing hands. The multitudes are shouting, laughing, applauding, laying wagers and swearing by their gods. The successful competitors approach the royal booth, receive their garlands and pass out.

The trumpet sounds again, and wild beasts are pitted against each other; lions, tigers and leopards tear each other to pieces. The people are tasting blood and whetting their appetites for still more brutal contests to come.

The trumpet sounds once more, and a company of gladiators march in—each man armed with net and dagger and shield. They lift their faces to the emperor and cry, "*Morituri, te Salutamus!*" They meet each other, hand to hand, in the arena; it is a struggle to the death. The vanquished plead for mercy. "*Habet! Habet!*" is the cry. The thumbs of the people are reversed; they roar for blood. The bodies are dragged out with hooks by Nubian slaves; dragged into the death chamber, still palpitating with life. The arena is strewn with fresh sand. On with the Saturnalia! The audience is frenzied with a thirst for blood. Meanwhile, as Ovid says, "The love-making in the upper booths goes on." "Pompa Diaboli!" Blood! blood! blood! And this was the great festival of the Augustan Age.

Look on that picture and then on this:

The home is decked with evergreen and filled with life and laughter. Last night "the stockings were hung in the chimney with care," and the children are rejoicing in their gifts. The members of the household gather about the board; the absent are remembered, and the past is revived in joyous reminiscence. The grandparents are there, their eyes shining and their youth renewed. Then at the family altar the goodness of the Heavenly Father is remembered in thanksgiving. All join in the glad songs of the Christmas tide;

> God rest ye, merrie gentlemen,
> Let nothing you dismay;
> For Jesus Christ our Saviour
> Was born on Christmas Day.

What makes the difference between the Saturnalia and our Christmas festivities? *The shining of the Day Star.* The world has been moving grandly on during these Christian centuries. Give God the praise!

The Star has shone into our home-life. The word *familia* used to mean merely a retinue of slaves; the family now suggests a circle of tender ties; mother and father, son and daughter, brother and sister. If these are sacred names, it is because Christ has sanctified them.

It has thrown its light into the work-shop. The Third Estate is the product of Christian civilization. The term "sweat-shop" suggests one of the modern evils of our municipal life. But there was a time when the whole industrial system of the civilized world was one great sweat-shop. There were no strikes, there were no labor guilds, there was no contest of labor with capital, because the handicraftsman was a hopeless serf. The Carpenter who toiled in the shop at Nazareth, has dignified labor the whole world over. If it be true that "the heart of the toiler has throbbings that move not the bosom of kings," it is due to Jesus, who was a fellow-craftsman with all the honest toilers of the earth.

It has thrown its radiant influence into the larger forms

of our commercial life. What could a man do with his savings nineteen hundred years ago, but wrap them in a napkin and bury them in the earth? There was no confidence between man and man. There were no savings banks, because, as King Henry said, "oaths were straws, men's faith as wafer cakes." The banking system of to-day is a tribute to the power of the gospel; the logical sequence of the angels' song, "Good will to men." The man who has saved a golden eagle may, with reasonable confidence, now commit it to the care of a trust company; or, if he prefer, can send it around the world to Hong Kong by a chain of connections every link of which speaks of mutual confidence and bears the name of the Lord Christ.

Its light has gleamed upon all the institutions of our political life. The man who most aptly represented the governmental system of the olden time was the publican sitting at the raceipt of customs. He stood for extortion, for blackmail, for blood-money. Here and there the plague spot still lingers; but we recognize it as a belated barbarism, and are moved to eradicate it. The words, Liberty, Equality, Fraternity, which pass current as the shibboleths of popular government in our time, had little or no place in public affairs at the beginning of the Christian Era. The truth enunciated by St. Paul on Mars' Hill, "God hath created of one blood all nations of men," has come to be a controlling influence among all nations lying within the charmed circle of what we call Christendom.

To what shall we attribute this onward movement of the years? To the fact that *Jesus Christ came to dwell among men.* How far yon Star of Bethlehem casts its beams! Our Lord proclaimed his purpose in the synagogue when he opened the book and read, "The Spirit of the Lord is upon me, because he hath anointed me to preach the gospel to the poor; he hath sent me to heal the broken-hearted, to preach deliverance to the captives, and recovering of sight to the blind and to set at liberty them that are bruised."

III. *It was the Star of Empire.* It foretokened a perpetual improvement of the affairs of nations and men. It prophesies for us that what our Lord has done for Christendom, he will do for the whole world. The Star that shook the corners of Moab, shall shake the remotest corners of the earth until, to use the Psalmist's figure, as the house-wife shakes the crumbs from a napkin, so shall it shake all evil out of it.

Our Lord was born between the hemispheres. Tradition says that he was crucified with his face towards the west; westward the star of empire takes its way. He is the cosmopolitan Christ. His kingdom is from the river unto the ends of the earth.

A coin was found at Clunia, in Spain, bearing the image of Diocletian and the date Anno Domini 300. On the obverse was the hand of Hercules strangling a hydra, and over it the inscription, *Deleta Christianitas.* Thus to the mind of that haughty emperor the power of paganism was destined to strangle the gospel of Christ. Nay, strangle the sun! Strangle the atmosphere! Strangle the springs that gush out of the hills to feed the unfathomable sea! Christianity is an all-pervasive and universal power. The royal ensigns onward go.

> For, lo, the days are hastening on.
>   By prophet bards foretold,
> When with the ever circling years
>   Comes round the Age of Gold;
> When Peace shall over all the earth
>   Which now the angels sing.

All other stars shall fade. The sun shall be changed into darkness and the moon into blood, and the stars of heaven shall fall as when a fig-tree is shaken of its untimely figs. But the Star of Bethlehem will shine on forever. The zeal of the Lord of Hosts shall accomplish it.

IV. *It is the Star of destiny.* Napoleon was wont to speak of his star of destiny which set, alas, at Waterloo. But this is the star of destiny which leads all pilgrims, if they will, to the joys of the endless life.

Somewhere, for every man, the light of God's mercy is shining. It may be in the memory of a face crowned with silver and hands now folded under the sod. The light of reason, of memory, of revelation, all point to Bethlehem. O foolish Magi, had they stayed in the fields doubting, wondering, hesitating and making excuses! It was a far journey from Chaldea to Bethlehem, requiring ten times as long as to cross the Atlantic in these days. But these were wise men, and they said, "Arise, let us follow the star until we find him."

In the folk-lore of Russia it is said that as these Magi were journeying, they passed through a village where a woman was scouring her door-step. "Come with us," they said to her, "for we have seen the King's star, and we go to find him." "Not now," she answered; "my house must first be set in order; then will I follow after you." But when her work was finished, it was too late. And now the children of Russia look for the Baboushka—an old woman with a troubled face, who is said to go in and out among them at Christmas-tide, scanning the faces of the children in hopeless quest for the Christ-child.

If the call comes to-day, dear friend, heed it. God points so clearly to the desire of our hearts. Ring out, O bells of hope and promise! Ripple on, O laughter of the children! Burn clear all lights in the windows of happy homes, and lead us to Christ! The wise men are on their way. Cold unbelief looks on and moves not. The wise men are on their way to Bethlehem. Arise, my friend, and journey with them, and God's blessing be with you along the way.

ONE THING.

"If any other man thinketh that he hath whereof he might trust in the flesh, I more: circumcised the eighth day, of the stock of Israel, of the tribe of Benjamin, an Hebrew of the Hebrews; as touching the law, a Pharisee; concerning zeal, persecuting the church; touching the righteousness which is in the law, blameless. But what things were gain to me, those I counted loss for Christ. Yea, doubtless, and I count all things but loss, for the excellency of the knowledge of Christ Jesus my Lord; for whom I have suffered the loss of all things, and do count them but dung, that I may win Christ, and be found in him, not having my own righteousness which is of the law, but that which is through the faith of Christ, the righteousness which is of God by faith: that I may know him and the power of his resurrection, and the fellowship of his sufferings, being made conformable unto his death; if by any means I might attain unto the resurrection of the dead. Not as though I had already attained, either were already perfect: but I follow after, if that I may apprehend that for which also I am apprehended of Christ Jesus. Brethren, I count not myself to have apprehended: but this ONE THING I do, forgetting those things which are behind, and reaching forth unto those things which are before, I press toward the mark for the prize of the high calling of God in Christ Jesus."—PHIL. iii. 4-14.

Here is the secret of a great life. The secret of a noble life is always a great thought. The great thought which made the Apostle Paul what he was, was this, to know Christ. To know about Christ is one thing; to know him vitally, experimentally, that is another thing. The ambition of Paul was to know Christ in such a manner as to enter into the fellowship of his sufferings and be made conformable unto his death; so that he might be able to say, "I no longer live, but Christ liveth in me."

At this point the ambition of Paul was in line with the purpose of God concerning him; as he says, "I follow after, if that I may apprehend that for which also I am apprehended of Christ Jesus." The word "apprehend" is significant. It means to lay hold on; as when an officer apprehends a fugitive from justice, laying his hand upon him. Everybody knows how and when Jesus laid hold of Paul. That was a momentous day for him when the great light above the brightness of the sun smote him. Not many words were spoken. "Who art thou?" "I am Jesus." "What will thou have me to do?" Thereupon the mind of Jesus respecting Paul was made known to him. And from that moment the great thought of Jesus concerning Paul became the purpose and ambition of Paul respecting himself, namely, to know Christ, to know the power of his resurrection, to know the fellowship of his sufferings, to be made conformable unto his death, and so to apprehend that for which Christ Jesus had apprehended him. This meant life, character, usefulness, influence, manhood; for the true measure of manhood is the stature of Christ the ideal Man.

We are interested to know the measure of Paul's success. For this also is the purpose of every true Christian, to know the Master and to be like him. Here we have his report of progress: "I have not attained neither am I already perfect; I count not myself to have apprehended." As he utters this humble and regretful confession of shortcoming, two pictures present themselves before us: one is Paul in prison; aged, infirm, chained to his guard, and poor as poverty, sending for the cloak which he had left at Troas, to protect him from the cold. He had given up everything for Christ. Here is the inventory: as to his birthright, he was an Hebrew of the Hebrews; as to his standing under the law, he was a Pharisee of the straightest sect; as to his zeal, he was a zealot persecuting the church; as to his ceremonial purity, he was blameless. No man in Jewry had a brighter future before him; "but what things were gain to me, those I counted loss for the excellency of the knowledge of Christ Jesus my Lord; for whom I have suffered the loss of all things, and do count them but dung, that I may win Christ and be found in him." And what had he to show for this abandonment of all? "I count not myself to have apprehended." Failure? O no, the end is not yet. He still cherishes his high ambition. Thirty years have passed since Christ apprehended him on the way to Damascus, and he still follows after, that he may apprehend Christ.

The other picture is one that glows in the eyes of the aged prisoner. He is back again in Tarsus, the home of his boyhood. He has followed the stream of spectators to the Poseidonium and from the great galleries looks down upon the Isthmian games. He sees again the runners at the crimson line. They have trained away every ounce of superfluous flesh; they are stripped to the waist and bound tightly about the loins; their best foot is forward; their eyes are on the marble goal; every muscle is tense. Thus they stand in line awaiting the signal. The trumpet sounds, once, twice, thrice, and they are off like the wind. Their bodies are bending forward; their feet spurn the sanded course; no glance is thrown backward or upon the great cloud of witnesses about them. One thing! One thing they do! The Apostle has his figure; he grasps his stylus and writes, "So run I, forgetting the things which are behind and reaching forth unto those which are before, I press toward the mark for the prize of the high calling of God in Christ Jesus."

It would appear that he is really doing two things; forgetting and reaching forth. In fact, however, the forgetting is merely incidental to the reaching forth, which is the one thing. We, like Paul, have little or nothing to do with the things which are behind. The race which is before us must engage our thought. As to past sins, they are forgotten by the grace of God; lost in oblivion as in a boundless sea. As to past sorrows, let the dead past bury its dead. As to past failures and shortcomings, we "rise on stepping-stones of our dead selves to higher things."

In forgetting the past, however, we must not dishonor it; for the things which are behind have a most vital bearing on the things which are before. To-day is what yesterday has made it. We forget as nature forgets, in order to growth. We leave the past, as a river leaves the fountain hastening towards the sea; as the oak forgets the acorn—though the acorn makes the oak—and the sunshine and the beating storms, in the stretching out of its strong arms to furnish a shadow for the passer-by. We forget, as Quentin Matsys forgot his apprenticeship in the blacksmith shop, when he began to paint Christs and Madonnas for cathedral walls, though the forge and the hammer were in every stroke of his brush; or as Franklin forgot his kite, though the kite-string was father of the electric wire; or as men forget their alphabets, though the alphabet enters into every line and utterance of after life.

The old year is dying.* We utter a tender fare-

---

* This sermon was preached at the beginning of the year 1897.

well, because we believe that all the experiences of the twelve months have been working together for our good and for our further growth in grace. And then, girding ourselves, we turn our faces to the front and bravely forget. So writes the Apostle, "Leaving the principles of the gospel of Christ, let us go on unto perfection." He broke with the past, and so must we, because the future is before us. Let us reach forth unto the things which are before.

And what are the things which are before? The impenetrable curtain falls. God only knows the future; its tasks and sorrows, Giant Grim and Giant Despair, trials and tribulations; they are kindly hid from view. We pass into the new year as Abraham set forth by faith to journey into a country that he knew not.

But as we are followers of Christ Jesus, there are some things in the future which lie in clear view, to-wit: *the course, the mark,* and *the prize* of our high calling.

1. *The Course.* There is a race set before us—the straight path of the Christian life,—the path to manhood and character and usefulness. Are we in the lists? What is our high purpose at the opening of the year? Is it to get and hoard and spend upon ourselves? Is it as votaries of pleasure to chase butterflies and thistle-down? Is it to climb another round on the ladder of fame and position? Not if we are Christ's. One thing we do.

We are made for two worlds, like water-beetles that swim on the brooks in quiet places in summer. Dull creatures they seem, and yet among the cleverest, for they have two sets of eyes; one pair below watches for prey ; another pair above guards against the foe or looks toward the blue sky and the sunlight. So amid the sordid cares of earthly life we look toward better things. We seek, if we are true followers of the Nazarene, first of all the kingdom of God.

> The soul of man is like the rolling world,
> One-half in day, the other dipt in night ;
> The one has music and the flying cloud,
> The other, silence and the wakeful stars.

2. *The Mark.* Our eyes are toward the marble goal; that is, Christlikeness,—nay, more, oneness with him ; that we may know Christ and be found in him, not having our own righteousness, which is of the law, but the righteousness which is by faith in him.

We speak of the mystical union of the believer with Christ. In fact, however, there is no mystery here at all. Nor shall we attain our high ambition by dreaming and philosophizing about it. We shall not become Christlike by gazing upon the crucifix. It is a matter of plain common sense. To follow Christ, however difficult, is as simple a matter as for a child to follow in its mother's steps. He lived without guile ; so must we. He went about doing good ; so must we. He accepted truth as the chiefest thing ; and, without murmuring, so must we. To think his thoughts after him, to obey his precepts, to do his work, to spread his evangel, to reflect the moral beauty of his character, this is to win Christ and be found in him. This is the one thing which is worth doing, the one thing that needs to be done, the one thing that must be done. Is it the one thing I do ?

The " one thing " suggests an absolute concentration and unity of purpose. This is necessary to success in any ambition whatsoever of material or spiritual life. The "flying wedge" has been ruled out of amateur athletics, because it is an irresistible combination. It is energy with a point to it. It is avoirdupois piercing like a spear. It did not originate, however, with our football athletes; it was known to the ancient Romans and used as a mighty stratagem in battle. Nor did the Romans originate it. You may see the same manœuvre in a flight of wild geese. There is no resisting the onward movement of a man who has converged all his energies to a single point, and who can say, "One thing I do."

The Apostle Paul had *three callings*. (*a*.) He was a *tent-maker;* this was his trade. A livelihood is necessary to life. Paul took his needle with him wherever he went. All honest men do likewise. (*b*.) He was *a philosopher;* this was his profession. He had been trained in a school of the Rabbis. He had attended the University of Jerusalem, where he sat at the feet of Gamaliel, called "The Flower of the Law." He was familiar also with the learning of the philosophic schools of Greece. (*c*.) But all this accomplishment was subordinated to high spiritual uses. He was pre-eminently *an Apostle of Christ;* this was his business. He was "sent," as all Christians are sent, to seek the kingdom in doing the Master's will. And this was always supreme. This was the one thing which he did. In this he was a single-hearted man.

3. *The Prize;* namely, the high calling of God in Christ Jesus. The proudest moment in the life of an ancient athlete was when, victorious in the Olympic race, he went up higher to receive the laurel wreath

from the king's hand. A year ago the Olympic games were revived in Athens. When they were over, the victors in the various contests passed in procession around the arena. I have seen a photograph of that scene. A sea of faces is looking down from the galleries. The people have risen to their feet, and are shouting forth their acclamations. The group of victors are passing along the course over which they had just before run so strenuously. Among them are three American youths carrying flags and with their right hands uplifted. Proud and happy are they? O this is but child's play! What will heaven be, think you, when the race is run? This was in the mind of the Apostle when he said, "The time is at hand; I have fought a good fight, I have finished my course, I have kept the faith; henceforth there is laid up for me a crown of righteousness which the Lord, the righteous Judge, shall give me in that day."

There are two ways of living. One is to go along the dead level of sordid life; shoving the plane, preparing briefs, engaging in household tasks, sewing on buttons, pursuing handicraft, day after day grinding like Samson at the mill with no elevating thought of future blessedness, no high ambition—just trudging on, staff in hand, to the end of the journey—and then a blank wall of darkness. The other is climbing a steep path up the hills, higher and higher; wondering with each new attainment if this is the last, if this grace will complete character, if this task will round out the record of duty, if this cross shall bear the inscription, "It is finished!"; only to find at each summit that there are new summits rising into the sky, new paths to climb; the air growing purer and the sun shining clearer all along the way; until one day we come to a mountain-top where there is nothing beyond but heaven; as Moses ascended Nebo and saw the land that flowed with milk and honey. The golden gates of heaven opening like a sunset! And a voice, the welcoming voice of the Master, calling still, "Higher! higher! higher!"; and then the transport to heavenly tasks and duties in the kingdom of God.

Is it worth while? Ask the multitudes of saints triumphant. "Earth seems so little and so low when heaven shines full and bright." The domes of the celestial city ring with the shout of high ambition and eternal progress; "Higher! higher! higher!" For this we may cheerfully suffer the loss of all things. Forgetting, remembering, repenting, rejoicing, striving, hoping ever, we press toward the mark for the prize of the high calling of God.

> Awake, my soul, stretch every nerve,
>   And press with vigor on:
> A heavenly race demands thy zeal,
>   And an immortal crown.
>
> Tis God's all-animating voice
>   That calls thee from on high;
> 'Tis His own hand presents the prize
>   To thine aspiring eye.
>
> A cloud of witnesses around
>   Hold thee in full survey:
> Forget the steps already trod,
>   And onward urge thy way.

CAIN.

"They have gone in the way of Cain."—EPISTLE OF JUDE, 11th Verse.

The Epistle of Jude is called "catholic" because it is addressed not to any particular church, but to all generations, to all churches, to all sorts of men. It has to do with certain sins which prevail everywhere and always, and it denounces errors which are found under all conditions and in every period of time. It seems to have been called forth by the appearance of false teachers whose specific errors are not here exposed, but who are characterized as "trees without fruit, twice dead and plucked up by the roots"; as "clouds without water"; as "wandering stars reserved for the blackness of darkness." There are false teachers in every age, and history is always repeating itself in the ebb and flow of the tides of error.

The author of this Epistle characterizes these false teachers briefly in the phrase, "They have gone in the way of Cain." What was the "way of Cain"? In order to arrive at a definite determination of this, we must go back to the infancy of time. I wonder why my mind and conscience were directed to Cain in the early part of the week, when I was wondering what would be profitable for me and my people? I think it was the impression which had come to me, that we sometimes deal unfairly with this man.

There is something to be said even for Cain, although his is a most repugnant figure. We scarcely like to mention him, but there is something to be said even for him. A legend which prevailed among the early Christian fathers says, that as Jesus was going to the Temple one day he drew near to the Gate Beautiful, and there in the market-place a mad dog had been killed. A crowd of the people stood around reviling it; one saying one hard thing about the poor creature, and another saying another hard thing. The Teacher Jesus presently said, "What beautiful teeth he has!"

It is a simple legend for the children of the early days, but it illustrates the fact that there is something good everywhere if we will only find it, and there is no man so abandoned, and never has been, but that there was some lingering remnant of the spark of divineness in him.

Now observe that Cain was *the first victim of the law of heredity*. On the day when he was born his mother cried in the delight of the moment, "I have gotten a man from Jehovah"; the same joy that all mothers have when they hold their first-born in their hands. "I have gotten a gift from Heaven!" And she called him "My Treasure"—for that is the meaning of Cain—just as mothers call their children treasures at this day. She looked down into his face and dreamed dreams about him and wondered—for he was the first child ever born into the world—and saw visions of bright coming days. But disappointment awaited her; when another brother was born she called him "Disappointment"—for that is the meaning of Abel: "Vanity," or "Disappointment." Something had come in between which had dashed that mother's hope. What was it? The one constant factor in human nature and history; to-wit, sin! Sin had somehow developed already in the heart of her treasure. He had inherited it.

We speak of "original sin." You may call it whatever you please. If you have a prejudice against the doctrine of original sin, call it "heredity." It is bad enough anyway. It means simply that the blood of our fathers and mothers, with all its lading of sin and habit and shame, comes surging down through successive generations, and is flowing through us. Heredity!—he inherited sin.

What do we mean by the law of heredity? What is a law? It is the resultant of observations of phenomena. Here is a universal phenomenon. You never saw a child that did not, approaching the time of thoughtfulness and self-dependence, reach the condition of a sinner; you never knew one. You never saw a righteous man. There is the universal phenomenon. There is no qualification; we are all sinners. Wherever it came from, it is here. Heredity is a fact, and the statement of the result of the observation of this universal phenomenon is the law of heredity: or, as I prefer to call it—because I want to honor the orthodoxy of the Fathers,—original sin. No better philosophic expression has ever been found for it in science or theology than in the New England Primer:

> In Adam's fall
> We sinnèd all.

Observe, next: Cain was *the first heir of the covenant of grace.* As he was the first victim of the law of heredity, so he was the first heir of the covenant of grace. He had the Bible and he had the Cross. No sooner had Adam sinned than the Bible came, the protevangel. God said to him, "The seed of the woman shall bruise the serpent's head, and it shall bruise his heel;" that is to say, the seed of woman was somehow to redeem the fallen race, and in doing so there was to be the shedding of his blood. Now, that protevangel was the Scripture of those days. It was the nucleus of all the Scripture we have now. Holy men wrote, until the close of the sacred canon, all around that earliest evangel. "All scripture given by inspiration" is but the accumulation of God's Word; the heart of it all is the protevangel, in which came the announcement of the Christ.

Along with that protevangel came the altar. The altar is there with the very opening of history,—as the rabbis say—" close by the gates of Paradise"; for the family were now dwelling in Eden, just outside the Paradise from which they had been expelled. To use the symbolism of the Book, the angel with a flaming sword stood yonder at the gate to prevent their return to their primeval joys. The angel with the uplifted sword, God's ambassador of mercy as well as of justice, will yet open the gate, but now he keeps it closed during the prevalence of earthly sin. In that angel standing by the gate with flaming sword, the token of God's abiding presence in both justice and mercy, we have the earliest appearing of the Shechinah, or the glory of God: the luminous cloud which afterwards led the children of Israel, a pillar of cloud by day and of fire by night; the same token of the divine presence which afterwards hovered above the ark of the covenant and its golden cover, the mercy-seat, which was sprinkled with the blood of the sacrificial lamb; the same Shechinah that was seen on the Mount of Transfiguration; the Shechinah which still shines in the effulgence about the Cross, and illuminates the nations. There by the gate of Paradise stood the altar with the blood flowing over it, the symbolic fulfilment and presentation of the truth of the protevangel,—"the seed of woman shall bruise the serpent's head, and it shall bruise his heel:" that is to say, "Without the shedding of blood there is no remission of sin."

Observe, next, that Cain was *the first neretic*. He took issue both with the protevangel and with the altar. He said substantially that he would have his own way of thinking, and so far forth he was right. But every man ought to be a free thinker within the prescribed limits of thought; otherwise he becomes a wild rover of the seas. Cain said, "I will do my own thinking. Why should there be blood in my religion? Why shall I bring the first-fruits of the flock? I will bring the first-fruits of the field;" and he brought the first-fruits of the garden and of the field and laid them upon his altar. There stood Abel's altar with its bleeding lamb, and here was Cain's. He was simply a self-willed man, determined upon having his own way. He had rejected revelation; he had turned his back upon the protevangel; he had resolved that God can ask nothing more of a man than that he shall give his best, that he shall love righteousness and observe truth—what more can God ask? There was no atonement upon his altar; there was no recognition of the fact that "The blood of Jesus Christ cleanseth us from all sin."

There is no heresy, beloved, except in the antagonism to Scripture and the rejection of the Cross, and there in embryo was the rejection of both Scripture and the Cross. For that reason God took cognizance of Abel's sacrifice, and preferred it to the other. It was a token of absolute loyalty to the revelation of his mercy in the foregleam of the Cross of our Lord and Saviour, Jesus Christ.

And observe, next, that Cain was *the first murderer*. The murder began by the side of that altar, when as it is written, "He was wroth, and his countenance fell." Then he lifted the bludgeon to kill his brother: as the Scripture saith, "He that hateth his brother is a murderer." Envy, jealousy and bloody wrath were born within him at that moment. The murder was not consummated, it may be, for years afterwards. It is said that as they went out together in the field on some occasion, long after perhaps, he "smote Abel that he died." The rabbis say that the suggestion came from the enemy of souls, who went before him and smote a goat with a stone that he fell dead. In any case, Cain as yet knew nothing of death. There had never been any such thing in the history of man.

Cain slew his brother, and then, as the legend says, he put the dead body upon his shoulder and went hither and yon, not knowing what to do with it. As there had never been death, so there had never been burial. A raven came and buried its mate in the earth, and so Cain perceived how he might put the dead away out of his sight. With that load lifted from his shoulder, but the spectre still before him, he went on crying, "My punishment is greater than I can bear."

Observe, next, that Cain was *the first enemy of missions.* He stood beside the first grave that ever was digged upon the earth, and God spake to him: "Where is Abel, thy brother? His blood crieth unto me from the ground, which hath opened her mouth to receive it." And Cain answered, "I know not; am I my brother's keeper?" He was the father of all the misanthropes, and selfish people on the earth, who say, "I have all I can do to take care of myself and my kinsfolk. I am not going to worry about other people"; of all who say, "My neighbor is the one who lives only next door: I have nothing to do with the Chinaman who lives the other side of the earth"; the father of the man who said recently in an editorial in one of our leading papers against missions: "We have so many poor, hungry, suffering people at home—why should we give money to Borria-boola-gha?"

A solidified body, no matter how solid it is, has motion continually going on within it. A block of granite is simply a mass of motion; every particle is moving upon its neighbor. That is human society. You touch your remotest neighbor somehow or other. We say, "*noblesse oblige*,"—that is to say, "a noble birth has its responsibilities." To what? You are born of God, the universal Father of the race, who hath "created all men of one blood for to dwell upon the face of the earth." That makes you neighbor to every man: *noblesse oblige*—this is your responsibility, and you must carry it. There is the word of the Master: "Thou art thy brother's keeper; go thou to the remotest part of the earth and preach the Gospel to every neighbor of thine."

And observe, next, that Cain was *the first vagabond.* He went out curséd from the earth to be a wanderer and a vagabond upon it. God said, "Thou art curséd from the earth." God did not curse him. He simply stated an eternal fact. The man whose hands are stained with bloodguiltiness, as every man's hands are stained if he hateth his brother, or has in him the essence of selfishness, is curséd from the earth. And every such man is a wanderer from the face of God.

The curse was a self-imposed curse. The only hell there is in the universe is the hell that a man makes for himself, and upon which God puts the seal of eternal justice when he says, "Depart from me," The only hell there is in the universe is to be without God, and so without hope; to wander away from the luminous cloud that hung yonder above the gate of Paradise; to pass forever out of sight of it and feel that there is to be no Paradise Regained. The undying worm is true; the fire that never is quenched is true: but no worm can gnaw like the remorse of the soul that is exiled from God; no fire can burn like the despair of a man who has fled from before the face of his God. That was in the cry of Jesus, when in the consummation of his death agony he cried: "Eloï, Eloï, lama sabachthani?" going out himself as a wanderer and a vagabond, as the representative of all the lost and ruined human race, into the blackness of outer darkness, away from the face of God: "My God, my God, why hast thou forsaken me?"

Here the curtain falls upon Cain. We are told only a little of the sequel. Why was not capital punishment inflicted upon Cain beside his dead brother that day? Why? Because that man, and all other men, must have another chance. God bears with us to the uttermost limit of our probationary life, and gives us full warning of the dead line. Let Cain go yonder bearing the spectre of his pain and punishment with him. God will go with him. God puts a mark upon him. We speak of the mark of Cain as if it were a curse. It was the mark of God's mercy. If there were any visible mark on the man's forearm, as the rabbis say, or on his forehead, I know what it was : it was the mark of the Cross. He went out, away toward the East, to bear with him the assurance that God was still ready to forgive—for there is no limit to his mercy, and even bloodguiltiness cannot stand as a barrier between a guilty soul and the peace of God—he went out and built a city, unable to bear his solitude. He became the father of enterprising men, the Cainites, the handicraftsmen of those days. I wonder if ever he built an altar. There is a glimmer of hope for Cain in the fact that he called his firstborn "Enoch"— "Consecration ; " and that he called the name of his city, "Given to God," and that he had another son, "Methusael"—" The Champion of God." He had apparently not forgotten the meaning of the mark or sign, whatever it was, that God was ready to forgive that him.

Here we leave him. But, beloved in Christ, let us take heed and beware of the way of Cain. Go back far enough now to remember this: that the whole trouble came from his rejection of the protevangel and the altar. Let us believe in God's revelation, and not interpose our own vain reason betwixt our welfare and the wisdom of God. Let us accept the Christ, the Lamb of God, slain from the foundation of the world. The blood of that early sin crieth still from the ground, but "the blood of Christ speaketh better things than that of Abel."

At the very moment when Cain was contemplating his crime, when he was wroth and his countenance fell, the voice of God said, "Why art thou wroth? If thou doest not well, if thine altar is not right, if there is no blood in thy faith, if there is no atonement in thy religion, if thou hast rejected Christ thus far—why art thou wroth? A sin-offering lieth at thy door": as if a lamb were there bound and ready for the altar, and all that Cain needed to do was to displace the first-fruits of the field—the religion which he had made out of his own fancy and reason— and place the lamb upon the altar, and render unto God a just sacrifice in the acceptance of the Lord Jesus Christ, who appeared thus early in this foregleam and silhouette of the Cross.

That altar, the Cross of our Lord Jesus Christ, still stands close by the gate of Paradise. He who believes in Christ, though he may wander far eastward, as Cain did; though he may have followed his own devices all through a long lifetime; though his hands be red with bloodguiltiness—if he believes in Christ, the Lamb of God, slain from the foundation of the world, shall enter in, and have a right at last to the tree of life which is in the midst of the Paradise of God.

THE ELOQUENT SILENCE OF JESUS.

"If it were not so, I would have told you."—JOHN xiv. 2.

It is a little thing to say of Jesus that he was an honest man. And yet there is much in that; for "an honest man's the noblest work of God." Moreover, there is nothing so rare. The rule among men is masks and disguises. Not one of us would be willing to have a window in his breast through which our neighbors might see the secret imaginations of our hearts.

An honest man is a two-sided man; that is, his silence is as honest as his speech. It is customary in Siam to punish an incorrigible falsifier by sewing up his lips. But the cure is inadequate; for a lie may be told by the lifting of the eyebrows, or the pointing of a finger. It is possible "to convey a libel with a frown, or wink a reputation down." Indeed, a falsehood may be told by making no motion at all. A gossip comes to you with a scandalous story which you have reason to believe is false; in common honesty you should make an indignant denial, but you utter not a word. Speak up, man! Silence gives consent. Silence is a liar, a slanderer, a forsworn enemy to friendship and truth and righteousness.

Let us say then that Jesus, the divine Teacher, was absolutely honest. There was no guile on his lips; there was no guile in his heart. His life was as transparent as his utterance; his silence was as candid as his speech.

There are those who insist upon having no creed save the teachings of Christ. If that statement may be accepted in its full significance, we shall not dissent from it. The teachings of our Lord had to do with all the great problems and verities of the endless life. But when we speak of his teachings, we must be permitted to include his eloquent silence. For in many ways his silence was more eloquent than his words. He found his disciples in possession of certain views respecting truth, of which, had they been false, it was his simple duty as an honest Master to dispossess them. It is with this consideration in mind that we turn our attention now to his assurance, "If it were not so, I would have told you."

First, with respect to himself. The world had been looking for the coming of Christ. This feeling of expectancy was universal, but the Jews in particular were on the *qui vive*. The coming of Messiah was spoken of as "The Consolation of Israel." They had been led by their prophets from time immemorial to believe, that in the fulness of time one would appear who should restore the glory of their nation. His nature and character were predicted in minute detail. This was "The Hope of Israel." The disciples of Jesus as Jews shared in the common expectancy. In their familiar intercourse with Jesus, listening to his sermons and beholding his wonderful works, they came to believe that he was the long-expected Christ. Let it be observed, that he permitted them to entertain that view and uttered no word against it.

At the beginning of his ministry he was announced by John the Baptist as the Lamb of God. The term had no significance whatever, except as it pronounced Jesus to be the antitype of all the sacrifices which the children of Israel had been wont to offer in expiation of their sins. John meant, if he meant anything, that Jesus was "the Lamb of God slain from the foundation of the world." It was so understood by the disciples, though with only a dim apprehension of the manner in which that intimation was to be ultimately fulfilled. And Jesus allowed his disciples to rest in that view of his office and work.

As he was once journeying through Cæsarea-Philippi, he made inquiry of his disciples, "Who do men say that I am?" And when they answered, "Some say one thing, and some say another," he further inquired, "But who say ye that I am?" Then Peter witnessed his good confession, "Thou art the Christ, the Son of the living God." Not only did Jesus make no disavowal, but he distinctly consented in the words, "My Father which is in heaven hath revealed it unto thee."

In the upper room he met his disciples after his resurrection, and bade doubting Thomas thrust his fingers into his wounds in evidence of his triumph over death. Then the skeptical disciple fell before him, crying, "My Lord and my God." Had Jesus been less than very God of very God, he must, in common honesty, have said in that very moment, like the angel in the Apocalypse, "See thou do it not." But he permitted this act of divine homage, and so by his silence distinctly avowed his equality with God.

There are moments when all believers are tempted to doubt. How could it be otherwise, when the great verities lie in the realm of the invisible, and we have only fleshly eyes? We walk by faith. Our faith as Christians rests upon the testimony of our Lord. We stand at the manger, bewildered by the mystery of the incarnation. How can it be that he whom the heaven of heavens could not contain, lies here, wrapped in swaddling bands? We stand under the cross and say, "How can it be that the Sovereign of Life should thus bow to the King of Terrors?" We stand at the open sepulchre and say within ourselves, "How can it be that one whose helpless hands were folded over his breast, should by his own power break these bands and take captivity captive?" At this point the silence of Jesus is as convincing as his speech. "Ye believe in the incarnation, ye believe in the atonement, ye believe in the resurrection, and ye rightly believe; for if these things were not so, I would have told you."

Second, as to Scripture. At the time of the advent, the Jewish people had the most implicit faith in their oracles. The Scribes were an order of Biblical experts, set apart to the study of the Scriptures. They would not touch the parchment with unwashen hands; they weighed and measured the relative value of its doctrinal truths and precepts. If ever "Bibiolatry" prevailed on earth, it was in those days. The people regarded the Scripture as the whole truth, and nothing but the truth. They taught it to their children; they committed it to memory; they bound it as frontlets between their eyes.

The disciples of Jesus, as loyal Jews, shared in the common belief as to the infallibility of holy writ. In determining upon his Messiahship, their only question was whether or not he adjusted himself to the prophecies. Like ourselves, they received the Scriptures as their infallible rule of faith and practice. If they were mistaken in this opinion of Scripture, Christ as their honest teacher should have told them so.

It was charged that he opposed himself to the Scriptures because he had denied the traditions of the elders. In refuting this charge he repeatedly announced his loyalty to "the Law and the Prophets," that being the technical title of the Scriptures at the time. He said, "I am not come to destroy the Law, but to fulfill it"; and, "Not one jot or tittle of the Law shall pass away until all be fulfilled." He said again, "Search the Scriptures, for in them ye think ye have eternal life, and these are they which testify of me." In his sacramental prayer for his disciples he said, "Sanctify them by thy truth, thy word is truth." He referred with approval to many of those particular portions of Scripture which in some quarters are now alleged to be fabulous and false. He made reference to the story of Lot's wife, the destruction of the cities of the plain, and the deluge. He referred to Jonah in the whale's belly as a prophetic type of his resurrection from the dead, and, in a manner, adventured the genuineness of his mission and work upon the truth of it.

At this point we find ourselves in a serious dilemma. If the Scriptures are not true, our Lord either knew or did not know it. In the latter case he was manifestly not qualified to be a teacher in spiritual things. To say that Jesus, in emptying himself of the form of his divine attributes went so far as to become ignorant in matters supremely important to spiritual life, is to rob him of all that should constitute a true Saviour of men. To say that he was not so wise in his acquaintance with the great doctrines of the spiritual world, or with the oracles that reveal them, as some of our modern Biblical experts, is to blaspheme the incarnate Son of God. It is difficult to see how any who accept that view, should profess to receive him as Prophet, Priest or King.

But the alternative is worse. If Jesus was aware that the Scriptures were not true, as his disciples received them, but in fact largely a collection of myths and traditions in many points untrustworthy and false—this being the position which many of our destructive critics have assumed—and by his silence allowed his disciples to rest in their fetich worship, their faith in falsehood, their misapprehension of alleged truth, then it is impossible to regard him as an honest man.

The great body of Christian people in these days have an implicit faith in Scripture. They mean what they say when they profess to receive it as the infallible rule of their faith and practice. Many of them "just know, and know no more, their Bible's true." The very air is full of insinuations against the book. Have we been mistaken in our confidence? Have we been affixing our faith to a redactor's collection of myths and fables? It is impossible to believe that Christ who has promised to direct his people, as he led his disciples into truth, should have permitted us to rest in such a calamitous misapprehension. We believe in the Scriptures because we believe in him. Our faith in the oracles rests upon the honesty of our great Teacher. There is infinite assurance in his word, "If it were not so, I would have told you."

Third, as to the "Larger Hope." The Jews believed in Gehenna. Their thought of eternal punishment found its illustration in a deep ravine called Hinnom close by the temple, where the offal of the sacrifices was thrown. There the fires were always burning, and decay was a continuous process. From this came the phrase, "Their worm dieth not, the fire is not quenched." The Jews believed in a future life. They believed furthermore that the present life is probationary and that the future state must be determined by character formed here and now. "As the tree falleth so shall it lie." And they believed also in the eternity of punishment. To these views which were shared by the disciples Jesus gave the weight of his authority again and again. He spoke of the separation of the wheat from the tares; of the goats from the sheep; of Lazarus from Dives. He spoke of hell as a place of weeping and wailing and gnashing of teeth. He used the phrase *aion ton aionon*, "forever and ever." He said, "If thy hand offend thee, cut it off: it is better for thee to enter into life maimed, than, having two hands, to go into hell, into the fire that never shall be quenched; where their worm dieth not, and the fire is not quenched. And if thy foot offend thee, cut it off: it is better for thee to enter halt into life, than, having two feet, to be cast into hell, into the fire that never shall be quenched; where their worm dieth not, and the fire is not quenched. And if thine eye offend thee, pluck it out: it is better for thee to enter into the kingdom of God with one eye, than, having two eyes, to be cast into hell-fire; where their worm dieth not, and the fire is not quenched."

It thus appears that the direct teaching of Jesus was most positive as to the matter of eternal punishment for unforgiven sin. The suggestion that his warnings were not founded upon an actual danger, but merely intended to frighten the indifferent, is not for a moment to be allowed. He found his disciples and the people generally believing in an awful truth, and he left them there. Had there been a "Larger Hope," a reasonable ground for the thought of another probation in the future life, he must have suggested it. He was the kindest soul that ever lived on earth, yet by his words, and still more by his silence with reference to the common belief, he taught that the only hope of salvation is in repentance in this present life. The belief of the universal church of Christ is the same; and if it were not true he would have told us.

Fourth, as to heaven. His disciples had given up all to follow him. For their devotion to his Messianic claims, they were cast out of the synagogues and persecuted in many ways. The axe was always gleaming before their eyes; but they believed in the compensation of a blessed future. They looked forward to a gladsome day, when abundant restitution should be made for all their privations and sufferings. We entertain the same hope. We reckon that the sufferings of this present time are not worthy to be compared with the glory that shall be revealed in us.

The teaching of Jesus with reference to heaven is most comprehensively found in his words, "In my Father's house are many mansions, if it were not so, I would have told you; I go to prepare a place for you." It is a prepared place for a prepared people. It is a home where the redeemed shall meet in joy unspeakable and full of glory.

One of the most frequent questions with reference to heaven is, Shall we know each other there? It is inconceivable, in view of the relation of the disciples to each other and Christ, that they should not have entertained that view; and they must have been unspeakably encouraged in that belief by the words of Jesus in this connection: "If it were not so I would have told you."

Our view of heaven changes as our years increase. I can remember when my conception of heaven was chiefly associated with the glowing descriptions of the Apocalypse. It meant gates of pearl, and golden streets, and multitudes of white-robed angels hymning a perpetual song, "Holy, holy, holy Lord God Almighty!" But there came a time when a beloved sister fell asleep, and thereafter her face was always associated with every thought of that celestial city. Then the dear father went, and then the first-born of the household, and then another " with folded hands and dreamy eyes went through the gates of paradise." And now all heaven is full of faces, and there are hands beckoning and voices calling. So, more and more, as the years pass, do I realize the joyous significance of the Master's word, "My Father's house." Heaven is home.

> So part we sadly in the wilderness,
> To meet again in sweet Jerusalem.

This is the glorious hope which dwells in the hearts of God's people everywhere. We look for a gladsome day, when we shall see the familiar faces of those who have gone before us, and clasp hands in the unutterable joy of re-union, and shall go out no more forever. The words of the Master, so far as he spoke directly with reference to the unseen world, are all in harmony with this belief. Still more convincing, however, is his assurance, "In my Father's house are many mansions; if it were not so, I would have told you."

What then is our conclusion? Be not faithless, but believing. We are often tossed about in doubts and misgivings as the disciples were in their little boat on Gennesaret when Jesus came to them walking on the waves. "It is I," he said; "be not afraid." And Peter answered, "If it be thou, bid me come to thee upon the water." The Lord said: "Come." Peter set forth bravely until, as the billows surged about him, he began to sink and cry, "Lord save me or I perish." The hand of the Master was stretched forth with this word, "O thou of little faith, wherefore didst thou doubt?" Aye, beloved, wherefore did we ever doubt? Our faith is buttressed by the teachings of our Lord in his word and in his silence. The pagan Pythagoras said, "If God were ever to render himself visible among men, he would choose light for his body and truth for his soul." He has made himself visible among men in the incarnate form of Jesus, which shines ever upon us through an atmosphere of truth. Let us believe. This is the peace of Christian living, to believe in the absolute candor of the incarnate Son. "Ye believe in God," he said, "believe also in me. The things which I have taught you abide in infinite truth and wisdom. If it were not so, I would have told you."

I.—IN THE PORCHES OF BETHESDA.

"Now there is at Jerusalem by the sheep market a pool which is called in the Hebrew tongue Bethesda, having five porches. In these lay a great multitude of impotent folk, of blind, halt, withered, waiting for the moving of the water. For an angel went down at a certain season into the pool and troubled the water. Whosoever then first after the troubling of the water stepped in, was made whole of whatsoever disease he had."—JOHN v. 2-4.

[The statement about the angel, as everybody knows, is a gloss, and does not properly belong here. It crept in, perhaps at the hand of some monk who was copying the manuscript and put this explanation into the margin; whence it found its way into the text.]

The Feast of Purim did not belong to the ceremonial religion of Israel. It was distinctly a secular feast: that is to say, it was not by divine ordinance. There were three annual religious festivals · Pentecost, Tabernacles, and Passover; but the children of Israel celebrated the Purim with the greatest enthusiasm, because it commemorated their deliverance from the awful massacre which had been planned by wicked Haman, the prime minister of King Ahasuerus. After the people were saved through the intercession of Esther, the three days' fast beginning with the 14th of Adar was changed into a three days' festival, and it is celebrated among the Jews to this day.

I.—IN THE PORCHES OF BETHESDA.

During this feast Jesus came down to Jerusalem. No doubt he betook himself first of all to the Temple, for his heart was always there. If so, he heard the priest reading from the book of Esther, and observed the people, at every mention of the name of Haman, their persecutor, all with one accord stamp their feet and cry, "The name of the wicked shall rot!" He saw there the offering of the sacrifices, and heard the thanksgivings. But this was in the decadence of Israel, and he knew that while the people were worshiping God and rejoicing with their lips, their hearts were far from him. The atmosphere of the temple was stifling to this Son of Man, so he betook himself into the streets of Jerusalem. The people were waving green branches, masquerading, singing, and making merry, in every way: and the Lord's heart was out of sympathy with it. Where should he go? His soul was burdened with the thought of an agonizing humanity and with a desire to deliver the children of men.

He turns his steps toward the booths and the tables by the sheep market, and so reaches Bethesda —the House of Mercy—a pentagonal booth with five porches, wherein lie many incurables—impotent folk, cripples, the halt and the withered, who have been forsaken of their friends and have given up hope. Here they lie about the central pool, watching, waiting, for the moving of the water when an angel shall come down and brush the water with his wing. It was an intermittent thermal spring, and it was thought that whosoever first entered into the water when it should be moved was delivered from whatsoever disease he had. So these forlorn folk were watching for the ripple upon the pool. Many of them were suffering from nervous maladies, as seems to be suggested in the words "impotent folk;" and people who suffer in that way are oftentimes cured even by superstition. There is no more potent remedy in all the materia medica than the imagination. Ask Christian Science if that be not so. Poor, suffering folk! The whole world was a Bethesda in those days.

A few years ago a pamphlet appeared with this title: "The Bitter Cry of Outcast London." It was an awful picture of the shame and the suffering of that populous city. Then, presently, there came a book written by General Booth, of the Salvation Army, with this title: "In Darkest England." People now began to think about the great unseen multitude who were suffering all about them, and a new word came in,—"Slumming." It became the proper thing to do; and respectable people went about visiting among the distressed of that metropolitan city. It is about the thing represented in that word that I wish to speak to you. I like better an expression that came in with the Lord Jesus Christ. "Slumming" is good; "evangelizing" is better.

I. Note, to begin with, as we are here together in Bethesda, "*man's inhumanity to man.*" For that is what this means—the sufferers lying friendless and forsaken, while all Jerusalem is celebrating its Saturnalia; while the people are laughing and singing and making merry in the streets. Here they lie—the lame, the withered, and the halt, the friendless, and the despairing, waiting for the moving of the pool.

> Man's inhumanity to man
> Makes countless thousands mourn.

Do you remember Landseer's picture of the

wounded stag creeping with trembling steps toward the edge of the pool for his last refreshing draught before he dies, while off yonder the herd are fleeing across the hills? It is a picture of common life. Here they are—the forsaken. Where are their friends?

> O, it is pitiful,
> Near a whole city full,
> Friends they have none.

Selfishness is born in us. Here it is: two children and two apples on a plate; the boy says to his little sister, "You choose." That is magnanimous. She chooses the larger, and he says to her, "You selfish thing! I meant to choose that myself." It is born in us. "The carnal mind is enmity against God," and is enmity against man.

Out in Bombay they are suffering from the plague and are probably going to suffer more and more. To-day when one is stricken, his pagan friends forsake him. While we sit so comfortably in the sanctuary, the dead are lying in the streets of Bombay unburied. Little children are abandoned by their mothers, and wives are forsaken by their husbands. It is so the whole world over, and it is too much so, alas! among those who profess to be the followers of Christ, the elect of the world. Selfishness is still in us.

If I were to speak of "the Tenderloin" here, you would resent the word; but you cannot do better than face the fact, for it is close to us. This church elbows it—a great, surging world of shame and unspeakable vice; vice of men and women of high degree and low degree; shame unspeakable; crime everywhere, hiding behind the doorways; political and social vice just beside us. We would rather not hear about it. God pity them, and God pity us, unless, like the Lord Jesus, we find our way to our Bethesda and relieve it! Whether it is right here, or out on our frontiers, or by the banks of the River Congo, the word of the Master is always the same. "Ye are the salt of the earth." Salt sweetens; salt purifies. "But if the salt have lost its savour, wherewith shall it be salted? It is thenceforth good for nothing but to be cast out and to be trodden under foot of men."

II. But now consider *the philanthropy of Jesus*. He comes to Bethesda. He is ever walking in the porches by the pool. If he were to come to New York to-day, would the churches receive him? I do believe they would—if they knew him. If he were to come into this aisle to-day, not a pew door would be closed against him. You who profess to follow the Lord Christ would all fall at his feet and kiss them in gratitude and love—if you knew him. But, alas! you might not know him, for perhaps he would come as a carpenter, clothed in homespun, and with horny, toil-worn hands. If he were to walk down the Avenue or Broadway, would all the people receive him? Yes, all—if they only knew him. But, alas! they might not know him. I doubt if those sufferers in Bethesda knew him as he walked in the porches that day; but he was the ideal philanthropist, who set a pattern for all who love him.

Observe the marks of philanthropy in him:

First, *he sought the sufferers out*. He went with willing feet to Bethesda to find them. So must we. The beggars who meet us along the streets; the poor, sodden women with red faces and brows seamed and scarred with vice, and shawls drawn about their shivering forms, begging for a penny; the tramps who want their supper, and waylay us along the street —they have their claim upon us,—but, after all, those are not the people whom primarily we are bound to help. There is a world of shame and anguish and suffering that never comes out on the street to stretch out its hands, but hides away and says, "In God's name, come and find me"; poor seamstresses making shirts at thirty cents a dozen, and working seven days in the week to keep soul and body together; men with proud spirits dying to-day and asking no help; little children famished to skin and bone,—poor innocents who are above begging! Oh, if the roofs were lifted! If we could see into the attics! If we could look down into the basements! If our eyes could but gaze upon the "submerged tenth"! Our hearts would go out toward them.

God be praised for our Associated Charities! If we will not go to the suffering, our Associated Charities will go for us and find them out. But, after all, we cannot shift the burden that way. We must go to Bethesda ourselves. We must seek the suffering, that we may help them. That is the foundation of foreign missions as well as of city missions. "Go ye everywhere, evangelize, help as you can, the children of men."

Then observe, in the second place, that *Jesus looked on the sufferers.* He sought them out, and looked on them. Now, that is a great thing. There are multitudes of good people who are willing to help, but they do not want to look on suffering. "Don't harrow my soul with the story of pain. Here is my purse. Take all you want and give relief. My heart is bleeding; the tears are rolling down my cheeks. Take what you want, but don't talk about it any more. It rends me." O, the quackery of such charity as that! Go, look on the suffering! Look on it! See the shame and the hunger, the crime, the pain, the anguish! See it with your own eyes if you want to help it.

You can see pathos in the theatre. You love it there. You read it in the last novel. You will go clear through to the last chapter to find the climax of agony. But you turn your eyes from it in real life. The tenderest-hearted man that I ever knew was a surgeon whom I am glad to number among my cherished friends. I have seen him stand with knife in hand above the body of a man under anæsthetics, whom he counted as his brother. While we who stood near were all quivering at the sight, his hand was without a tremor; and as he cut close to the heart there was no sign of a tear falling from his eye. He had to look in order that he might help; so must you and I.

The third token of the real philanthropy of Jesus lay in the fact that *he pitied the sufferers.* There was one who for thirty and eight years had been impotent, hoping against hope, feeling all the while that there was nothing but misery awaiting him. The Lord looked on him and pitied him. You and I might have said, "It serves him right!" for the narrative tells us that this man was suffering for his sin. His vice had gotten into his flesh and bones, and he was reaping what he had sown. "Let him bear it!" That is the way we treat men. The Lord be praised that he does not take us at our word, for we are all suffering from our sins, and there is something to be said for the worst of us; but he pities all. He pitied the worst man that was in Bethesda that day.

Not long ago in an elevated train I was holding by a strap, and I saw a curious thing in front of me. There was a young man, and just behind him a young woman. I could not see her face—her back was toward me;—but with her left arm she clung to the young man's waist, and with her right hand she patted him on the shoulder now and then in a most affectionate way. It seemed to me and to others that she was doing an unseemly thing. But all at once she turned toward me, and I perceived that she was blind! It was her sense of utter dependence that made her cling that way. So we pass judgment behind people's backs.

> Then at the balance let's be mute
> We never can adjust them.

Then, note the fourth token of the real benevolence and philanthropy of Jesus in the fact that *having come and seen and pitied, he helped.* He administered relief to that worst man. He said to him, "Wilt thou be made whole? Take up thy bed and walk." Benevolence is not a sentiment; benevolence is a principle. Philanthropy is not a sentiment that finds its expression in mere tears and words of compassion. Philanthropy is a duty.

A traveller relates, that on the banks of the Nile, he saw multitudes of poor, sore-eyed, half-clad, wretched beggars who ran along crying for help in the name of God; and the captain of the boat, a Moslem, scarcely taking pains to turn his eyes toward them, kept repeating over and over again, "God pity you! God pity you! God pity you!" That is the way we do. A warm hand, with a penny in it, is worth all such expressions that a man can utter in a long life. The Lord Christ proved his compassion in that he administered help to those who needed it.

Dear friends, let us praise God that we have no Bethesdas in these days. You go to any of our hospitals and mark the cleanliness and sweetness there. See the physician with his skill, and the nurses in their white aprons, with soft words, soft steps and gentle touch: that is the Bethesda of Christendom to-day. O, there is an infinite gulf between Bethesda in old Jerusalem and our hospitals! What makes it? Jesus has been walking in the porches all through the ages, and the hospital, which is peculiar to the charméd circle that we call "Christendom," is a fruit of the philanthropy of the historic Christ. He is the divine patron of all the beneficence which distinguishes our modern civilization.

He has been walking among the nations, also. Is not your heart glad to-day because of the arbitration treaty? Are you not praising Jehovah because the two great Anglo-Saxon peoples have clasped hands and said, "There shall be no more garments rolled in blood." What does that mean? It means that Christ has been walking through the porches, and that at last the sword that maims and cuts and kills is sheathed. Swords shall be beaten into plowshares, spears into pruning hooks, and Shiloh shall come.

We are moved to-day with a sense of obligation toward all the suffering children of men. Let me admonish you before you leave this sanctuary that *it is a great mistake to go slumming without God.* There are people who do it, but it is an awful thing to pass out amid the shame and suffering of the world, to see the gaping wounds, the breaking hearts, the suffering children, poor, desolate, friendless humanity, so overwhelming, so multitudinous, everywhere, and not to feel that God rules. If there is no God, what is the sufferer to me, or I to him? Let him suffer on. Let him bear his anguish to-day; tomorrow he will be gone, and there is an end. If there is a God—O, if there is a Father, and I am his son—and if he has a great family of people who are bound together in a mighty, organic unity which we call the Church of God—and if the world rolls around every day further into his light, and he is having his way among the children of men, then I can go with my message, believing that in the fulness of time he will heal all. "The hills and the mountains shall break forth before him into singing, and the trees of the field shall clap their hands." "He shall wipe away the tears from all faces." All is right if God be in the reckoning; all is wrong, forever, horridly wrong, without God.

One thing more, and then we are done with Bethesda until to-night. *It is a dreadful mistake to go slumming with nothing but bread;* for down below the hunger, and deep under the gaping wound, there is a longing for something better than that. Man is made in the divine likeness, with a longing for joys and hopes that reach out into an endless life. If we go out to save and deliver and help, let us go not only with bread, but with absolution ; with the message of the Lord Jesus Christ, "Come unto me, all ye that labor and are heavy laden, and I will give you rest ; " rest from your wounds, and your heartaches, and your hunger; rest from your despair and fearful looking forward to judgment ; " for the Son of Man hath power on earth to forgive sins."

II.—IN THE PORCHES OF BETHESDA.

"And a certain man was there which had an infirmity thirty and eight years."
—JOHN v. 5.

It was a desperate case. Observe some of the unfavorable symptoms.

To begin with, *the disease was chronic;* the man had been thus afflicted for thirty and eight years. O, what a story of suffering and hope deferred! If all the pains and weariness and disappointments of those thirty-eight years could be bound together, what a bundle of sorrow they would make! Thirty-eight weary years he had been waiting for relief, and waiting in vain.

Then, also, *his disease was self-imposed.* Vice had brought it upon him. There are some ills that we inherit from our forebears. I think my father must have exposed himself somewhere on a wet day, and given me this twinge of rheumatism which I feel occasionally in my right shoulder. Your mother before your birth was frightened at something, by reason of which you were always a timid child, and are now, perhaps, afflicted with nervous debility. Our convivial ancestors sat up at late suppers, over-drank and over-ate, and we have inherited dyspepsia. Thus many of our ills are heirlooms; we call this fact "heredity." No doubt the man at Bethesda had inherited much, but this particular disease was definitely his own. I saw a skeleton a little while ago in the office of a physician; and on one of the bones was a very manifest scar, a circular indentation. "What is that?" I asked. He glanced at it, and said simply, "Vice." And I remembered what the Good Book says: "The bones of the wicked are full of the sins of their youth." This cripple had reason to be the more hopeless because he had made his own bed and doomed himself to lie in it.

Moreover, it was probably *a repulsive disease;* for his friends and kinsfolk had abandoned him. He was here so absolutely friendless and alone that he had none, when the water was moved, to put him down into it. Did you ever hear of a more pathetic case? "For while I am coming, another steppeth down before me." No doubt I am looking into the faces of men and women who feel desperately lonely and friendless. There are multitudes of young men and young women, here in New York, growing up with the enterprise of the great city, who have left the memories and delights of home behind them. One said to me the other day, "I have been here a year and a half, and I have not made a single friend." But there is One that sticketh closer than a brother—One who will come to you in the little hall bedroom alone at night, and stay with you there, closer than touching or seeing, who will commune with you and delight your soul. There is no friend so near, so kindly, so always true and helpful, as my Lord and Saviour, Jesus Christ. But this man in Bethesda knew little or nothing of him.

There were, however, some favorable symptoms. His case was by no means as desperate as it might have been.

First of all, *he knew his condition.* There are some diseases that dull the consciousness; they are so insidious and deceptive that a man, though he feel the cold fingers of death close to his heartstrings, will not acknowledge his danger. Palsy is one of them, consumption is another. I had a sad duty to perform a while ago. A friend said to me that his eldest son was dying of a pulmonary trouble; he was not aware of his true condition, and would I tell him? I went into the room and said, "Good day; how are you?" "O, I shall be around in a few days," said he. His hands seemed as thin as a wafer; his poor face was pinched, and his eyes growing dull. I went over and laid my hand on his, so cold and clammy, saying, "My good fellow, you cannot live twenty-four hours." He looked up pathetically and asked, "Did the doctor say that?" "He did; this is your last day." He gazed straight at me for half a minute, and said, "I suppose, then, I ought to be getting ready to go."

Sin is one of those diseases, so insidious and deceptive that people will scarcely allow that they have it. The trouble is, that while our first impressions of guilt are deep enough, we harden our consciences against them, as a blacksmith hardens his arm amid the flying sparks of the forge, until we cease to feel them. We grow "immune," as physicians say. In Paris a year ago I saw the funeral of Pasteur moving through the city with great pomp and circumstance. He was buried with all the honors that the French people could lavish upon a distinguished citizen, because he had discovered the process of inoculation against certain sorts of diseases. But the honor was not Pasteur's. The snake charmers of India knew how to make themselves "immune" by inoculation long before Pasteur discovered it. The men who handle cobras are not afraid of the virus, because they have gradually inoculated themselves with the virus until the striking of a serpent's fang—which would be fatal to an ordinary man in six hours—is no more dangerous than an insect's sting.

The time was when you were sensitive to every appeal of the Gospel. If you were called upon to stand at the foot of Mount Sinai, under the lightnings and thunders of divine justice, you shook and trembled like an aspen. When you were urged to repent and to believe in the Lord Jesus Christ, you said in your heart, "I will, but not now. It is the right thing to do; I will only wait for a more convenient season." When you were exhorted to abandon certain of your darling sins, and you knew very well what those darling sins were, you said, "I will, but not just yet." Now you have grown immune. Sin dulls the conscience, pollutes the reason, makes null and void the power of the moral sense and delivers a man over unconsciously to spiritual death. The gospel phrase is, "dead in trespasses and sins." It may be that one of you, looking at me with two bright eyes this moment, is "dead in trespasses and sins." What is death? If I bend over a lifeless body and lift the eyelids, there is no responsive light. If I call for the sweetest music that ever was sung, there is no token of appreciation there. If I sear the white flesh, it will not shrink. That is death! A man may move about his ordinary occupations while his soul is dead. Dead men walk along our streets. Dead men are busy on the Stock Exchange. Dead men and women go about their common tasks, laughing and making merry; their souls as dead as if their grave were marked "Hic jacet." Their spiritual natures make no response to the great verities, God, Immortality, Judgment, Hell, Heaven. This is death.

But the man of Bethesda knew what ailed him. He looked with self-pity on his poor, shriveled limbs. He heard the footfall of those who passed by outside the porches, the romping children as they ran past, and said, "O, if I had but their strength, paralytic that I am!"

Then, secondly, *he wanted to be well.* O, if he might only be made whole. There was energy, if nowhere else, in his despair. There comes a time in similar cases when longing ends, but it was not so here. No doubt in these porches he and his fellow-sufferers spoke oftentimes of the moving of the water. He looked for the time when perhaps he would be enabled to receive its benefits, but it came not. Nevertheless he hoped against hope. I like the pluck, the courage, of this poor sufferer; after thirty-eight years of hope deferred he was still lying there, waiting to be healed of his infirmity.

Now and again some man who is burdened with the cares and troubles of life takes the short cut out of it—hangs himself to a rafter, or drowns himself in the river. The charitable version of suicide is, that the man went daft before he did it. The only alternative is to pronounce him a coward. The meanest man that lives is he who runs from the struggle of life, and perhaps leaves a wife and children behind to bear the strife and burden after he, with despicable cowardice, has fled from it

This man lay in the porches and heard of the

Wonder Worker who was going about healing desperate cases. He wist not who he was; but doubtless he heard them speaking of him. One said : "There was a nobleman in Capernaum who came to this new Prophet pleading that his son was in the very throes of death—would he come and heal him? and the Prophet spoke the word, and his son was made whole." Another said: "Yes ; and there was a leper standing afar off as he journeyed, with his finger on his lip, crying, 'Unclean ! Unclean !'—and they say that this Prophet spake the word, ' Be clean !' and the flesh of the incurable leper came to him like the flesh of a little child." And another of those sufferers said: "I hear that there was a man possessed of an unclean spirit, who came into the synagogue one day when the Prophet was there, and uttered lamentable cries, and the Prophet said to him, 'Come out, thou unclean spirit!' and a moment later the man, in his right mind, lay sobbing before his feet." Another said: "Up in Capernaum a few days ago there was a paralytic carried on a mattress to the place where this Prophet was preaching, and four of his friends bore him upon the roof, and let him down at the feet of the great Teacher and Wonder Worker ; and he, seeing the man lying helpless and incurable, said to him, 'Take up thy bed and walk !' and as the man arose he added, 'Thy sins be forgiven thee.'" Such rumors as these the man at Bethesda heard; and doubtless he said in his heart: "If he would but come ! Thirty and eight years have I suffered; thirty and eight years have I lain helpless and hopeless. O, if this healer of desperate cases would but come this way !"

A third thing in his favor is that *he had a will to be healed.* He knew his condition, he longed to be better;

and when the important moment came, he *willed for it*. The word of the Master, who walked through Bethesda that day, "Willest thou to be made whole?" inspired him with confidence. He did not know Jesus by name, but it may be there was something in the face of this visitor that led him to surmise. Then at the word of encouragement his will rose up and pleaded for healing. He willed. His will reached forth, like a stretched out hand, to grasp the proffered gift. So must yours, if you ever enter into life. If you are ever saved, it is because you meet Jesus half way; it is because your sovereign will, made like the will of your Father, with power to refuse or to accept his eternal grace, shall go out to accept it.

A man strangling in the river sees a rainbow. He remembers that the rainbow is the bow of promise, the token of the covenant of God. He remembers how it was said, "I do set my bow in the heavens as a sign that the earth shall no more be overwhelmed with a flood." But that does not help him. What he wants is a rainbow of his own. What he wants is to get hold of that rainbow, so as to be upheld by it. What he wants is to be brought into personal contact with that covenant, or it will never help him. The Cross saves no man. There is more blood in the fountain that was opened for uncleanness at Calvary than there is water in all the oceans; but there is not blood enough to save a man who will not wash and be cleansed in it.

Next, observe that *this man obeyed the injunction of the Lord immediately*. When Jesus said, "Arise; take up thy bed and walk!" he arose *straightway*. If ever there was a case of infirmity, moral or physical, where there seemed good reason to hesitate and argue before resolving, it was the case of this paralytic; for he was impotent. "'Arise; take up thy bed and walk!' What? Walk with these shriveled limbs that have not served me for thirty-eight years? Take up my bed with these arms that have lain so long numb and helpless beside me! Does this man mock me?"

Our fathers used to talk about "inability." Moral inability in consequence of sin is just as real as the impotency of that paralytic. The will is palsied. Mind, conscience and heart are palsied. Now, are you going to wait and question, and deliberate, and argue that subtle doctrine, while the Master stands by, saying, "Repent! believe! be baptized, and enter into life"? The power was given to the paralytic in the act of obedience. The power will be given to you in the same way. God works within you, and God helps those who help themselves straightway. Repent!—that is his word. You and I are sinners. Let us be frank with ourselves and him. Believe!—that is, stretch forth your hand. The will is the hand of the heart reached forth to take the gift of God. Be baptized!—that is to say, as an honest and grateful man, having accepted Christ, prove your sincerity by making an open confession of your loyalty to him.

One thing more about this paralytic: *he followed Christ*. As he left Bethesda, carrying his bed, the Pharisees met him. They said, "It is the Sabbath; it is not lawful for thee to carry thy bed." He was in no mood to discuss an abstruse question in ethics or theology just then. His answer was: "He that made me whole said to me, 'Take up thy bed and walk.' That is enough for me. He has put me under an eternal obligation. The word of the Man who made me whole is my court of last appeal." So is it for every Christian man. No church, no manifesto of any ecclesiastical judicatory can stand between a shriven and redeemed soul and the Master who said, "Arise; take up thy bed and walk—walk in the way of my commandments—walk on till thou pass through heaven's gate!"

A little later this happy man met Jesus—for this was during the Purim feast, when all the people were dividing portions in gratitude, and giving remembrances to friends, as we do at Christmas-tide— and Jesus gave him a Purim gift. He said, "Go, and sin no more, lest a worse thing come upon thee!" And he never spoke a better word than that to a redeemed soul. All the glory of Christian growth and character is in that word, "Go, and sin no more!" And the man went, telling about Christ, telling everywhere that it was Jesus of Nazareth, the great Prophet and Wonder Worker, who had healed him.

Is there an unshriven man or woman here? Is there one who has not accepted Christ? Is there one who has felt that his case, protracted through many years, and grown into a sort of moral indifference and stupidity, is almost beyond cure? Let me commend to you the case of the paralytic of Bethesda, and beg you, in this blessed hour, to meet the Master's overture of mercy as he met it.

In a fishing town on the southern coast of France, there was a great iron chain, fastened on the beach, and stretching out to an anchor in the bay. The skipper of a little fishing boat, while hurrying along the shore, accidentally stepped through one of the links. It seemed a small matter; but all efforts to extricate his foot were vain. The more he struggled, the worse his plight became. The foot was now chafed and swollen. He said to a comrade, "Go to the nearest village and bring the smith to saw this chain, for the tide is coming in." The smith was three miles away, and before he came the tide was at the skipper's feet. Then he said, "Bring a surgeon, I must lose my foot or my life. And make haste; the tide is coming in." But the surgeon was miles away, and the waters crept up, and were cold at his loins, at his waist, at his throat. It was too late for smith or surgeon. The minister of the little village came and offered a prayer, while death in the white foam kissed the man's lips. Nothing could be done for him.

We speak of desperate cases. There is not a foot-fast sinner whom Jesus cannot save. He is smith, surgeon and minister in one. He is able to save unto the uttermost all who will come unto him. There is no conceivable reason, except in the stubbornness and inactivity of our wills, why any man or woman should pass through those doors unsaved to-night. Some of you have grown gray in sin. Like the paralytic, you have waited, lo! these many years for healing. Here is the Great Physician, walking in the porches. Will you accept him? The reaching forth of the will, an immediate response to the Master's word, "Repent, believe and be baptized," will save you.

He spoke a word of immediate salvation to the woman who pressed upon him in the crowd, saying, "If I may but touch the hem of his garment, I shall be made whole;" and when she touched him she felt the warm currents of health flowing fast through her veins. Then Jesus turned and said, "Daughter, thy faith hath saved thee."

In like manner he spoke to the Magdalen who had spent her life in sin, but repented at last, breaking the alabaster box of precious ointment upon his feet: "Daughter, go in peace; thy faith hath saved thee."

Such a word of mercy he spoke to the blind man of Jericho, who cried as the Master was entering into the village, "Jesus, thou Son of David, have mercy upon me." And Jesus said, "What wilt thou?" "O, that I might receive my sight!" "Receive thy sight; thy faith hath saved thee." Faith saves! "He that believeth shall be saved." "Believe in the Lord Jesus Christ." Only believe!

WANTED : A NEWSPAPER.*

"And he sent letters by posts."—Esther 8, 10.

The progress of the centuries is seen in all the enlarged and improved activities of the race; but in nothing more conspicuously than the better facilities for disseminating news.

In early times the herald went about with his pack of tidings from hamlet to hamlet. The herald, the pursuivant and the courier, were the Mercuries of those days.

In the court-yard of Shushan is gathered a company of footmen stripped to the waist and girt about the loins, and of horsemen ready to mount at the signal. A royal proclamation giving immunity to the Jews who had been previously doomed to death, has been signed and sealed by Ahasuerus and must

---

*At a union meeting of ministers of the six leading evangelical denominations of New York City, on December 7th, 1896, a committee was appointed to consider the relation of ministers and Christian people to the newspaper press. The committee was thus constituted: Rev. J. M. Buckley, D.D., Rev. Wesley Johnson, D.D , Rev. J. B. Remensnyder, D.D., Rev. Robert S. MacArthur, D.D., Rev. William T. Sabine. D.D , Rev. John Hall, D D., Rev. David James Burrell, D.D. The report of this committee was heard at a similar meeting on January 25th. The recommendations were as follows:

" First—That, whatever the sentiments of publishers and editors, religion should be treated by the press as a factor of prime importance in the life of the country, should be men-be carried with all haste to the utmost borders of his realms. Yonder through the gates they pass. Speed ye! Rest not night nor day! The lives of a nation depend upon your faithfulness.

The herald was in process of time succeeded by the "post," so-called from *positus;* a reference to the fact that relays were placed at intervals that the riders might be expedited on their way. Hence the nomenclature of our present postal system. The messenger was a "postman," the station was the "post-office" and the superintendent in charge was a "postmaster" whose business was to receive packets and provide horses for a continuance of the journey. The man who stood by the gate of Jerusalem to receive the tidings of the battle of the Wood of Ephraim was to all intents a postmaster; and Ahimaaz and Cushi, whom he saw approaching with all haste, were postmen.

But many things have happened since those days. It could not be that the herald and the post should outlive Lawrence Coster, Watt and his tea-kettle, Franklin and his kite. "The old order changeth." Out of the logic and necessity of events has come the

---

tioned respectfully, and that the reports of religious enterprises, special services, and local progress should be made as full as their significance properly demands.

"Second—We regard Sunday newspapers as tending to break down the distinction between Sunday and other days; impairing the spirit of devotion: often superseding the family reunions at the altar of prayer; consuming the time necessary to prepare for the house of God, and pre-occupying the minds of those who attend, so as to render them impervious to spiritual influences.

"Third—We appeal to the people of the churches to consider prayerfully their responsibility in these premises. They can, by combining, exert an irresistible influence upon the character of the secular press.

"Fourth—We urge upon them the importance of patroniz-

newspaper. Its evolution from the past, is indicated in such titles as "The Post," "The Herald," "The Courier," "The Messenger" and "The Mercury." It was regarded as a marvellous thing that the Emperor Dionysius was enabled as he sat in his throne room to hear through a system of brazen pipes the gossip of his entire palace. In our time it is the privilege of every man to sit thus at an electric focus and listen to the story of events transpiring at the uttermost parts of the earth.

It is not uncommon to see a contrast drawn between the power of the Pulpit and that of the Press. In point of fact, however, there is no ground of comparison, for the following reasons:

First: The Church is of divine ordinance; in it God has promised to manifest his personality and power in a peculiar manner. Of all the lights that shone in old Jerusalem—sunlight, moonlight, starlight, and the shining of innumerable lamps in happy homes—there was none to be compared for a moment with the glory that was seen between the wings of the cherubim above the golden cover of the ark. This was the Shechinah from which God had prom-

---

ing only such newspapers as manifestly aim to be clean and wholesome, and such as support the principles which subserve the highest welfare of the community.

"Fifth—We suggest that if any one of the leading newspapers should withdraw its Sunday edition, it should have such immediate and general support as will unmistakably manifest the moral sentiment of the community.

"Finally, in the name of our common country, in the name of humanity, in the name of the homes of the land, and in the name of religion, we appeal to the press of the city to use the great powers in its hands to help men to do right, and to make it hard for men to do wrong, and not to lower the moral tone and degrade the life of the homes that, because of its merits, admit its issues, by inserting in its columns matter of a kind that, judged by any candid standard, can only exploit vice."

ised to show himself and commune with his people. It was the "pillar of cloud by day and of fire by night."

Second: The function of the Pulpit is to declare the saving power of the gospel of Christ. We have nothing to do with secular truth as such. All truth is important; in science, in philosophy, in art. But the truth with which men are vitally concerned is that which points the way to the endless life. If a man has fallen into an abyss, he may be greatly interested in what his neighbors, leaning over the edge, shall say about the weather and the gossip of the town, but a rope let down for his deliverance will be of incomparably more importance to him.

Third: The Church is a living organism through which the divine energy is being applied to the ultimate regeneration of the race. Its symbol is in the vision of Ezekiel:—the appearance of wheels; wheels within wheels; a living engine of power pervaded by a divine spirit, so that "whithersoever the Spirit was to go, the wheels went, for the Spirit was in them." Here is the great propaganda. Here is a foregleam of the Master's word, "Go ye, into all the world and evangelize." By the foolishness of preaching the nations of the earth are to be brought to the knowledge of Christ; that so the whole round world may every way be "bound, as with gold chains, about the feet of God."

But while we thus magnify the power of the Christian pulpit—which, by reason of the omnipotent God who ordained it, has more strength in its little finger than any secular institution has in its loins—we may not depreciate the magnificent power of the press. Of all secular energies it stands easily first.

So much has been said upon this point, however, in the columns of the newspapers themselves, that it will not be necessary here to emphasize it.

It is a pleasure to pay tribute to the magnificent service rendered by the *New York Times* in the overthrow of the Tweed regime. It seized upon that great evil power as a man grasps a serpent by the neck and strangles it. So Theseus set forth under black sails to slay the Minotaur; he followed the monster through the intricate windings of the Cretan labyrinth until he accomplished his purpose, and won the acclamations of his people. That was in legend; but the strangling of this monster of municipal corruption is matter of history. Honor to whom honor is due.

The *New York Tribune* some years ago placed the church under obligation by giving an extended report of the transactions of the Evangelical Alliance, which held its international convention in this city. It was a verbatim report; column after column, page after page; a triumph of stenography and the printer's art. The churches have not forgotten it, nor will they.

Aye, the press is a great power, for good, or for evil. This is the sorrow of it. One of the newspapers just mentioned for noble service done in the interest of truth and righteousness, showed an equal spirit of enterprise in publishing the most notorious divorce case that has ever occurred in our annals. Day after day it sent the reports of that case into Christian homes. The details were as vile and hateful as the plague of frogs that came up into the bedchambers and kneading-troughs of Egypt. It is impossible to calculate the far-reaching influence of that record of shame. The press is, indeed, a tremendous power, an incalculable power—for good or evil. Its influence is like that of wealth, of which Hood wrote:

> Gold! gold! gold! gold!
> Good or bad a thousand-fold;
>   How widely its agencies vary,—
> *To save, to ruin, to curse, to bless,*
> *As even its minted coins express,*
> *Now stamped with the image of good Queen Bess,*
>   *And now of a Bloody Mary.*

One of the weighty sayings of John Foster was this: "Power to the last atom is responsibility." Our friends of the newspapers will not be able to escape responsibility by saying that the press is merely a colorless reflection of public sentiment. The question is not to be determined merely by the law of demand and supply. We regulate the trade in the common commodities of life; we do not allow the sale of watered milk, or poisoned beer, or unmarked oleomargarine. Men and women want opium and arsenic, but they are not permitted to purchase them at will. There are some things which cannot be left to the law of supply and demand, but which must be determined under a higher law; to wit, the public good. *Salus populi suprema lex.* It is to be hoped, moreover, that newspaper men themselves do not take this view of their vocation. Are they content with the parrot-like function of echoing the public mind? Nay, rather, they make public opinion—they create sentiment. On this ground only can the press claim to be a great public educator; but upon this ground it must also meet the other tremendous fact that responsibility is ultimately bound to face the judgment bar of God.

It is not my purpose here, however, to dwell on the moral obligations of the editorial fraternity. I wish particularly to emphasize the duty of Christian people with respect to the press. Much is being said just now as to "the Ideal Newspaper." An impression is given that Christian ministers are calling for that. Let us not be side-tracked in this way. The "ideal" is that which we have not and are not likely to get. We are not trying to reach the unattainable. We are not making unreasonable demands. We simply ask that Christian people may have a newspaper which they can read with impunity and safely introduce into their homes. Is that too much? There are hundreds of thousands of Christian people in this city. They belong to the reading class. Their relation to the press is purely voluntary. They cannot lay hands on the editor and require him to honor God. They cannot stop the wheels of the presses; but they are numerous enough to get what they desire, if they rightly set about it.

I. *We want a newspaper that shall be abreast of the times.* It must publish the news. Christians above all are interested in current events. To them history is the massing and combining of energies in the interest of the kingdom of Christ. Events are the rumbling of his chariot wheels. We are interested in the Arbitration Treaty because of its bearing on the coming of Christ. We want to know about the Nicaragua Canal because it must be a thoroughfare for the propagation of the gospel. We are profoundly concerned in the suppression of the Armenian persecution and in the overthrow of Islam; in the development of Japan; in the opening up of the dark continent; in the Tripartite Alliance and the Eastern question, because these events are marks of Christian progress. We must keep track of legislation in our national congress and in our various commonwealths, of municipal reform and of quick local transit, because they all have a more or less important bearing upon the great ultimate event. We must have the news. Wherefore " prithee," good editor, as Shakespeare says, "take the cork out of thy mouth that we may drink thy tidings."

II. *Our newspaper must be truthful, clean and wholesome.*

It must tell the truth. Time was when the business of lying was sensational; but it has been done to death. The white lie and the black lie, cant, humbug, exaggeration, mealy-mouthed pretence, understatement, overstatement and polite misrepresentation, all have been worn to the marrow of the bone. Hence the proverb that "If you see it in the newspaper, it's not so." The reading public want the truth—plain, unvarnished truth. This would be in the nature of a novelty; but the other is flat, stale and unprofitable.

As matters are, no character is safe. Though a man or woman be chaste as ice, pure as snow, he shall not escape calumny. Let him pray the hyena to deliver him from the sensational reporter.

Who said that a man's house is his castle? The youth who covets promotion on the reportorial staff on some of our great newspapers must pass through an apprenticeship of prurient exploration, casting about for skeletons in closets, prying into confidences, pumping at domestic cesspools, and measuring success by the number of reputations he ruins. Not all are so; but there are more than enough to warrant plain words. These are a generation of Peeping Toms, who glory in their shame.

And if by mischance a man is in public life, let him ask and expect no mercy. The Philistines—the breath of whose nostrils is falsehood and the light of whose eyes is misrepresentation—are always upon him. It would appear that citizens in public life are as much entitled to fair treatment as any other. They may as reasonably claim the benefit of the Ninth Commandment and the Golden Rule. But the vials of vituperation are so lavished upon them that politics itself becomes a stench. The people say: "There must be fire where there is so much smoke"—forgetting that it is the business of certain newspapers to make smoke without fire; and honest men, fitted to lead in public affairs, loth to expose themselves, suffer the government to go by default into the hands of lewd fellows of the baser sort.

But there are newspapers and newspapers, and "we must discriminate." Granted. Nevertheless, the best is a sinner; and the fact remains that anything which is not actionable in law passes as truth in the usual politics of the press.

The newspaper for Christian people and Christian homes must also be clean and wholesome. When Charles Dickens returned from his visit to America, he took occasion to speak in his American Notes of the shameless character of some of our newspapers. He represented the newsboys calling, "Here is your New York Sewer!" and "Here is your Key-hole Reporter!" The American people were, at the time, indignant beyond expression. Since then, however, the public taste has been greatly depraved, and lo, the New York Sewer and the Key-hole Reporter are here. It is not necessary to give them their proper names. One of them was apparently anticipated by Shakespeare when he wrote:

> Her tongue
> Outvenoms all the worms of Nile; her breath
> Rides on the posting winds, and doth belie kings, queens,
> Maids, matrons, nay, the secrets of the grave.

And Spenser was manifestly thinking of the other when he wrote:

> Her face was ugly and her mouth distort,
>   Foaming with poison round about her gills,
> In which her censéd tongue, full short and sharp
>   Appear'd like asp his sting, that closely kills
>   Or cruelly does wound whomso she wills.

These are not newspapers; they are scavengers. And the others are not blameless. Is there one that can consistently say, "We print all and only the news that is fit to read"? The smell of the clothes-hamper is more or less delicately over them all. We have supped full on gossip! We are weary unto death of the co-respondent. Why should we be obliged to walk through the columns of the newspaper, rather than anywhere else, arm in arm with men of the town and their concubines? Why must we breathe the odors of garbage and coagulated blood? Is it the function of "the great public educator" thus to pollute the air? Must it needs pander to the lowest and basest?

An American, resident for many years in Paris, recently said to me: "I am amazed that you permit such personal scandals. The worst of our Parisian papers, in comparison, shines like a good deed in a naughty world! We do not profess a Christian civilization in France; neither do we allow such license of the press."

III. *The newspaper we want should be non-religious.* We do not ask a religious paper, nor do we expect it. We may reasonably ask, however, that the papers to which we give our voluntary patronage, should treat with ordinary respect the great truths which lie close to the centre of our hearts. God and the Scriptures, the atonement of Christ, the influence of the Holy Ghost, revivals, home and foreign missions, these are as our very blood and the marrow of our bones. In self-respect we are bound to insist on a courteous attitude toward them. If a newspaper were to impugn the fair name of my mother, would I complacently suffer it? But Christ and his religion are dearer than any earthly relationship. If we admit that our newspaper need not be religious, we demand, without any equivocation, that it shall not be anti-religious. It must not in any wise oppose the gospel which is so dear to us.

In this view it would appear that the newspaper which shall commend itself to Christians shall honor the Moral Law. The Fourth Commandment is part and parcel of that law. There is not a morning newspaper in New York City which does not habitually, flagrantly, defiantly violate the Sabbath. It is not my purpose to speak just now of the Sunday newspaper at any length; it will suffice to say that it stands as the head and front of the whole offending in the matter of current and increasing Sabbath desecration. We are asked by newspaper men to lend them our influence to make the Sunday newspaper a cleaner, better sheet. But they overlook the fact that our objection is made not to the character of the Sunday newspaper, though that is bad enough at the best, but to the institution *per se*. It is not possible to publish seven issues of a secular newspaper without seven days of continuous work. Nor can any secular newspaper be published on the Sabbath which shall not by the introduction of secular news antagonize the fundamental principle of Sabbath rest. It secularizes our holy day. But while we thus strenuously object to the Sunday newspaper, weare, under present conditions, forced to be *particeps criminis*. We are obliged to take six issues of a morning newspaper, which has a Sunday edition, or fall behind the times.

What shall we do? No proposition has been made to start a new paper; but stranger things have happened. All enterprises have a beginning. If a millionaire can come across the continent to New York City and invest his money in a newspaper with an apparent purpose of making it a great power for evil, is it preposterous to suppose that the heart of some Christian millionaire, who holds his money in trust for God, shall be moved on occasion to make a corresponding investment in the interest of truth and righteousness? But a more immediate possibility is that one of our present newspapers may withdraw its Sabbath issue in deference to the sentiment of a multitude of people who reverence the Lord's Day. Should that occur, it would be the manifest duty of Christian people, other things being equal, to lend their united support. It is a good rule to honor those who honor God. If the women of the Christian churches would take cognizance of those merchants who do not advertise in the Sunday press and give them preference in their patronage, that would be an argument of great weight. And Christian people would accomplish a great deal if they would support such enterprises as manifest a desire to honor the fundamental precepts of morality and so subserve the public weal.

(1) It should be the part of every Christian to attend to his individual duty. Let him do right precisely as if he were the only living man. "One with God is a majority." To assume that, because the newspapers have "come to stay," we had better accept the situation, is to reason without regard to the first principles of Christian ethics. " Ye are the salt of the earth, but if the salt have lost its savour, it is thenceforth good for nothing but to be cast out and trodden under the foot of men."

> If every one would look to his own reformation,
> How easy it would be to reform the nation.

(2) Let us unite and act. "*Eendracht Maakt Macht.*" If I throw a thousand pounds of iron filings into the air, they will descend as gently as snow flakes ; but if I weld them into a cannon ball, back it with a charge of powder, and fire it from a columbiad, I can sink a man-of-war with it. The people of the churches have illimitable power, if they choose to use it. So long as we are willing to patronize the newspapers as they are, we shall get nothing better. The sentiment of right-thinking people should make itself heard and felt. Almost any suggestion is better

than none. Let us purge our consciences. We are strong enough to have our way in New York City; and New York pitches the tune for the other cities of the land. Let us unite and act! "We must hang together," said John Hancock, in the Continental Congress. "Aye," responded a voice, "or we shall hang apart." Wherefore, let those who are like-minded in this matter unite and act.

> The flighty purpose never is o'ertook
> Unless the deed go with it.

FISHERS OF MEN.

"Fear not; from henceforth thou shalt catch men."—LUKE v. 10.

The scene is in the early morning by the Lake Gennesaret. The breath of the diurnal resurrection is over all. Far to the east the glory of the sunrise is on the hills of Bashan. The waters of the lake ripple and sparkle in the early breeze. You may see yonder through the garden mist Tiberias and Magdala. A fleet of fishing boats swings at anchor here in the bay; some are fastened to the shore. In one of these the old fisherman Zebedee and his sons are mending their nets. In the boats some are washing their nets; others on the beach are stretching their nets in the sun.

It was upon such a scene and under such circumstances that Jesus appeared. Early as it was, he was followed by a considerable company who desired to hear him discourse on the truths of the endless life. The little boat swinging by the shore afforded him a suitable pulpit. A blessed matin service that! And when the service was over, and the congregation dismissed, he turned to the fishermen and said, "Launch out into the deep and let down your nets for a draught." The reply of Peter savored of disappointment and weariness, of loyalty and faith: "Master, we have toiled all night and taken nothing; nevertheless at thy word I will let down the net." It was done; and behold "they inclosed a great multitude of fishes, and their net was breaking." And they were astonished, Peter above all. But Jesus said to him "Fear not; from henceforth thou shalt catch men."

We cannot regard this as a mere episode in the common-place life of a few fishermen. It was a great event and the opening chapter of the story of a vast enterprise.

I. We see behind this group on the shore of Gennesaret *the outline of the universal Church of God.* For what is the Church indeed but a guild of fishermen? Up and down the centuries the little boat has cruised, now over calm and prosperous seas, and anon beaten by contrary winds; but always under the divine protection—the prayerful crew letting down the nets here and there, taking sometimes a waterhaul and mourning, "Alas! hath God forgotten to be gracious?" at other times letting down the net on the right side of the ship, with the Master standing by, and blessing God for a multitude of great fishes. And so will it be year after year, the toilers an increasing company, the songs of success waxing louder and more joyous, until all the souls of the children of men shall be made prisoners of hope and the glory of the Lord shall cover the earth as the waters cover the sea.

The early Christians made more of the symbol of the fish than we do. In the story "Quo Vadis," a young Roman tribune makes an unseemly address to a Lygian slave girl, and is puzzled by her reply; for with a reed she draws in the dust an outline of a fish. The young tribune learned later that she meant by this sign that she was a follower of the Lord Christ. The symbol gets its significance from the word *Ichthus*, a fish; the letters of which form the initials of Iesous Christos Theou Huios Soter, that is, Jesus Christ, Son of God, Saviour. The symbol may still be seen in the catacombs, for it was used to disguise the sepulchres of Christians to prevent the desecration of their sleeping dust.

It suggests our personal "call" to the service of Christ. Here is Peter, a great soul if ever there was one, endowed with magnificent gifts and possibilities of usefulness. He is part owner of a little sloop; he cruises up and down Gennesaret for fish, carries them to the market-place at Capernaum, and chaffers there with housewives for a few paltry pence. It is an honorable calling, for

> Who sweeps a room as to God's law
> Makes that and th' action fine.

All honest toil is honorable. But is the making of a livelihood, a competence or a fortune, the consummation of life's purpose? Is this the best that Peter shall hope for? Early to bed, and early to rise, and down to the boats, and battling with the winds and waves, day in and day out, until the years are gone, and the limbs tremble, and the eyes are dim, and the hands are folded—O Peter, with thy mighty soul! is this all? And is life worth the living if this is all?

Here is John; his great eyes are full of dreams and visions and apocalypses; the hiding of power is there. He busies himself with dragging the nets, mending their meshes, hanging them in the sun. Is there no larger place for John in the busy world than yon little fishing boat? Shall all his energies be exhausted in the reefing of sails and the dragging of nets? Alas for a man whose soul is imprisoned in secular life! Alas for the lawyer who never gets above his briefs, the physician who knows no more than "laudamy and calamy," the carpenter who is satisfied with the shoving of his saw and plane, the housewife whose soul is absorbed in her needlework! We are made in God's likeness. Shall the eagle be tethered to a stake? Shall a lion be harnessed to a cart? An honest lark-pie is worth a shilling, but a lark's song—as he rises from the meadow with the dew of the morning on his wings and pierces the ether and gazes toward the sun—O, a lark's song cannot be valued with the gold of Ophir. *Sursum corda!* Up with your heart, O son of the living God! Make your secular business as honorable as you please; yet your life will be a failure if it exhausts itself upon that.

But the Master comes this way. "Follow me," is his word, "and I will make you fishers of men"; that is, "I will not turn you aside from the familiar methods of your occupation; fishers once, fishers ever. But ye shall be promoted to a higher sphere; as apostles, missionaries, evangelists, teachers, ye shall turn your skill to the betterment of the world." We also are in the apostolic succession. The apostles are "sent ones"; so are we. For did not the Master say, "As the Father sent me into the world, so have I sent you"? For what? To deliver the world from its shame and sin. Blessed calling! The Master speaks. Bring all your energies of body and soul to the propaganda of truth and righteousness. Seek first of all the kingdom of God.

II. Here also is *an unveiling of the secret of power.*

The words of Peter are significant: "Master, we have toiled all the night; nevertheless, at thy word I will let down the net." The key of the whole matter is in that word, "Master." What shall we call him? Christ—the Anointed One, of whom all the prophets spake? Jesus—so called because he should save his people from their sins? Aye; but above all, Lord. Our Lord Jesus Christ. "Ye call me Master and Lord; and ye say well, for so I am."

It is remarkable, when we stop to reflect, that these men should have given heed to the Master's words, "Launch out into the deep and let down your nets." Who is this man, so ready with his counsel? They knew all about the business of fishing. They were born here at Gennesaret. They had floated their toy boats along the edge of the water and fished with crooked pins when they were lads. They knew the haunts and habits of all the fishes. They knew the weather signs. They could call the name of every wind that blew across the waters. And who is this that offers advice? A carpenter of Nazareth. He had served his apprenticeship with saw and plane; he knew how to mend ploughs and furniture; but what did he know about fishing?

Ah, but he was their Master. That tells the story. There was no reservation in their submission to him. Their acquaintance with this man was but slight as yet; they had met him at the banks of the Jordan, when the prophet of the wilderness said, "Behold the Lamb of God!" But they were ready to accept his counsel in things temporal as well as in things spiritual. There was no questioning, no hesitation, no reserve. We know more of Jesus than they did. We have a deeper personal experience of his power to save. We have seen him controlling the affairs of men and nations,—the commanding figure in the history of these nineteen centuries. If John and Peter and James could say, "Master, thy word is ultimate," how much more should we!

His mastery is over every department of life. His counsel is for the market-place as well as the sanctuary. These are troublous times in the business world; men are worrying all day, and passing sleepless nights. Are you, my friend, in financial trouble? Go to your Master with it. Is not he the silent partner in your affairs? He knows all, is interested in all that concerns you. It was for men under such circumstances that he spoke this word: "Consider the ravens; for they neither sow nor reap; which have neither storehouse nor barn; and God feedeth them; how much more are ye better than they?"

He is Master, also, with reference to the duties of the religious life. You are a member of the great fellowship; you have entered into covenant with him in the service of the kingdom of God; you want to know what to do. "I am a fisher of men, but where shall I cast the net?" Ask, and he will direct you. The beginning of all spiritual usefulness is in the word of Paul: "Lord, what wilt thou have me to do?"

> If you cannot speak like angels, if you cannot preach like Paul,
> You can tell the love of Jesus, you can say he died for all.
> Let none hear you idly saying, There is nothing I can do,
> While the souls of men are waiting, and the Master calls for you;
> Take the task he gives you gladly, let his work your pleasure be;
> Answer quickly when he calleth, Here am I, send me, send me.

"And whatsoever he saith unto you, do it." Do it at any cost of personal convenience. Do it, however his counsel may seem to conflict with your own ideas of prudence and propriety. Do it without delay or questioning. Do it because he is Master, and his word is ultimate. The best offering that a man can make to his Lord is absolute obedience. All the trophies of wealth and honor that the most distinguished of mortals may bring, cannot supply the lack of it. The best of the fatlings, with King Agag in bonds, could not prevent the prophet's word, "To obey is better than sacrifice." Therefore, having submitted your life to the Master, whatsoever he saith unto you, do it.

III. Here also is *the suggestion of the penny at evening*. We toil for wages. Jesus himself was not above it, for is it not written, " For the joy that was set before him, he endured the cross, despising the shame, and is now set down at the right hand of the throne of God"?

We sometimes think of heaven as the reward of service; but this is not so. It is indeed our El Dorado. When Godfrey, having brought his crusaders through storms and scorching suns, at length saw in the distance the glowing domes of Jerusalem, he turned to his men with this exclamation, "Who will not strive for such a city!" But heaven is not to be had for striving. Heaven is of grace. The qualifications for entering that city are on the one hand pardon through the blood, and on the other sanctification by the Spirit. And pardon and sanctification are both of grace.

What then is the reward of service? Fruitfulness. The husbandman is patient in scattering the seed, because he sees aforetime the golden fields and hears the creaking of the loaded vans. It was a right prayer that Moses made: "Let thy work appear unto thy servants, and thy glory unto their children. And let the beauty of the Lord our God be upon us; and establish thou the work of our hands upon us; yea, the work of our hands establish thou it."

But alas for the discouraged ones! How many there are who say like these weary fishermen, "We have toiled all night and taken nothing." It is the cry that goes up from the closets where parents have been pleading for the wandering these many years. It is the prayer of the missionary who toils alone in the regions of darkness and the shadow of death. Carey and Morrison, Allen Gardiner and Adoniram Judson—they dragged their nets year after year in vain. It is not toil that tries the soul of man, but toil without fruit.

What do we need? Patience? Yes, truly; but faith above all. Faith is the mother of patience. He that believeth, shall not make haste. It was faith that said, "*Nevertheless*—at thy word I will let down the net." We can afford to wait, so long as we believe. Bide a wee and dinna weary. The kingdom of heaven cometh not with observation. The mustard seed grows in the night. Toil on and trust God. In due time we shall reap, if we faint not.

At this point we note the astonishment with which Peter regarded the great draught of fishes. All were astonished, but Peter was overwhelmed. He cast himself at Jesus' feet, saying, "Depart from me, for I am a sinful man." Should we not rather have expected him to clasp his hands in adoring wonder and renew his vows of faithful service with great joy?

But in that moment he saw that which thrilled him through and through. A miracle! But why should a miracle have amazed him? We live in the midst of marvels. Every throb of our pulse is a miracle; every breath we draw is a miracle. All providences are special providences. It is as extraordinary for God to turn a snowflake from its course, as for the sun to stand still on Gibeon. Nothing is too hard for him.

But the wonder of the miracle in the case of Peter was its revelation of God. He saw in this Jesus of Nazareth an unveiling of the mighty God. At the same instant he saw himself a sinner. And between him and that Incarnate God a gulf opened that seemed vast and bridgeless. A moment later Jesus stretched his hand over that separating gulf and drew Peter toward him, saying, "Fear not." He drew him into fellowship, friendship, copartnership with himself, in the things of the kingdom of God—"I will make thee a fisher of men."

This was but a prophetic silhouette of Pentecost. On that memorable day these fishermen again let down their nets, and when they drew them in they caught three thousand souls for God. Again they were amazed. The lambent flames rested upon their brows. The miracle was wrought which is wrought again and again in every outpouring of the Spirit of God.

The Master is not far from any one of us. He is here as really as he stood with the disciples in the little boat that day. "Follow me," is his word, "and I will make you fishers of men." "Go ye, evangelize; and lo, I am with you alway, even unto the end of the world." "He that goeth forth and weepeth, bearing precious seed, shall doubtless, *doubtless*, DOUBTLESS, come again with rejoicing, bringing his sheaves with him."

"BEHOLD, THY KING COMETH UNTO THEE!"*

"All this was done, that it might be fulfilled which was spoken by the prophet, saying, Tell ye the daughter of Sion, Behold, thy King cometh unto thee, meek, and sitting upon an ass, and a colt the foal of an ass."
—MATT. xxi. 4, 5.

It was a bright spring day in the year 29. The city of Jerusalem was crowded with worshippers who had come up to the celebration of the Passover from every part of Palestine. As they looked toward the East, they saw a company of pilgrims rounding the spur of Olivet, waving palm branches and crying, "Hosanna to the son of David!" In front rode the prophet of Nazareth who was by many believed to be the long-looked-for Messiah. A rumor of his approach had reached the city, and many, seeing the procession coming, set out to meet him. The two streams met on the slope of the mountain, and came on down toward the Kedron; those going before and those following after joined in the cry, "Hosanna to the son of David! Blessed is he that cometh in the name of the Lord!" They crossed the ford, ascended the opposite road, and passed through the gates and along the street, still shouting, waving palm branches, and casting their garments before Jesus in the way.

---

*This discourse was preached on Palm Sunday, 1897.

There were people looking down from the housetops, others peering through their windows of lattice-work, still others looking on from the doorways of bazaars. Those who were abroad in the streets turned aside to let the strange procession pass. "Who is this?" was heard on every side. "This is the son of David," they answered. "Hosanna, hosanna, blessed is he that cometh in the name of the Lord!" So they proceeded to the Shushan gate of the temple and passed in.

I. Let us observe, to begin with, *the importance of the triumphal Advent of Jesus as an isolated fact.* This was the first Palm Sunday. The hosanna of those who led the prophet of Nazareth to the temple was the first Christian hymn. What was the meaning of it?

The hour had come for Jesus to declare himself. His purpose in making himself one among the children of men was to set up his kingdom of truth and righteousness on earth. He was to be its king, and was to reign ultimately from the river unto the ends of the earth. He had spent thirty years in preparation for his work. All this time he had been a king in disguise. He had grown up from childhood in no wise distinguished from the other lads of Nazareth. He had served his apprenticeship as a carpenter and had shared the common lot of toiling men. It was three years now since he had crossed the threshold of the carpenter shop, closed its door, and entered upon his formal ministry. During that ministry he had worn no halo, displayed no insignia of office, but rather kept himself under a constant reserve. Now and then he spoke briefly of his hopes and purposes, but as one who was aware that a precipitate unveiling of his divine royalty would thwart his plan. He could afford to wait in confidence. "He that believeth shall not make haste."

In the temptation of the wilderness his adversary, who was called the "prince of this world," had offered him universal dominion in return for a single act of homage. He knew, however, that a holy kingdom could not come to him in such a manner, and he refused it.

By the shore of Gennesaret, after a day of preaching and wonder-working, the people put their heads together and said, "He is indeed the son of David who will restore the glory to Israel. Why should we not lead him to Jerusalem and place him upon the throne?" He knew what was passing through their minds; had he been less or lower than himself, he would have accepted their homage, for he knew that the Jews would hail him with acclamations if he gave promise of deliverance from the hated yoke of Rome. But again he knew that the kingdom could not come in this way. So it is written, "He departed into a mountain himself alone."

On the Mount of Transfiguration he revealed to the chosen disciples a passing glimpse of his glory. His face was like the sun, and his garments were white and glistering. They would have set up his royal establishment then and there, saying, "Let us make here three tabernacles; one for thee, one for Moses, and one for Elias." But the glory vanished, and he straightly charged them that they should tell no man.

Tell no man! So did he counsel the leper who was healed at the foot of Olivet, the blind man who received his sight at Bethsaida, Jaïrus, whose daughter was restored from death. So did he enjoin upon Peter when he cried, "Thou art the Christ of God!" "See thou tell no man."

But now the hour has come. There is no longer any occasion for withholding the truth concerning his personality and his purpose. He will announce his Kingship to-day; yet in a peculiar manner. It would be wholly unworthy of him to celebrate a triumph like the princes of this world. It is for Cæsar, Alexander, and the mighty conquerors of Egypt and Assyria, to ride on war-horses that prance and champ their bits, with noble guards and armies of defenders, captives in chains, and long processions of slaves. The procession of this King of kings and Lord of lords shall be a protest against the vain and vulgar fashion of sordid ambition. "Thy king cometh unto thee, meek, and riding upon an ass." So, too, the judges of Israel in old times rode about on their errands of truth and judgment. This very day, the tenth day of the month, marks the bringing in of the paschal lamb for the sacrifice. The King Messiah is also the Lamb slain from the foundation of the world. What a preposterous triumph this would have been had Jesus been only a man! How far short of the glory of all earthly potentates! But if Jesus be the very Son of God, then how unworthy would it have been to ape the affectations of the mighty of the earth! He comes to die, to triumph in death, to triumph over death, to triumph in behalf of all the children of men.

> Ride on, ride on in majesty!
> In lowly pomp, ride on to die!
> O Christ, Thy triumphs now begin
> O'er captive death and conquered sin.

> Ride on, ride on in majesty !
>   The wingèd squadron of the sky
> Look down with sad and wondering eyes
>   To see the approaching sacrifice.
>
> Ride on, ride on in majesty !
>   Thy last and fiercest strife is nigh !
> The Father on His sapphire throne
>   Expects His own anointed Son.
>
> Ride on, ride on in majesty !
>   In lowly pomp, ride on to die ;
> Bow Thy meek head to mortal pain,
> Then take, O God ! Thy power, and reign.

But let the pageant pass ; of itself it means but little. It is a foregleam, a silhouette ; it has a bi-frontal eloquence pointing backward into prophecy, forward through history, and ever declaring the Kingship of Christ.

II. *It points backward to prophecy.* "All this was done that it might be fulfilled which was spoken by the prophet, saying, Tell ye the daughter of Sion, Behold, thy King cometh unto thee, meek, and sitting upon an ass, and a colt the foal of an ass."

Who said this ? The prophet Zechariah, during the building of the second temple, when the Syrians and Philistines were oppressing the Jews. This prophet saw the coming King with clear eyes. He spoke of him with the utmost particularity. He bore witness five centuries before the event to Christ's coming, his suffering, his betrayal, the purchase of the potter's field with the thirty pieces of silver, and other incidents relating to Christ's passion. It was meet that he should also predict his triumph.

It is not in Zechariah alone, however, that clear prophecies of the Messiah are found. They are everywhere in the Old Testament, running through it like a golden thread. The first word of promise that ever was spoken, "The seed of the woman shall bruise the serpent's head," had reference to him. He was to go out as a knight-errant, like St. George against the dragon, to deliver the race from sin. He is spoken of continually as the seed of David—"Great David's Greater Son." To a Jew this meant everything royal and magnificent; for David himself was at the very centre of their hearts. What could be more vivid than the prediction of Isaiah: "For unto us a child is born, unto us a son is given; and the government shall be upon his shoulder; and his name shall be called Wonderful, Counsellor, The mighty God, The everlasting Father, The Prince of Peace."

He is seen on the far heights beyond the Jordan approaching the Holy City. "Who is this that cometh from Edom, with dyed garments from Bozrah? this that is glorious in his apparel?"—"I that speak in righteousness, mighty to save."—"Wherefore art thou red in thine apparel, and thy garments like him that treadeth in the winefat?"—"I have trodden the winepress alone; and of the people there was none with me; and I looked, and there was none to help; and I wondered that there was none to uphold; therefore mine own arm brought salvation unto me; and my fury, it upheld me."

The visions of Daniel portray the Christ sitting upon a throne, which supplants all the visions of earthly dominion, high and lifted up. His worshippers are coming from afar, and magnates are bringing their tribute unto him.

Or shall we ask David himself to sing of his royal Son? "The kings of the earth set themselves, and the rulers take counsel together against the Lord and against his anointed, saying, Let us break their bands asunder, and cast away their cords from us. He that sitteth in the heavens shall laugh ; the Lord shall have them in derision. Then shall he speak unto them in his wrath, and vex them in his sore displeasure. Yet have I set my king upon my holy hill of Zion. I will declare the decree: the Lord hath said unto me, Thou art my Son ; this day have I begotten thee."

I am aware that in some quarters prophecy is regarded as mere guess-work, and, as a rule, *ex post facto*. The supernatural is eliminated from it. One by one the predictions which have been supposed to refer to the coming of Christ—even such as Christ himself interpreted in that way—have been torn asunder to make way for a thousand gratuitous and unfounded conjectures. Men who call themselves Christians, and claim to be experts in Biblical exposition, have stretched these prophecies on the rack and claim to have forced from them under torture a protestation that they have made no reference to Christ at all !

But there is a larger view of this matter. The reverent eyes of those who believe that Scripture was written by holy men who spake as they were moved by the Holy Ghost, can see everywhere in these oracles a majestic Figure, looming up in the twilight of the early dawn and coming into clearer and ever clearer light, until the Sun of Righteousness ariseth with healing in his beams. We are always in danger of losing a mighty truth when we speculate too closely as to the relative value of the jot and the tittle. Men who spend their lives in spectral analysis are not likely to see nature glorified by the sun.

But let the panorama of visions pass. Close the book of prophecy, open the book of history, and consider the logic of events.

III. *The triumphal advent in history.* We mark a continuous procession from the foot of the cross to the throne of heaven.

It is significant that on this occasion our Lord on reaching Jerusalem went up immediately into the temple. So David sang, "Behold, I have set my king upon my holy hill of Zion!" The progress of Christianity is identified with the history of the Church.

On leaving this world, our Lord committed his work to the Holy Spirit. The Holy Spirit was to be thenceforth the administrator of the affairs of his kingdom until his throne should be fully established among men. The Holy Spirit works through the Church, touching the lips of its ministers with fire, building up its people on their most holy faith, and regenerating the hearts of the children of men. The Spirit is in the wheels of the great organism, so that it goeth whithersoever the Spirit taketh it. We are living in the dispensation of the Spirit, whose function it is to take of the things of Jesus and show them unto us.

It is written that the whole city was "moved" when Jesus drew nigh to it. The people are moved to-day by the presence of Christ. The nations of the world are moved by the story of the cross.

The men of Jerusalem were "moved." They saw the influence of this strange and unique personality. In our time it is seen yet more distinctly. The influence of Christ means the overthrow of caste and the setting up of the brotherhood of man. The world is old enough now to have established the fact that Jesus has come to break every chain and bid the oppressed go free. He has dignified labor, for the shadow of the carpenter shop of Nazareth has fallen over all. He has more and more dispelled ignorance as the centuries have passed by. The lands where Christianity prevails are dotted with schools and institutions of learning. He stands in history for Liberty, Equality, Fraternity. He has proven himself to be the Prince of Peace. To-day he is breaking the spear asunder. All Christendom is moved with indignation at the "concert" of the great powers who have undertaken to protect the unspeakable Turk and suppress the Cretans in their struggle for rights and freedom. Shiloh is ruling more and more in the hearts and consciences of men.

The women of Jerusalem were "moved" that day. Their clear voices joined in the "Hosannas" that greeted the Christ. At that time woman was a household drudge; a toy for the zenana. But under the influence of Christianity during these nineteen hundred years she has been delivered into a glorious liberty. The Magnificat was the first outburst of gratitude for this splendid service of the Christ: "My soul doth magnify the Lord, because he hath exalted the estate of his handmaiden." Wherever Christianity prevails, there mother, sister, daughter, wife are sacred titles; there polygamy is a memory, the home a paradise. Let Mary break her alabaster box and pour the ointment on the head of Jesus, and let all her sisters sing, Hosanna to this son of David.

And the children of Jerusalem were "moved."

Little piping voices joined in the acclamations. Of all the sacred teachers that ever lived, there was not one who like Jesus stretched out his arms to the children, saying, "Suffer them to come unto me." Nor was there one who so clearly perceived the philosophy of the proverb, "The child is father of the man." That was a great saying of the Master, "Except ye become as little children, ye shall in no wise see the kingdom of God." "Rabbi, rebuke them," the Pharisees said, "Hearest thou not? Bid them keep silent." And he answered and said, "If these should hold their peace, the stones would immediately cry out."

The Messiah is bound to have his welcome. The world is moved more and more to receive him as the centuries pass. All history is paying tribute to him. The Church, for the nucleus of which he chose eleven men, has passed through persecution after persecution, and from Pentecost to Pentecost, until at length there are hundreds of millions who cry, "Hosanna, hosanna, blessed is he that cometh in the name of the Lord!"

But Jesus was not dazzled by this homage. He knew what was to follow. He heard the mutterings of hatred beneath this chorus of welcome. At one point in his journey he paused and surveyed the Holy City. Tears came into his eyes. "O Jerusalem! Jerusalem!" he cried, "how often would I have gathered thy children together, even as a hen gathereth her brood under her wings, and ye would not! And now, behold, your house is left unto you desolate." He foresaw the long succession of calamities; the wars and rumors of wars, the centuries of waiting; but he knew the end from the beginning. It was for the joy set before him in the prophecy of his ultimate triumph that he was enabled to endure the cross, despising the shame. All things must work toward the final consummation until he shall be king over all and blessed forever.

Now let us roll up the chronicles, close the pages of prophecy and history alike, and gaze for a moment toward the heavens.

IV. *The consummation.* "I saw heaven opened," wrote the Evangelist, "and, behold, a white horse; and he that sat upon him was called Faithful and True. His eyes were as a flame of fire, and on his head were many crowns. He was clothed in a vesture dipped in blood; and his name was called The Word of God. And the armies of heaven followed him upon white horses, clothed in fine linen, white and clean. And he hath on his vesture and on his thigh a name written, King of kings and Lord of lords."

"And I saw and, behold, Satan, went forth to gather the nations together, Gog and Magog, to battle. And the fire of God came down from heaven and devoured them. And I saw and, behold, Satan was bound and cast into the bottomless pit. And I saw the holy city, new Jerusalem, coming down from God out of heaven, prepared as a bride adorned for her husband. And I heard a great voice out of heaven, saying, Behold, the tabernacle of God is with men, and he will dwell with them, and they shall be his people, and God himself shall be with them, and be their God."

We are not left in doubt as to this restitution of all things. The only question is, What are our personal relations to this ultimate fact? There were four classes of people who on the first Palm Sunday looked on Jesus as he entered the Holy City.

There were the inquirers, who as yet were ignorant of the claims and character of this Jesus. "Who is this?" was their question, and they were ready to learn of him.

And there were the indifferent; shop-keepers who looked out of their doorways, and others who regarded with a complacent smile this strange display. They were intent upon secular affairs; they did not know how closely this coming of the Christ to Jerusalem was related to their own need and destiny. Or, if they were told, they cared little or nothing for it.

Then too there were the opposers, the enemies of Christ. The Pharisees were baffled and angry; they uttered no hosannas; they hated this Jesus of Nazareth. While men thronged about him as he preached in Solomon's Porch, they had retired to the hall Gazith, and taken counsel how they might destroy him. Destroy him! He that sitteth in the heavens shall laugh.

And there also were his friends. There were some whom he had healed of mortal maladies, some who had learned from his lips the great truths of the spiritual life, and many who had faith in his power on earth to forgive sin; these cast their garments in the way before him.

We cannot close this brief study of the triumphal advent without calling attention to the strange manner in which the Lord secured his beast of burden. "Go ye into the village," he said, "and ye shall find a colt tied, whereon man never sat; loose him and bring him. And if any man say aught unto you, ye shall say, The Lord hath need of him." He knew that the question of ownership would be likely to arise. We raise the question of ownership constantly; as to our time, our energy, our treasure, ourselves. There is one word that solves the question, The Master hath need.

Was it true that the Master had need of an ass's colt for that occasion of triumph? Aye; and for the advancing work of his kingdom he has need of our time, energy, possessions, all that we have and are. "I beseech you, brethren, that ye present yourselves, which is your reasonable service." The things that we call ours are of value only as they can be applied to the uses of his kingdom. He makes a mighty claim because he is our King. All that we have belongs to him, because we ourselves are his. So, my friend, if you would make the most of life, put everything at his disposal. If you would make your influence tell, put the kingdom above the shop; the triumph of Christ above all temporal well-being. He is marching straight on through the years from the cross to his throne. The royal standards onward go. Fall in! Fall in! Lift up your voice with the voices of the multitude and cry, "Hosanna, hosanna to the Son of David!" On to the heavenly Zion, whose gates are lifted up for all who bear palm branches in the company of the Mighty One! On to Zion with the multitude of the redeemed, who shall enter in with songs and everlasting joy upon their heads!

CITIZEN GEORGE WASHINGTON.

"And there was not among the children of Israel a goodlier person than he."
—I. Sam. ix. 2.

In the year 1643 Laurence Washington, rector of the parish church of Purleigh, was dispossessed of his living by order of Oliver Cromwell, on the ground that he was "a public tippler, oft drunk and loud to rail against the Parliament." The right or wrong of the matter does not concern us. A rector without a living has a struggle against fate. There were thirteen years of it, and then the family broke up. The eldest son, John, sailed for America as "second man to Edward Prescott," owner of the ship that brought him across the Atlantic. He settled on the Northern Neck, as it was called, between the Potomac and the Rappahannock; and there John begat Lawrence, and Lawrence begat Augustine and Augustine begat George, with whom we have to do.

We speak of him fondly and reverently as "the first American." But why? To ascribe to him transcendent genius or character unparalleled, would be to wrong the memory of not a few Americans who, in both natural gifts and accomplishments, have towered head and shoulders above him. Nevertheless, when you have named them all, lo, Washington stands *facile princeps*—" first in war, first in peace, first in the hearts of his countrymen."

I. He is entitled to this pre-eminence, at the outset, because *he was so distinctly a man of the people*. The best political type of man in America is *the average man*. If you want his picture, you must take a composite photograph of the whole people. At no point, in qualities natural or acquired, must he be colossal. His greatness is a symmetry of commonplaces. No segment of his character is far above mediocrity, but the circumference is perfect. This is the ideal in American citizenship. And because our hero stood so splendidly for that ideal he was pushed to the front as " Citizen George Washington."

We " reformers " are apt to forget this thing. The rule of the best is our ambition ; but popular sovereignty means the rule, not of the best, but of the average. Let us spare our lamentations. All goes well. *Vox populi, vox Dei.* The country is safer in the hands of John Plowman than in those of the most select oligarchy. Let that be remembered when our ward goes wrong. It has (say) 3,000 voters ; of whom fifty are men of means, culture and good morals. You say those fifty must march in the van of the 2,950, or else the community is in danger. God forbid ! The man who in our ward as elsewhere must " bear the gree an' a' that," is the average man. Reformers must take their places, and wield their influence, in the rank and file. The " rule of the best," so-called, has ruined all the alleged republics of history. Tarquin the Proud, walking with his prime minister in the royal gardens, was asked, " Which is the strongest form of government?" He said not a word, but with his staff whipped off the heads of the tallest poppies. That was a wise answer. Abraham Lincoln was of the same mind: "Have faith," said he, "in the people." In any case, whether we like it or not, this is the theory of our government. For want of apprehending it, reformers become pessimists and political preachers develop into common scolds. *Level down!* is the word; and *Level up!* is the word; and *Strike the average!* is the secret of our political life. So long as the average man is true to his responsibilities God reigns and the country is safe.

So much for citizenship; but what about rulers and magistrates? Shall they not be skimmed from the top? Not if representative government is wise. The average man best represents the people. In point of fact our rulers and magistrates, from George Washington to William McKinley, and from the White House to the City Hall, have been average men. As for such as boast their millions, wear university honors and delight themselves in the shadow of venerable family-trees, verily they have their reward, but not in political preferment. Washington the farmer, Lincoln the rail-splitter, Grant the tanner—this is the way Democracy works itself out. The village blacksmith is the stuff that sound governments are made of.

But here again, the reformer is in danger of losing both his philosophy and his temper. Because he cannot agree with current political methods, he concludes the system is bad; and because his confrères are not at the helm, the ship is little better than a nest of pirates. His vocabulary is inadequate to a just characterization of politics and politicians. Not one of our public men has escaped the tongue of well meaning calumny. George Washington, during his administration of public affairs, was charged with lying, malfeasance and misappropriation of public funds. Shamed by the obloquy which was heaped upon him, he expressed the wish that he had been carried to his grave before consenting to participate in public affairs. "Such indecent terms," he cried, "could scarcely have been applied to a common pickpocket." On one occasion he prepared an elaborate defence and read it with these prefatory words, "Gentlemen, you will permit me to put on my spectacles; for I have grown not only gray but almost blind in the service of my country." It is easy to see, through the years, the injustice of it all; but surely there is a lesson for us. Who among our public functionaries has escaped the bitter sting of partisan passion? If what we hear is true, they have all gone astray and wrought wickedness, there is none that doeth good, no, not one. By long persistence in this sort of judgment, we have succeeded at length in making politics so disreputable that self-respecting gentlemen are loath to have anything to do with them.

The whole method rests on a misapprehension. There is no such thing as natural leadership. Neither is a man entitled to it because he is wise, wealthy, or surpassingly pious. The average man, who, separating himself from the mass, forces his way by personal energy and with popular consent, to the top, is the man who belongs there. Any other view savors of the divine right of kings. Louis XIV. said, "I am the state." Washington ruled as one of the people, *primus inter pares*, vindicating his right to leadership not so much by a personal assurance of competency as by a determination on the part of the people that he should lead.

II. Another reason for assigning to Washington the first place in American Citizenship is the fact that *he was in perfect sympathy and accord with the underlying principles of the republic.*

(1) *The love of Freedom* was as the breath of his nostrils. He believed in the dignity of manhood, as a reflex of the sovereignty of God.

> O mighty brother soul of man,
> Where'er thou art, or low or high,
> Thy skyey arches with exultant span,
> O'er-roof infinity!

This means that mind, conscience and will are subservient only to the divine behest. No power, civil or ecclesiastical, must be permitted to forge fetters for the freeman whom the truth has made free.

(2) And then *Equality.* This is the obverse and complement of liberty. A man, sovereign in his own right, is of necessity the equal of every other man.

Such adventitious circumstances as blue blood and yellow dust have nothing to do with it.

> The rank is but the guinea's stamp ;
> The man's the gold.

When you have traced your genealogy, my friend, back to William the Conqueror, it will be wise to go further still, in the genial company of any chance acquaintance, until you find your noblest birthright in the saying that is written, "He was the son of Seth, who was the son of Enoch, who was the son of Adam, who was the son of God." Then come to Areopagus and hear Paul's manifesto to the proud Autochthenes, "God hath made of one blood all nations of men for to dwell on the face of the earth." And by that time we shall be ready to go down—as Washington went down from New York to Philadelphia in June, 1776—to hear the clangor of old Liberty Bell, ringing and swinging round and round to tell the world that "all men are created free and equal and with certain inalienable rights." There is not the width of a mountain brook betwixt those two great doctrines, liberty and equality. Out of the way, then, George the Third! and up with the Third Estate!

(3) But given liberty and equality, we are bound to add *Fraternity*. " Let us hang together," exhorted John Hancock in that Continental Congress. "Aye," responded a voice, "or we shall hang apart." The normal expression of this fact is universal suffrage. Liberty and Equality are mere high-sounding words, except as they are guarded and defended by the ballot—

> A weapon stronger yet,
> And better than the bayonet,
> A weapon that comes down as still
> As snowflakes fall upon the sod,
> And executes a freeman's will,
> As lightning does the will of God.

The French, therefore, were right. The triad of principles, "Liberty, Equality, Fraternity," are the sustaining pillars of popular constitutional government. To each of these the heart of Washington responded, *Yea* and *Amen*. "Aristocrat?" Not he. By birth, breeding and conviction, he was a republican; own brother to him who, a century later, besought his countrymen to "highly resolve that a government of the people, by the people and for the people, shall not perish from the earth."

It is regarded as greatly to Washington's credit that, when the sceptre was placed within his grasp, he refused it. "Be assured, sir," he wrote, "no occurrence in the course of this war has given me more painful sensations than your assurance that such ideas prevail in the army. I am much at a loss to conceive what part of my conduct could have given encouragement to an address which seems big with the greatest mischiefs that can befall my country. If I am not deceived in myself, you could not have found a person to whom your schemes could be more disagreeable Let me conjure you, therefore, if you have any regard for your country, concern for yourself and posterity, or respect for me, to banish these thoughts from your mind." But why should this be regarded as a strange thing? It was just like Washington. It was precisely what we should expect from such a man.

III. And this leads to a further reason for his undisputed primacy, to wit, *his glorious patriotism*. A man may be intellectually drenched with political truth, and still false to the body politic. The entire consecration of Washington—body, soul and estate—to the cause which he espoused, made him the Father of his Country.

At the drum-beat he was ready. Every drop of his blood throbbed hot for "the independence of these colonies." The die once cast, no doubts or misgivings restrained him. On hearing that his nephew had entertained a company of British officers at Mount Vernon in his absence, he wrote, "It would have been a less painful circumstance to me, had they in consequence of your non-compliance with their request, burnt my house and laid the plantation in ruin."

There was no reserve in his consecration to the cause. Did he in the fervor of war exceed the bounds of prudence? "My excuse," he wrote to Congress, "must be a character to lose, an estate to forfeit, the inestimable blessing of liberty at stake, and a life devoted."

Here is the secret of his military success—"liberty at stake and a life devoted." The Museum of Art in this city has recently been enriched, through the generosity of a fellow-townsman, by the addition of an historic masterpiece known as "Washington Crossing the Delaware." It tells a story of unswerving and indomitable courage. Ten hours on a storm-swept river, wrapped in the darkness of an Egyptian night, forcing a way through fields of floating ice ; then the dreary march to Trenton through driving sleet. "The guns are wet," complained General Sullivan. "Use the bayonet," said Washington ; "the town must be taken!" The town was taken. Then on to Princeton after Cornwallis. "An old-fashioned Virginia fox-hunt, gentlemen," said our hero, bending in his saddle to shout the view-halloo. This was the movement which Frederick the Great pronounced to be "the most brilliant campaign of the century."

But a true patriot loves better to sheathe his sword than draw it. The mark of great generalship is in the words, "Let us have peace." At the close of the Revolution the commander in-chief retired to Mount Vernon. His mind, at this period, was unveiled in a letter to Lafayette: "At length, my dear Marquis, I am become a private citizen on the banks of the Potomac. And under the shadow of my own vine and fig-tree, free from the bustle of the camp and the busy scenes of public life, I am solacing myself with those tranquil enjoyments of which the soldier who is ever in pursuit of fame, the statesman whose watchful days and sleepless nights are spent in devising schemes to promote the welfare of his own and perhaps the ruin of other countries—as if this globe was insufficient for all—and the courtier who is always watching the countenance of his prince, can have very little conception. I have not only retired from all public enjoyments, but am retiring within myself. Envious of none, I am determined to be pleased with all. And this, my dear friend, being the order of my march, I will move gently down the stream of time until I sleep with my fathers."

A pleasant picture this; the weary veteran, "first in peace," going the rounds of his plantation, casting up accounts, or gossiping with Jack Custis' little lad —"a very little gentleman with a feather in his hat, holding fast to one finger of the good General's remarkable hand"—but it passed like a pleasant dream.

There were problems to be solved more difficult than the crossing of swords. The Colonies were bound together by a rope of sand. Their credit was utterly broken down. Their various interests were pulling them asunder. The mind of Washington swept the future; he saw a continental empire threaded by ways of commerce which, like an arterial system, should find a common centre. But the drift was toward chaos. The Planter of Mount Vernon wrote to Henry Lee, "I know not where that influence can be found which shall be a proper remedy for our disorders. Influence is not government. Let us have a government by which our lives, liberties and properties shall be secured, or let us know the worst at once."

Aye, by all means *let us have a government!* But who shall lead the way? Cincinnatus must be called from the plow. "We cannot, sir, do without you," said Governor Johnson; "and I and thousands more can explain to anybody but yourself why we cannot do without you."

Never was a more unwilling candidate for the high honors of state. "My movement to the chair of government," he wrote, "will be accompanied by feelings not unlike those of a culprit who is going to the place of execution." But his love of country constrained him. Farewell to the restful pleasures of Mount Vernon! The journey was a triumph all the way from the banks of the Potomac to the ferry-stairs at the Battery. There were arches and garlands; mounted escorts and processions of children; salvos of cannon and martial music and vociferous cheering. It was on the 30th of April, 1789, that, facing the people from the balcony of Federal Hall, in Wall Street, Washington said, "I do solemnly swear, that I will faithfully execute the office of President of these United States, and will to the best of my ability, preserve, protect and defend the Constitution"; then added, as he kissed the Bible, "So help me God!"

IV. And here we come upon the full and final justification of his civic primacy; namely, *he believed with all his soul in the God of Nations.* No atheist, no infidel, no rationalist could have occupied his place. Thomas Paine, champion of human rights; Jefferson, architect of the nation's framework; Franklin, farseeing prophet of its destiny—all were incompetent to lead the way. There must be faith to follow the pillar of cloud. God's hand has been manifest in our history ever since Columbus planted the red-cross banner on the shore and christened the new-found continent "Land of the Saviour." Not all Americans are Christians; but thrice over it has been determined in our National Court of Last Appeal, that Christianity is an organic part of our common law.

Washington believed in God and made no scruple to avow it. He struck the key-note of our national welfare and prosperity when in his inaugural address he said, "The smiles of heaven can never be expected to rest on a nation that disregards the eternal rules of order and right which heaven has ordained." And again when he resigned his commission to Congress: " I consider it my indispensable duty to close this last solemn act of my life by commending the interests of our dearest country to the protection of Almighty God and those who have the superintendence of them to his holy keeping."

He believed in "God Manifest in Flesh," as the teacher, liberator and unifier of the race. He conceived of the Brotherhood of Man as proceeding from Christ's doctrine of the Fatherhood of God. He said, "It is my earnest prayer that God would incline the hearts of our citizens to cultivate the spirit of subordination and obedience to government; and that he would be most graciously pleased to dispose us all to do justice, to love mercy, and to demean ourselves with that charity, humility, and pacific temper of mind, which were the characteristics of the divine Author of our blessed religion, without a humble imitation of whose example in these things we can never hope to be a happy nation."

He believed in the Bible. He referred to it as

"the pure and benignant light of revelation." He loved it; he searched it as for hid treasure. He believed that he found in it the inestimable riches of the endless life.

He believed in the Church as God's temple. He shared with the other framers of the Constitution in a profound abhorrence of a national establishment of religion. In this he quite agreed with that distinguished Irish orator who characterized the union of Church and State as "a foul and adulterous connection, which corrupts the purity of heaven with the abominations of earth and hangs the tattered rags of political piety on the insulted cross of a crucified Redeemer." He was himself a Churchman—no wizened stickler for sectarian pre-eminence—but a believer in the goodly fellowship of that Holy Catholic Church, whose rock-rooted power is the franchise of national greatness and continuance. To his mind, Church and State were co-ordinate powers,—independent, interdependent, and both alike ordained of God.

He was a praying man. On his leaving home in early boyhood his mother said, "My son, never neglect the duty of secret prayer." Nor did he. It was his custom to rise at four in the morning for devotions. It is known to every one how a certain Quaker, while walking along a creek near Valley Forge, heard a voice from a dense thicket, pushed his way through and found Washington upon his knees. His face was uplifted and suffused with tears. The Continental cause was then at the last extremity. The troops were barefoot and hungry, the treasury depleted, and all hearts sick with hope deferred. The Commander-in-chief was making a mighty appeal to God for the triumph of right and freedom. The great leaders in the historic struggles for human rights have been praying men, such as Cromwell, William Prince of Orange, and Gustavus Adolphus, who entered battle with a *Pater Noster* on his lips.

The religion of Washington was more than an outward profession. It had the savor of salt. In a copy-book used in his boyhood is this sentence writ large, "Labor to preserve in your bosom that lingering spark of heavenly fire which men call conscience." That maxim was ever his guiding star. His life was marked by an enlightened probity. The flour manufactured at Mount Vernon and bearing the Washington mark, was passed without the customary inspection in West Indian ports. The name of Washington was voucher for truth, honesty, genuineness. He had learned the Master's word, "Let your light so shine before men that they may see your good works and glorify God."

It may be profitable here to call attention to a striking historical parallel. The cause of freedom was fought out almost contemporaneously in America and in France. When the hour struck in our country, the man was forthcoming—Washington, a man who thoroughly believed in God. When the hour struck in France, also, the man was forthcoming—Napoleon, who followed his star of destiny. While our people were nerving themselves in prayer and consecration for the approaching struggle, the mobs were gathering in the streets of Paris; they were writing "Liberty, Equality, Fraternity," across the dead walls and on the doors of Notre Dame. The Continental Congress was opened with prayer; but in the Corps Legislatif a resolution was offered and passed, "There is no God!" The wives and children of the Colonies, while their husbands and fathers were enduring the rigors of war, bore hunger and privation with humble patience. The women of France marched out to Versailles and interrupted the National Assembly, crying, "This is no question of politics ; this is a question of bread." While the fabric of constitutional freedom was rising on this side of the sea, the sharp blade of the guillotine on the other was decapitating the bravest and noblest of France. And when our nation was rejoicing in the ultimate success of its glorious struggle for human rights, and giving praises to God, the disappointed people of France were in unspeakable despair because their hopes were extinguished and their ill-founded temple of freedom had gone down in fire and blood. So true is it, that the nation that will not serve God shall perish. Of men and nations alike Jehovah has said, "If ye seek me, I will be found of you; if ye forsake me, I will cast you off."

Let it be observed that, in commemorating the civil virtues of Washington, we inadvertently weigh and measure his religion. For his life was moulded by his faith. We must, therefore,—unless our reverence for him is mere fruitless sentiment,—pay tribute to the God in whom he believed, the Saviour in whom he trusted, the Bible in which he had implicit confidence, the Church whose interests he espoused, the Sabbath which he scrupulously observed, the habit of prayer which he regarded as the bond of union between heaven and earth, and all those Christian graces which, making up a perfect character, find their realization in the divine Son of Man. So that the logical conclusion of the whole matter should be, "His God shall be our God, his Bible our Bible, and his Religion our Religion forever and ever."

THE SIGN OF THE PROPHET JONAS.

"Then certain of the scribes and Pharisees answered, saying, Master, we would see a sign from thee. But he answered and said unto them, An evil and adulterous generation seeketh after a sign; and there shall no sign be given to it, but the sign of the prophet Jonas: for as Jonas was three days and three nights in the whale's belly, so shall the Son of man be three days and three nights in the heart of the earth."—MATT. xii. 38-40.

No man ever made such extraordinary claims as this Jesus of Nazareth. Who was he? A man of the people who had received his education in a carpenter shop; yet he put himself forward as an infallible teacher in spiritual things. He touched the great problems of eternity with a fearless hand, and he taught as one having authority. The common people followed him in multitudes and heard him gladly. The scribes and Pharisees who were the accredited theologians of the time, looked on with amazement and envy. They inquired of him, "Whence is thine authority?" He answered, "From heaven." "Then give us a sign from heaven," said they, "to verify it."

He had wrought miracles among them. I do not say he claimed to work miracles, because his miracles were at that time undisputed facts. There were present in the popular assemblages those whose eyes had been opened, whose leprous scales had been wiped away, whose palsied limbs had been restored by his power. In the presence of such witnesses there was no room for denial or doubt. The only question was Whence did Jesus derive this power to work miracles? Was it from above or from beneath? The scribes and Pharisees intimated that it was from Satan. "No," said Jesus, "it is divine power. I can do nothing except the Father be with me. I and my Father are one." Then said the scribes and Pharisees, "Let us see your credentials. If this power be from heaven, show us a sign from heaven to attest it." But Jesus refused. He could say "No" on occasion, and there were special reasons why he should here refuse to give a sign.

(1) *Because it would have been of no use.* The trouble with the scribes and Pharisees was unbelief. A heavenly portent might convince their reason, but it could not change their heart. There was no adaptation of the means to the end.

The Hindoos tell of a famous conjurer who was commanded by his Rajah to gather peaches in winter. He said, "I will send up my little son to the orchard and see." He tossed a ball of twine into the air and ordered the lad to climb. The boy ascended hand over hand until he disappeared from sight. Presently a peach fell out of heaven, another and another; then came a bloody hand, a foot, a gory head, and trunk. The conjurer wailed, "They have caught my son and killed him. O Rajah, and good people, give me money to bury him." It was done. He gathered the severed limbs as if for burial, threw his cloak over them, waved his wand and, lo, his son walked forth. Now there was a sign from heaven apparently. It was possible beyond all doubt for Jesus to produce a marvel of that sort. But what then? It would only have convinced the beholders that he was a marvelous wizard, a master of his art. And nothing was further from the mind of Jesus than this. He came not to startle and bewilder men, but to save their souls from the power of death and hell.

A sign from heaven would have presented to the scribes and Pharisees no satisfactory argument for the validity of his religious teaching. It certainly could not have regenerated their souls, or brought them in humble penitence before God.

> A man convinced against his will
> Is of the same opinion still.

(2) He refused the sign, furthermore, *because they already had signs enough.* They had the Bible. This is the great miracle; the unveiling of the mind of God. It brought a message to the Pharisees concerning the Messiah which they refused to hear. His face was everywhere upon its pages. "Search the Scriptures," said Jesus, "for in them ye think ye have eternal life, and these are they which testify of me." It was their special business as religious teachers to know these Scriptures, and yet they had failed to discern their true significance. "If ye believe not Moses and the prophets," said Jesus, "ye would not believe though one rose from the dead." Still further, they had heard the discourses of Jesus, and had seen his wonderful works, but prejudice had blinded their eyes. They were given over to unbelief. They did not see, because they would not see.

But there was one sign which Jesus said these cavilers should have, to wit: The sign of the prophet Jonas. This was a sign, indeed, not from heaven, but from earth, from the darkness of the tomb, from the belly of hell. How runs the record? "*The word of the Lord came to Jonah the son of Amittai, saying, Arise, go down to Nineveh, that great city, and cry against it ; for their wickedness is come up before me. But Jonah rose up to flee from the presence of the Lord, and went down to Joppa, and found a ship going to Tarshish : so he paid the fare thereof, and went down into it. But the Lord sent out a great wind, and there was a tempest in the sea, so that the ship was like to be broken. Then the mariners took up Jonah and cast him forth ; and the sea ceased from her raging. Now the Lord had prepared a great fish to swallow Jonah, and he was in the belly of the fish three days and three nights. And he prayed unto the Lord out of the belly of hell, and the Lord heard him. And the fish vomited out Jonah upon the dry land. Now the word of the Lord came unto Jonah the second time, saying, Arise, and go unto Nineveh, that great city, and preach unto it the preaching that I bid thee. So he arose and went unto Nineveh. And he began to enter into the city a day's journey ; and cried, Yet forty days and Nineveh shall be overthrown ! So the people of Nineveh believed God and proclaimed a fast. And God saw their works that they turned from their evil way ; and God repented of the evil that he said he would do unto them ; and he did it not.*"

Now this is the sign which Jesus gave to those who refused to believe in him. A sign is something that signifies. What is the significance of the sign of the prophet Jonas? In other words, What did our Lord mean by it?

I. *It was a vindication of the truth of prophecy.* Our Lord said to his companions on his way to the village of Emmaus as he opened their understanding in the Scriptures, "Thus it is written, and thus it behooved Christ to suffer, and to rise from the dead."

It is the fashion in these days to make light of the story of Jonah. In some ecclesiastical quarters it is spoken of as a fable. Let it be understood, however, First, that *the Jews did not so regard it.* To them it was a record of an historical event. It was never called in question among those who accepted the Scriptures as the word of God. Second, *the early Christians believed it.* We find conclusive evidence of this in the fact that rude pictures of Jonah and the great fish are to be found on many of the graves in the catacombs. Here the early Christians laid away their dead and professed their faith in a final resurrection by the sign of the prophet Jonas. As the sea monster vomited forth the prophet, so should the grave give up the sleeping dust of their beloved to newness of life and immortality. And third, *Christ believed it.* He made this truth the guarantee of his own triumph over death. Had he regarded it as mere folk-lore, he could not have made such use of it. We do not use fables as guarantees of fact. Try it in a court of justice. As surely as Jason sought and found the Golden Fleece, so surely will I tell the truth! But that would scarcely answer. You must certify by an indubitable fact like this: As surely as there is a God in heaven I will tell the truth! Or try it in a common matter like the contract for a debt; make out your note on this wise: By the sign of Jack and the Beanstalk, or of Cinderella and her Crystal Slipper, I promise to pay when this obligation falls due. Does this seem preposterous? It is not a whit more preposterous than to allege that Jesus referred to a fable when he was called upon to produce a sign in verification of his claims as the only-begotten Son of God.

II. The sign of the prophet Jonas *was designed to verify and emphasize the Messiahship of Christ.* The antitype of Jonah and the great fish was the resurrection of Christ. This is the one pre-eminent miracle by which he verifies his claim. Thus Paul writes to the Romans: "He was declared to be the Son of God with power by his resurrection from the dead." This event proved his Messiahship with all that was involved in it.

It is a mighty claim, this claim that Jesus is the very Son of God. It covers his relations with his people every way.

(1) He presents himself *as our prophet or teacher in spiritual things.* He announced great truths. He stated them with authority; he did not hesitate to dogmatize with reference to them. Can we depend upon his word? Yes, if the sign of the prophet Jonas holds true. The poet Keats said, " My life is written in water." The authoritative teachings of Jesus of Nazareth were written in water indeed, if, like our fallible teachers, he succumbed to the power of death. But if on the other hand he conquered death, then every word of his presses itself upon heart and conscience with an irresistible force.

(2) He offers himself to us *as our priest.* He proposes to lay himself upon the altar as a living sacrifice in our behalf, to be wounded for our transgressions and bruised for our iniquities, that by his stripes we may be healed. He paid our ransom on the cross. But the proof of the payment of the debt is in the release of the debtor. He drew his bleeding hand, as he hung on Calvary, across the handwriting of ordinances that was against us and erased it. But we are still in the debtor's prison. In Joseph's garden the doors are flung wide

open; the seal of the satisfaction of justice is put upon the great sacrifice, and all the moral bankrupts of all ages and generations come forth by faith into the glorious liberty of the children of God. The sign of the prophet Jonas tells us that the ransom is accepted. To Mary weeping beside the tomb, because her divine Lord was dead, he suddenly appears and calls her by name; she falls at his feet and would embrace them, crying, "Rabboni!" He was dead and is alive again, and the word which he spoke to her is true, "Daughter, thy sins be forgiven thee!"

(3) He offers himself to us *as King;* as King to protect and rule over us. And with power he vindicates his claim by his resurrection from the dead. Who is the mightiest of earth? The King of Terrors. Is there any to dispute his power? Nay, there is no power like that of Death. Can the power of wealth equal it? Crœsus is reduced to dust. The power of glory? Nay,

> Imperious Cæsar, dead and turned to clay,
> Might stop a hole to keep the wind away.

The power of armies and navies? The shores of all the oceans are littered with shattered fleets and the hillsides are strewn with the dust of panoplied hosts. Who then shall dispute with death? On the pale horse, scythe in hand, he always has the right of way. At the door of the cemetery he laughs, and says, "I gather them in! I gather them in!" "My kingdom for an inch of time!" cries Queen Elizabeth. Fold her hands, cover her eyes; death is too much for her. "Fie! fie!" said Cardinal Beaufort, when they told him he had but a moment to live; "Wherefore shall death have me? Are my treasuries empty? Go bribe him!"

Fold his hands and carry him out; death has conquered. Death always conquers. Always? Nay, not in Joseph's garden. Here Christ meets the King of Terrors and vanquishes him—vanquishes him in behalf of all the children of men. In the darkness of this sepulchre, the bands and napkin, that never yet had been resisted, were as green withes in the grip of this Samson who rent them and came forth wiping the death dew from his face, saying, "O death, where is thy sting? O grave, where is thy victory?" And into the fellowship of this triumph he invites his people, following with them always after the bier and standing beside the open graves of their beloved saying, "I am the resurrection and the life; he that believeth in me, though he were dead, yet shall he live; and whosoever liveth and believeth in me shall never die."

III. The sign of the prophet Jonas *gives us a definite assurance of life and immortality.* It is written, "Life and immortality are brought to light in the Gospel." The world had always dreamed of immortality; had guessed and wondered and hoped. Now, however, the mists of doubt are lifted, the dream becomes a reality, the peradventure gives way to the "Yea" and "Amen" of the risen Son of God.

The relation of Christ to the believer in the matter of his resurrection is eloquently put by Paul in his Easter address to the Christians of Corinth: "*Now if Christ be preached that he rose from the dead, how say some among you that there is no resurrection of the dead? For if there be no resurrection, then is not Christ risen. And if Christ be not risen, then is our preaching vain, and your faith is also vain; ye are yet in your sins. Then they also which are fallen asleep in Christ are per-*

ished. If in this life only we have hope in Christ, we are of all men most miserable. But now is Christ risen from the dead and become the first fruits of them that slept."

There is a world of meaning in that word, "first fruits." It calls up the picture of a Hebrew farmer scattering his wheat in the furrows; then guarding his fields against drought and mildew and vermin and the fowls of the air; then watching for the first appearance of the green blade; praying for the dews and the latter rains; fearing, hoping until the green grows golden, and then going forth with sickle in hand to reap where the sun has fallen most benignantly, and bearing his sheaf to the temple—the first fruits, to wave it before the altar as prayer and prophecy; a prayer that God will guard the growing fields, a prophecy that the whole harvest shall be brought in. The great choirs of the temple sing the festival chorus, but there is an undertone which only the farmer hears; the joy of the hungry, the song of harvest home, the creaking of the heavy wains that bear the yellow harvest to the garners. So Christ is the first sheaf of the resurrection waved before the altar of God. His resurrection is both prayer and prophecy. "*Now is Christ risen from the dead and become the first fruits of them that slept. And behold, I show you a mystery: We shall not all sleep, but we shall all be changed, in a moment, in the twinkling of an eye: for the trumpet shall sound and the dead shall be raised incorruptible. Then shall be brought to pass the saying that is written, Death is swallowed up in victory. O death, where is thy sting? O grave, where is thy victory? The sting of death is sin; and the strength of sin is the law. But thanks be to God, which giveth us the victory through our Lord Jesus Christ.*"

TO THINE OWN SELF BE TRUE.

"So God created man in his own image, in the image of God created he him."
—Gen. i. 27.
"For thou hast made him a little lower than the angels, and hast crowned him with glory and honor."—Ps. viii. 5.
"How much better then is a man than a sheep."—Matt. xii. 12.
"Behold, now are we sons of God; and it doth not yet appear what we shall be."—I. John iii. 2.
"Let no man despise thee."—Titus ii. 15.

A man's opinion of himself has much to do with his manner of life. There are two extremes: On the one hand it is quite possible for one to "think of himself more highly than he ought to think." There is nothing which betrays itself more certainly than conceit. It is apparent even in the walk and the lifting of the eyes. An extreme case was that of Louis XIV., who, when reminded by his chaplain that he was a great sinner and in danger of eternal death, replied with a shrug of his shoulders, "All true, no doubt; but the good God will think twice before he casts out so good a prince as I am."

The other extreme is servility. This also manifests itself in unmistakable ways. What is more despicable than the fawning obsequiousness of Uriah Heep; the pale eyes, the clammy hand, the shuffling step, the cringing manner? But between conceit and servility lies the golden mean; to-wit,—self-respect. "This above all, to thine own self be true, and it must follow, as the night the day, thou canst not then be false to any man." The Scotch have a proverb of like import: "Be a friend to yersel and ithers will." It was a wise saying of John Milton, "The pious and just honoring of ourselves may be thought the fountain head from which every laudable and worthy enterprise issues forth."

But self-respect must have a solid basis. There are men who have no right to respect themselves. They should, in all reason, abhor and bemoan themselves in sackcloth and ashes. But there are others who, while suffering from the common malady, sin, are yet conscious of right purposes and noble aspirations. There is such a thing as a valid self-respect. It is grounded on self-knowledge. "Know thyself," said the Delphic oracle. Who am I? Whence came I? What do I? And whither am I bound?

I. *Know thy origin.* It is a great thing to be able to say with assurance, "I came forth from God. I was made in his likeness and after his image; his breath is in my nostrils."

Here is where the doctrine of evolution comes in. By evolution is properly meant the development of the highest form of being from the lowest, by the calm processes of natural law, without any necessity of interposition on the part of God.

(1) The Bible statement is very clear. There is no equivocation in the narrative of the creation of man. He came originally from the formative hand of God, full-grown, erect, intelligent and able to hold communion with the Being who created him. To those who accept the Scriptures as an infallible record, this should be conclusive. Those who take issue with their truthfulness, will attach little weight to it.

(2) But there is another source of information, namely, conjecture. It deals in theories and hypotheses, and arrives at *non sequitur* conclusions. An archæologist named Dubois recently unearthed, some yards apart, in the island of Java, a skull and a tibia. The skull belonged to an ape, the tibia to a man. Professor Dubois put on his guessing-cap forthwith, and said, "I guess these are about ten millions of years old," and again, "I guess they were parts of a single organism," and still further, "I guess I have found the missing link." And there are people who accept this sort of thing without a murmur!

(3) One voice, however, is still to be heard, the voice of science. The word science is from *scire*, to know. Science deals only in facts. What has science to say as an arbiter in the controversy between revelation and hypothesis? Only this, "I do not know."

Of course, if evolution is proven to be a scientific fact, we must accept it. Demonstration makes an end of controversy. But no scientist of any standing claims that evolution is a demonstrated fact. It is called now a theory and now a hypothesis. Darwin himself was frank to admit that its essential claims were unproven. It is only dilettanti scientists, and theologians in whom the wish is father to the thought, who assert otherwise. There are infinite gulfs which, by common consent, remain to be bridged; such for example as the gulf between nothing and something, and that between chaos and cosmos, and another between organic and inorganic matter, and still another between mere animal life and the divine soul. Until these and other chasms are bridged, it is manifest folly to accept evolution as a demonstrated fact.

For years there has been a continuous endeavor

to find the remains of a pre-Adamite man. It has been heralded once and again that a satisfactory refutation of the Mosaic anthropology had been found in fossil deposits. A few years ago, for example, a skull was found in the delta of the Mississippi at a point below the surface which seemed to demonstrate the most extreme antiquity. The scientists made a close calculation, resulting in the conclusion that the strata under which the skull was discovered could not have been formed in less than eleven millions of years. It occurred to them, that probably there were remains of still greater value to be found further down. The excavation was continued—and resulted in the finding of the remains of an old-fashioned flat-boat. Not all investigations of this character have ended in such sudden discomfiture; but all are alike in having fallen far short of proof. Whatever the future may bring forth, at this moment Adam remains the first man.

It passes understanding, under these conditions, how any man should be willing—and many seem not only willing, but eager—to accept as final a mere guess that man is descended from an anthropoid ape. It makes no difference, they say, whence we came, so long as we are here. But it does make a difference. It makes a great difference in the matter of self-respect. Blood is thicker than water. Ancestors do not go for nought. It is surely an easier matter to respect myself, if I believe as the Scripture says, that I am made "a little lower than the angels," than if I fall in with what Thomas Carlyle contemptuously calls "the religion of frog-spawn." It exalts me unspeakably to feel that my life is from God, for God, to God. As the skeptic Theodore Parker said, "The greatest star after all is that at the little end of the telescope; the star that is looking, not looked at."

> O mighty brother soul of man,
> Where'er thou art, or low or high,
> Thy skyey arches, with exultant span,
> O'er-roof infinity.

II. *Know the possibilities of thy life.* Not only do we come from God, but our kinship with him is manifest in many ways.

(1) *We can think God's thoughts.* In this fact lies the possibility of communion with him. We are able to contemplate the great verities which centre in him; such as life and immortality, judgment and glory. The fact that man can reason about the divine being, can pay tribute to moral responsibility, can determine "betwixt the worse and better reason," can argue *pro* and *con* as to retribution, is evidence of his kinship with God. "I thank thee, O Father," said Kepler, watching the stars at night, "that I am able to think thy thoughts after thee." It was this same feeling that moved David to exclaim, "When I consider thy heavens, the work of thy fingers, the moon and stars which thou hast ordained, what is man, that thou art mindful of him?" Birds and insects do not watch the stars. Dogs and horses have no apprehension of duty. Such experiences are not possible to the lower orders of life.

(2) *We can imitate the character of God.* This is, indeed, the rationale of all character. "Be ye holy, saith the Lord, for I am holy." To the end that this process of imitation might be made the more practicable, it pleased God to manifest himself in flesh and walk about among us. The Man Jesus is the fulness

of the Godhead bodily. The highest aspiration possible to a man is to be like him. In him we grow unto the full stature of a man. And herein we are infinitely exalted above all the lower orders. We do not speak of the character of a horse. We ask, "How many hands high is he? Is he docile and spirited?" and the like. But none of these requirements have any moral quality. Faith, virtue, knowledge, temperance, patience, godliness, brotherly kindness, charity—these things which find their fulness and perfection in God, are built into the character of man. To cultivate these is to realize the possibilities of our nature and make the most of ourselves. We are now sons of God, but it doth not yet appear what, in the processes of holy purpose and earnest endeavor, we shall be.

(3) *We are permitted to do the work of God.* He is setting up his kingdom on the earth. The average man takes little or no cognizance of it. The streets are filled with busy people engaged in sordid pursuits, most of whom appear to think that wealth, pleasure, and earthly distinction are the chiefest good. But these things pass away like mists before the morning sun. Here is our glorious franchise,— that we can stand beside the only-begotten Son of God in the great harvest field ; that we can thrust in the sickle and reap with him ; that after the labor of life we can enter into his joy. And, indeed, there is nothing higher than this possible to human nature. It is said that William Wykeham, who built a church for Edward I., carved over its doorway, "This work made William Wykeham." On being charged by the king with assuming an undeserved honor, he replied, "I meant not that I made the work, but that

the work made me; forasmuch as, having been poor when I began, I now have a fat and bulging purse." If ever we deem ourselves necessary to the work of Christ's kingdom, let us reflect how easily he could get along without us, and how much it means that he is willing to employ us. His work dignifies us infinitely; it makes us. It was one of the sayings of General Gordon, "If I were not permitted to participate in the work of Jesus Christ, I should be as worthless as an empty sack bumping on a camel's back."

III. *Know thy destiny.* Born of God, participating with him in his great thoughts and gracious work, it is ours to abide with him forever.

This means immortality. The argument for immortality has been made with success from many standpoints; but what need, if we believe the word that is written, "He breathed into our nostrils the breath of life." What can destroy the breath of God? When Marius, the great Roman, was confronted, unarmed, by an assassin with knife in hand, he repelled him with the word, "Dost thou kill Marius?" What can kill me if I am, indeed, a child of God? In the necessity of the case I share in the immortality of him who created me.

Here is heaven. We not only live forever, but we are to live with God. We are notified that the home has already been provided. "In my Father's house," said Jesus, "are many mansions; if it were not so I would have told you; I go to prepare a place for you." Thus, it appears, God's house shall be our house; and our Lord's joy shall be our joy for ever and ever.

And best of all, promotion. If we have loved our Master's work in this present life, we shall find the pleasure of eternity in the pursuit of nobler tasks. Of heaven it is written, "There his servants do serve him." There will be no withdrawing from responsibility, no drawing back from the behest of duty. Responsibility will be privilege. Duty will be pleasure. The answer to the Master's voice of command will ever be, "Here am I, send me"; "in the volume of the book it is written of me, 'I delight to do thy will.'"

We have indicated the grounds on which a valid self-respect must rest. There is only one difficulty in the way of realizing these possibilities; that is sin. It is not necessary to enter into a theological discussion about it. No matter whence or how or why sin came: here it is. Here it is; perpetually making trouble between me and my conscience, between me and my fellow-men, between me and my God. Sin is like virus poisoning the blood. It enfeebles body and soul, so that notwithstanding my high birth, my noble aspirations and my splendid dreams of destiny, there is no self-respect possible to me while I am under the dominion of it.

What shall I do then ? *Get rid of sin.*

(*a*) *Get rid of the record of the mislived past.* I have done those things which I ought not to have done, and left undone the things which I ought to have done. At this point, however, God has interposed. The cross stands before me. The piercéd hands of the Redeemer are stretched out. The blood cleanseth. Let us begin at the beginning; we can go no further until we have attended to this. An unforgiven sinner is like a convict wearing a ball and chain. Cut loose, dear friend, from the sin-stained past, that you may realize the possibilities of your nature. You can never stand erect and hold up your head with this fearful burden of shame and sorrow bearing you down. Ask Christ to forgive. It is said of Christian in the allegory, that when his bundle had rolled into the sepulchre at the foot of the cross, he "gave three leaps for joy and went on his way singing, 'He hath given me joy for my sorrow and life by his death!'"

(*b*) But when the past is cancelled we still stand in constant need of *help and inspiration.* Whence shall they come? To this end the Holy Spirit is given unto us. He delivers us from the bondage, as Christ by his blood delivered us from the penalty, of sin. Let us go on then under the influence of the Spirit and build up character. Everything depends on the influence of the Spirit. With Christ as your Saviour and the Holy Spirit as your Paraclete, who shall lay anything to your charge? What further shall stand in the way of self-respect? When Stephen of Colonna was led forth a captive from his ancestral castle, his enemy asked, "Where is your fortress?" He laid his hand upon his heart and answered, "Here!" Not until a man has discharged his duty to the very last atom, not until he has done to the very uttermost what he believes to be right, not until he has exhausted the last resource in delivering himself from sin, can he respect himself.

If Christ is the only deliverer, then am I not true to myself until I have accepted him. If the Holy Spirit is the only helper, in the large duties and responsibilities of life, then am I not true to myself until I have accepted him. Let us be honest in these matters and in everything else. Be true, my friend, to your convictions. Revere character. "Bring up the bottom of your life to the top of your light." Acknowledge the Christ who gave himself for you. Honor the Holy Ghost. Then you can reasonably respect yourself. Then will no man despise you.

THE CREED OF THE MOUNT.

"And seeing the multitudes he went up into a mountain: and when he was set, his disciples came unto him: and he opened his mouth, and taught them, saying."—MATT. V., 1-2.

We are thus introduced to the Sermon on the Mount which is spoken of as a wonderful sermon. Why not? It was uttered by the most wonderful of preachers, who spake as one having authority with respect to all the great problems of the eternal life. On one occasion a company of temple guards was sent to arrest him as he was teaching in Solomon's Porch. They came and listened, and returned without their prisoner. "Why have ye not brought him?" asked the Pharisees. Their reply was a tribute to the eloquence of Jesus such as was never paid to any other,—"Never man spake like this man!"

But wonderful as is this Sermon on the Mount, it is possible, nevertheless, to exaggerate its relative importance in the great body of moral and religious truth. Ian Maclaren errs in this respect in "The Mind of the Master," where he suggests it as a sufficient creed for an ecclesiastical body. His words are: "No church since the early centuries has had the courage to formulate an ethical creed, for even those bodies of Christians which have no written theological creeds, yet have implicit affirmations or denials of doctrine as their basis. Imagine a body of Christians who should take their stand on the sermon of Jesus, and conceive their creed on his lines. Imagine how it would read, 'I believe in the Fatherhood of God; I believe in the words of Jesus; I believe in the clean heart; I believe in the service of love; I believe in the unworldly life; I believe in the Beatitudes; I promise to trust God and follow Christ, to forgive my enemies and to seek after the righteousness of God.' Could any form of words be more elevated, more persuasive, more alluring? Do they not thrill the heart and strengthen the conscience? Liberty of thought is allowed; liberty of sinning is alone denied. Who would refuse to sign this creed? They would come from the east, and the west, and the north, and the south to its call and even they who would hesitate to bind themselves to a crusade so arduous would admire it, and long to be worthy."

In pursuance of this suggestion, a circular letter has been addressed to ministers generally, requesting them "to bring the Life Creed to the attention of their congregations." I desire now to give my reasons for personally withholding my endorsement of this movement, and to indicate why I for one am not willing to receive the Sermon on the Mount as presented in condensed and crystallized form in the "Life Creed" as a sufficient basis for a federation of believers in Christ.

I. *It was not so intended by Christ himself.* He came into the world to set up a kingdom of truth and righteousness. He was thirty years in preparation for his work. He then entered upon his ministry, and, at the outset, gathering his few disciples about him, he delivered his inaugural. The Sermon on the Mount is the inaugural address of the King. In it he sets forth certain principles which are to rule in the lives of all who shall be citizens in the commonwealth of God. They are to be poor in spirit, meek, merciful, nobly aspiring, pure in heart, peacemakers and patient sufferers for the truth's sake. "Ye are the salt of the earth," he says, "but if the salt have lost its savor, wherewith shall it be salted? it is thenceforth good for nothing, but to be cast out, and to be trodden under foot of men." And again, "Ye are the light of the world. A city that is set on a hill cannot be hid. Let your light so shine before men, that they may see your good works, and glorify God." It must be apparent, however, that important as these precepts and principles are, they do not exhaust the gospel and were not designed to do so.

On April 30, 1789, George Washington entered upon his first administration as President of the United States. In front of the national building at the corner of Wall and Nassau Streets, in this city, he delivered an inaugural address, which was full of sound political sense. If a man, however, were to suggest that his address upon that occasion contained all that was necessary to furnish the political standards of our Republic, so that the Declaration of Independence, the Constitution, the enactments of our legislatures and decisions of our courts are all unimportant, we should regard him as a foolish fellow. So, without minimizing the splendid significance of the Sermon on the Mount, we say that it is not enough to furnish an exhaustive and conclusive creed for the universal Church of God.

II. *It is too severe.* The friends of the new movement seem to suppose that the Sermon on the Mount is an expression of the divine love and tenderness. It is on the other hand distinctly legal. It is law, law, and only law from beginning to end.

It is spoken of as an "ethical creed." The phrase is incongruous. An ethical creed is a distinct contradiction of terms. A creed is one thing; a code is another. Doctrines and moral precepts are not identical. They run in parallel lines; they complement and supplement each other, but they are in no wise synonymous. Let that pass, however. The important fact is that a church founded upon a constitution of pure ethics would be a prison house of fear and sorrow.

The Sermon on the Mount is a clear echo of the deliverances of Sinai. "I am come," said Jesus, "not to destroy the law but to fulfill it." It places a startling emphasis upon the law. It is searching as fire. It is penetrating as acid. Listen to this: "Ye have heard that it was said by them of old time, Thou shalt not kill: But I say unto you, That whosoever is angry with his brother without a cause, shall be in danger of the judgment; and whosoever shall say to his brother, Raca, shall be in danger of the council; but whosoever shall say, Thou fool, shall be in danger of hell fire." And again, "Ye have heard how it was said by them of old time, Thou shalt not commit adultery: but I say unto you, That whosoever looketh on a woman to lust after her, hath committed adultery with her already in his heart." And again, "If thy right eye offend thee, pluck it out, and cast it from thee; and if thy right hand offend thee, cut it off, and cast it from thee; for it is profitable for thee that one of thy members should perish, and not that thy whole body should be cast into hell."

And observe, there is not one word of redemptive mercy in this sermon. If a man would live by the law, he must keep it. If a man break the law, he shall die by it. So far as we have to do with the Sermon on the Mount, there is no power of pardon in atoning blood, and there is therefore no deliverance from sin Here is the end of it: "Whosoever heareth these sayings of mine, and doeth them, I will liken him unto a wise man which built his house upon a rock: and the rain descended and the floods came, and the winds blew and beat upon that house; and it fell not; for it was founded upon a rock. And whoso heareth these sayings of mine and doeth them not, shall be likened unto a foolish man, which built his house upon the sand: and the rain descended and the floods came and the winds blew and beat upon that house, and it fell; and great was the fall of it."

III. *The Sermon on the Mount is a mere fragment of the teachings of Christ.* Why should we discriminate in favor of this sermon as against all his other words? Christianity means loyalty to Christ every way. The Christian is one who calls Christ his Lord and Master, and finds in him a tribunal of last appeal in all matters touching his faith and conduct. If we are moved by sound sense, and not mere sentiment, in saying that the words of Jesus shall furnish forth our creed, then why confine our devotion to this Sermon on the Mount? Why not include his address to the woman at the well? Or is there an offense for ritualists in the words, "I say unto you, The hour cometh when neither in this mountain, nor yet at Jerusalem, shall ye worship the Father; for God is a spirit; and they that worship him must worship him in spirit and in truth"? And why not receive his conversation with Nicodemus as an essential part of our creed? Is it because the two fundamental doctrines of regeneration and atonement are there? "Verily, verily, I say unto thee, Except a man be born again, he shall not see the kingdom of God," and, "As Moses lifted up the serpent in the wilderness, even so must the Son of man be lifted up: that whosoever believeth in him should not perish, but have everlasting life." And why exclude his arraignment of the scribes and Pharisees? "Woe unto you scribes and Pharisees, hypocrites! who make clean the outside of the platter; who pay tithe of mint, anise and cummin, and neglect the weightier matters of the law. Ye are as whited sepulchres; fair without, but within full of dead men's bones and all uncleanness. O generation of vipers! How shall ye escape the damnation of hell?"

And shall we exclude those parables in which our Lord sets forth the sterner side of the divine character; such as the parable of the talents, of the winnowing of the wheat, of the separation of the sheep and the goats, of Dives and Lazarus, of the ten virgins, of the man that had not on the wedding garment? These are fearful words, but the Master uttered them: "The worm that dieth not," "The fire that is not quenched," "The outer darkness where there shall be weeping and wailing and gnashing of teeth." Nor must we discriminate against the sermon in the upper chamber: "In my Father's house are many mansions." But if that be received, then the Arians must be ruled out of our Christian federation for it is in that discourse that our Lord says, "He that hath seen me hath seen the Father; and how sayest thou then, Show us the Father? Believest thou not that I am in the Father, and the Father in me?" Nor must we slight the sermon of Jesus on the Mount of Ascension in which he emphasized the importance of the great propaganda, saying, "All power is given unto me, in heaven and on earth. Go ye, therefore ; and evangelize ; and, lo, I am with you alway even unto the end of the world." All these and the other discourses of Jesus are to be received in the making of our creed if we are loyal to him. It will not answer to take a fragment of his teaching and build our faith upon it.

IV. *The Sermon on the Mount is worthless for practical purposes without a personal faith in Christ* We must believe that there is a God ; a personal Lawgiver behind the law. We must believe that Christ is his accredited ambassador, who has authority to declare the mind of his Father among men. We must believe also in the Holy Spirit as the Executive who transmits these truths through the centuries and propagates them through that great living organism, the Church, made up of all the followers of the Christ. Unless we have confidence in these verities, the Sermon on the Mount must be meaningless to us. Yet what are we saying? "I believe?" Credo? This is indeed the formulation of a creed, and ethics is valueless without it. "I believe in God the Father; I believe in Jesus Christ; I believe in the Holy Ghost"; this is substantially the Apostles' Creed, the historic symbol of the church of all ages. It is preëminently foolish to speak of ethics without a creed. We should by ethics alone be brought into legal bondage.

We would not think of making such a proposition in any other province than that of the religious life. There are those who call themselves "ethical Christians"; but the folly of their position is evident when we regard the character of certain "ethical" citizens with whom we are familiar in our civil life. There is a multitude of lewd fellows of the baser sort, who can only be kept in order by the restraints of law. You may find an illustration of ethical citizenship in the chain gang; men who work with a ball and chain upon their ankles, expiating the broken law. Let it be borne in mind continually that ethics makes slaves; it is the truth that makes free. Alas for a man who, in either church or state, is no better than the law makes him!

V. And, finally, we regard the Sermon on the Mount as in itself inadequate to meet the purposes for a creed, *because there must be outside of this sermon an ultimate authority somewhere.* We want verification. How do I know, indeed, that Jesus ever uttered the Sermon on the Mount?

There are four tribunals to which we may appeal for decisive authority. The first is *the Pope.* The decree of papal infallibility was required as a logical necessity in the Romish Church. The Pope is the court of last appeal in matters of faith and doctrine, and unless he is infallible, his power must inevitably pass from him.

The second is *the Church.* Prelacy holds that the voice of the Church is ultimate in all matters ethical and theological. But, unfortunately, the Church has no voice. Its voices in history have been like Babel. It was one section of the Church that protested against the error of the mass; and it was another section of the Church that pulled the bell-rope of St. Germain, and gave the signal on St. Bartholomew's night to massacre those who made that protest.

The third authority is *the inner sense*. This might answer if it were not a fact that no two have the same personal experience. It is not enough for me to say, "I feel that Jesus said it," because the next man may declare, "I feel that Jesus never said it." There is only one doctrine that is more preposterous than papal infallibility, and that is personal infallibility. Reason cannot stand alone; it must have something to lean on.

Fourth, *the Bible*. Here is a "Thus saith the Lord." The first thing for an earnest man to do is to satisfy himself whether the Bible is a true book or not. If that question be settled affirmatively, then he must needs take the Scriptures to be his infallible rule of faith and practice. The Sermon on the Mount will be a portion of his creed. All the other discourses of Jesus will have like importance, and will enter into his creed. All the remainder of the Book will have a corresponding value, because the entire Scriptures were written by holy men as they were moved by the Spirit of Christ. The words of Scripture are the breathings of Christ. We have no reason to say that the words that fell from his fleshly lips are more holy than the words which he has otherwise inspired. He holds himself responsible for all. The word is, "All Scripture is profitable for doctrine, for reproof, for correction, for instruction in righteousness; that the man of God may be perfect, thoroughly furnished unto all good works."

Here then we have our authority. Here is a complete creed, and here is a complete code of ethics. And here also is the living Christ, the Exemplar of truth and morals. On the seal of the Church of the Reformation is an open Bible, over it the name of

Jehovah with the words *veritate* and *pietate;* that is, a divine and, therefore, infallible rule of faith and practice. Our creed is the entire Scriptures; nothing more and nothing less. They were given for this very purpose. And the Master laid his most emphatic endorsement upon them in this relation when he said, "Search the Scriptures, for in them ye think ye have eternal life, and these are they which testify of me."

THE CHURCH.

"Ye are built upon the apostles and prophets, Jesus Christ himself being the chief corner-stone ; in whom all the building, fitly framed together, groweth unto a holy temple in the Lord."—Eph. ii. 20.

We are accustomed to think of Paul as a dry dialectician, a mere theologian or doctrinaire. It is a mistake. He was a splendid poet with an extraordinary development of the logical faculty. He could handle a metaphor with as much skill as a syllogism. Word-pictures bespangle his discussions of abstruse themes like stars on a deep blue sky.

He was familiar with the customs of the Roman soldiery, and accordingly he represents life as a campaign. It is a continuous succession of battles with the world and the flesh and the devil. "Put ye on the whole armor of God, therefore, that ye may be able to withstand in the evil day, and, having done all, to stand. Stand therefore, having your loins girt about with truth, and having on the breastplate of righteousness; and your feet shod with the preparation of the gospel of peace; above all, taking the shield of faith, wherewith ye shall be able to quench all the fiery darts of the wicked one. And take the helmet of salvation and the sword of the Spirit, which is the Word of God." Thus armed and panoplied,

> Fight on, my soul, till death
>   Shall bring thee to thy God;
> He'll take thee, at thy parting breath,
>   Up to his blest abode.

He had seen the Greek games; for there was a stadium in Tarsus which he must have frequented more or less in his early days. He paints life accordingly as a struggle for mastery. He sees the contestants stripped to the waist, their feet at the scarlet line, their bodies bent forward with every muscle tense, their eyes upon the distant goal. The trumpet sounds and they are off! "I count not myself to have apprehended, but this one thing I do, forgetting those things which are behind, and reaching forth unto those things which are before, I press toward the mark for the prize of the high calling of God in Christ Jesus." And again, "Let us lay aside every weight, and the sin which doth so easily beset us, and let us run with patience the race that is set before us, looking unto Jesus the author and finisher of our faith; who, for the joy that was set before him, endured the cross, despising the shame, and is set down at the right hand of the throne of God."

Paul knew about agriculture also and writes not unfrequently like a farmer's boy. To him life is sowing and reaping: "Ye are God's husbandry," he says; and, "Be not deceived; God is not mocked; for whatsoever a man soweth that shall he also reap." He dwells much on fruit and fruitfulness. The fifteenth chapter of First Corinthians—that wonderful chapter on the resurrection—has been characterized as an "Agricultural Allegory." He speaks of God's Acre as a field sown with the ashes of the sleeping dead who are to arise in newness of life. "But some man will say, 'How are the dead raised up?' Thou fool! that which thou sowest is not quickened, except it die: and that which thou sowest, thou sowest not that body that shall be, but bare grain, it may chance of wheat, or of some other grain: but God giveth it a body as it has pleased him. So also is the resurrection of the dead. It is sown in corruption, it is raised in incorruption; it is sown in dishonor, it is raised in glory; it is sown in weakness, it is raised in power; it is sown a natural body, it is raised a spiritual body." Ah, what a golden field is that and what a song of harvest home shall be heard on the resurrection morning!

In our context the artist betrays an acquaintance with the architectural methods of his time. Life is structural. He uses the word *edify* nineteen times in his epistles to the Churches. The word is cognate with *edifice;* its primary reference is to temple building, and hence its application to character. "Ye are God's building," the Apostle says. He is not speaking now, however, of the individual, but of the association of believers in the Church of God.

The Christians of Ephesus would instantly understand the reference here. They lived under the shadow of Diana's Temple, one of the seven wonders of the world. It was four hundred feet long and above two hundred feet wide, and was two hundred and twenty years in building. Its roofs were supported by sixty-seven columns of green jasper, eight of which of which may be seen to-day in the Mosque of St. Sophia. Its altar was designed by Praxiteles. Its walls were adorned by Apelles and Parrhasius. Its sanctuary was so safe that kings were wont to deposit their valuables there. Erostratus made himself immortal by setting fire to its dome. Alexander offered the spoils of an eastern campaign for the privilege of inscribing his name above one of the portals, and was refused. The title of *Neocorus*, or Sweeper of the

Temple, was coveted and competed for by various cities. The dome of this magnificent fabric was surmounted by an image of Diana catching the sunlight in her golden shield. In sight of this temple, within the hearing of its elaborate worship, dwelt a humble body of believers in Christ. To them the Apostle writes in terms of encouragement: "Ye are the living parts of a grander fabric, whose glory shall endure when the walls of the temple of great Diana have crumbled to dust. Ye are built upon the apostles and prophets, Jesus Christ himself being the chief corner-stone; in whom all the building, fitly framed together, groweth unto an holy temple in the Lord."

Here is the theme, therefore, which engages our thought: I believe in the holy Catholic Church, a spiritual house, a house not made with hands, built of God.

I. Observe, *the corner-stone is Christ.* The engineers of the Palestine Exploration Fund, by sinking shafts and opening galleries along the walls of the temple, came upon the original foundations. They are seventy feet below the surface, and rest upon the rocky slopes of Moriah. At the lowest angle of this temple area they discovered the corner-stone. It was four feet thick and fourteen broad, and its fine finish was almost unimpaired. It is not improbable that the prophet Isaiah had this very stone in mind when he uttered the Messianic prediction, "Behold, I lay in Zion for a foundation, a stone, a tried stone, a precious corner-stone." The first place, deepest down, most rudimental and fundamental, binding the walls together and upholding the whole,—this is reserved for Christ.

1. *The name of the Church is eloquent of this fact.* "What's in a name?' Everything here. Call the

Church whatever you please, it is Christian above all. All other names, Greek and Latin, Catholic and Protestant, Lutheran, Calvinistic and Wesleyan, are subordinate to that Name which is above every other that is named in heaven or on earth. All tribal banners are furled under the banner of the Lion of Judah.

Here is the touchstone of ecclesiastical legitimacy. It has just been decided in one of the Massachusetts courts—in a case brought by the Theosophists to secure exemption from taxation on their meeting-hall—that an organization, in order to be called "religious," must show that it believes in the living God. But with reference to the Christian Church the lines are drawn closer still. It is not enough that an ecclesiastical body shall be religious in order to justify its claim to the fellowship of the Holy Catholic Church; it must give evidence that it believes in Christ, that it accepts his divine birth, his Messiahship, his blood-atonement, his resurrection, and his word as law every way.

2. Here, also, is clearly indicated *the purpose or intent of the Church.* Why did Christ institute it? What is it intended for? It is not a social coterie, though many people make it so. Neither is it a benevolent organization, though the tendency of much of the sociological discussion of our time points that way. The primary purpose of the Church was not charity, caring for the poor, visiting the fatherless and the widows in their affliction. This is incidental; vitally so, to be sure, but merely incidental to a larger, nobler end. Nor is the Church a theological symposium. All Christians who are worthy of the name, are profoundly concerned to discover the truth. It is indeed

the noblest quest, but the purpose of the Church goes deeper and higher still.

What is this purpose? To set up the kingdom of Jesus Christ on earth. We believe that he came from heaven to suffer and die for the children of men; we believe that he rose triumphant, and now sits upon his throne high and lifted up; we believe that by the power of his Spirit he is working through this great living organism, which we call "The Church," for the restitution of all things; and we believe that in the fulness of time the heavens will part asunder, and he will come to reign King over all and blessed forever. To this end the Church was instituted; to this end its ministry was commissioned, "Go ye into all the world and evangelize"; and to this end the injunction is laid upon all Christ's people, "Let your light so shine among men that they may see your good works, and glorify God."

What shall I preach then? Christ, and him crucified. Nothing else? Nothing else. Whatever my theme, it must be like a thoroughfare leading to the cross. "The Jews require a sign, and the Greeks seek after wisdom; but we preach Christ crucified, unto the Jews a stumbling block, and unto the Greeks foolishness; but unto them which believe, Christ the power of God, and the wisdom of God." As an ambassador of Jesus Christ, my sole business is to magnify my Saviour's name, and to exalt him who said, "I, if I be lifted up, will draw all men unto me."

And how shall Christians live? As those whose lives are hid with Christ in God. Our religion is purely a personal relation with Christ. We have accepted Christ as the Jews in the wilderness, with the hot virus throbbing in their veins, looked to the brazen serpent for life. We have consented to cleanse ourselves from sin in the fountain filled with blood, as Naaman dipped in the Jordan seven times until his flesh became like the flesh of a little child. We have given ourselves to Christ in a consecration entire and unreserved, as the magi laid their golden myrrh and frankincense before him. We follow him as the sheep follows the shepherd, as a tourist follows his Alpine guide, as a child follows its mother, as a soldier follows his captain to the high places of the field. We abide in him as the branch abides in the vine, so that the parent life pervades and energizes it. We feed upon Christ as the Israelites fed upon the manna that dropped from heaven about their feet. For so it is written, "Except ye eat the flesh and drink the blood of the Son of Man, ye have no life in you." We receive Christ at his exact word in such a manner that his precepts are our last tribunal, and his promises are like the rounds of the ladder that Jacob saw, on which angels ascended with his prayers, and descended with blessings upon him. This is the significance of the primacy in our ecclesiastical and personal life. He is

> My Lord, my life, my sacrifice,
> My Saviour and my all.

II. *The foundation.* The Church is here said to be founded upon the apostles and prophets; that is, the Scriptures of the Old and New Testaments. It rests upon the truths handed down through the apostles and prophets from God.

I wonder whether those who are engaged in undermining faith in the Scriptures are aware what they are doing? "If the foundations be destroyed, what shall the righteous do?" The only Christ we have is the Christ revealed in the Scriptures. To impair their credibility, is to impugn the only historical witnesses that bear testimony to the religion of Christ. Some of these destroyers are among the professed followers of the Lord Jesus, but surely they do not follow him in this; for he never uttered a word in contravention of the plenary truth of the Bible, but was ever ready to vindicate and uphold it. "Search the Scriptures," he said, "for in them ye think ye have eternal life, and these are they which testify of me."

But how do the Scriptures serve as a foundation of the Church? In furnishing all that is needful for its organization and effectiveness every way. Herbert Spencer says that two things are necessary in order to a working Church, namely, creed and cultus. The Scriptures furnish the *creed*, the body of truth; they also furnish the *cultus*, or mode of worship; and this as given by inspiration is intensely simple. The beauty of holiness is the service of the heart; form is relatively of slight import. "When I make my prayers, shall I sit or kneel or stand upon my feet?' This is precisely like the question asked of Sir Thomas Moore by his executioner: "Sir, does your head lie right upon the block?" He answered, "No matter about my head so that my heart be right." Let us stand by Scripture in this matter of cultus, taking heed of unnecessary form and ceremony which is but superfluity of naughtiness. "For whatsoever is not of faith is of sin."

But something more than creed and cultus is needed in the making of a Church. We need a perfect *Code of Morals* and find it in the Decalogue and the Sermon on the Mount *plus* the personal example of Jesus the ideal Man. Also, a *Course of Action*, or campaign if you will. This is clearly marked out in the Scriptures. What is the business of those who belong to the Church of God? It is to seek first of all the kingdom of God and his righteousness. As we walk along the street, we mingle with two classes of people, who look alike but are separated by an infinite gulf; on the one hand those who are absorbed in the pursuit of wealth, pleasure or other personal emoluments, and know nothing higher than the things of this present life; who " forever hastening to the grave stoop downward as they run": on the other hand those who believe in the coming of the Son of Man and mean to do all in their power to hasten it. They also are engaged in bread-and-butter tasks, but the things of the kingdom are supreme, and their prime purpose is to hasten its coming on earth and in the lives of men.

By this it appears that the Church rests upon the trustworthiness of the Scriptures as the Word of God. No foundation, no house; no Bible, no Church. Stand by the Bible, therefore, my friend, even though others malign it. They are on the losing side. The old Book has stood like Gibraltar for thousands of years, and will stand for thousands more. It is not only the foundation of the Church, it is the hope of your personal eternal life. Stand by the Bible! John Knox spoke truly when admonished of the wrath of Queen Mary as he was going to Holyrood with a blue Genevan cloak over his shoulder and a Bible under his arm: "All hell," said he, "cannot prevail against the man that has in his left hand a candle to illuminate his right." Stand by your Bible! Read it, pray over it, love it and live by it. All dust is bad for human eyes, but the worst is that which gathers on our neglected Bibles.

III. *The Superstructure.* "Ye are built upon it"; that is, ye are the stones of the temple. At this point Peter comes to Paul's help—as he should indeed; for despite all differences of temperament and culture they were firm friends—saying, "Ye also as *living* stones are built up a spiritual house."

There were wonderful stones in the old temple of Moriah; Josephus mentions them in his Antiquities. Some of them, he says, were twenty-five cubits by twelve; that is, forty by twenty feet. It would seem incredible if it were not that some are still there. By what engineering skill were those ponderous masses lifted into place? Wonderful stones! But the stones of God's spiritual temple are more marvelous, for they are endowed with life. "Ye also as living stones are built up a spiritual house."

This means that Christians must do something more than merely lie in their places. It means that Church membership is not merely a name on a roster. There is nothing in the world more lamentable than a dead profession. A week ago our Navy Department sent out a message warning all outgoing ships against the derelict schooner which has recently been seen drifting about in the Northern Pacific. The name of this derelict is the "Siglin." She sailed with a crew of eleven and a cargo of valuable merchandise. Her masts are gone and, as the declaration says, "a dead man is lashed to her helm." Dead men down below, dead men lying on the decks, a dead man lashed to the helm! What a grim figure is there of a church devoted to the mere letter of truth or liturgy or ethics. Set over against that picture this temple of living stones. "I am come that ye might have life and that ye might have it more abundantly," said our Master. "And you hath he quickened which were dead in trespasses and sins."

The life here referred to is manifest in the relation of the Church member to Christ. Every stone of the temple pants toward him as if it had a heart within it. The bricks of the old Ninevite temple are all marked with the cartouche of contemporary kings, but the stones of this temple have been touched by the finger of their Lord, thrilled through and through with the electric power of his life.

It is manifest also in the fellowship of believers. The stones of the temple stretch forth hands inwardly as if to bear one another's burdens, as if to lay a benediction each upon the other, and all the temple rings with their sympathetic chorus, "Blest be the tie that binds our hearts in Christian love."

The life is also manifest in service. The hands of these living stones are stretched forth from the wall ontwardly to help a suffering, dying world, and voices are heard calling from the wall like voices of life-savers on the shore in a dark night, "Throw out the life-line!"

What a picture of a living church is this! Every part of the structure palpitates with life and energy. Every stone in the building calls out to Christ, to its fellows and to the world. The voice of praise, the voice of prayer, the voice of exhortation is here, and over all and about all is the atmosphere of heaven resonant with hallelujahs!

IV. And *the Church thus constituted "groweth"*— "groweth unto a holy temple of the Lord." The word is not such as was customarily used for a growing fabric; that is, one which grows by mere accretion, as thread upon thread in a loom, or stone upon stone in a building. But the word has reference to organic growth; that is, of vegetable or animal life. The temple is represented here as growing because it has life in it.

The growth of the Church is measured by that of the individual believers who constitute it. God's life is the germinating principle. This is the influence referred to by Paul where he speaks of the whole body as being fitly joined together, and compacted by that which every joint supplieth, according to the effectual working in the measure of every part, "making increase of the body unto the edifying of itself in love."

But apart from the growth of individual believers, there is a distinct growth of the mighty coherent unit which we call "The Holy Catholic Church." This growth is History. The ultimatum of history is the coming of the Son of God to possess his Church and reign through it. In the walls of the ancient temple of Jerusalem there are certain marks which indicate the successive periods of construction. The upper portions were built three or four centuries ago under the Sultan Suleiman, but below that, and clearly separated, are other parts running back to the fourth century of the Christian Era. Still farther down are portions which belong to the period of Herod, and lower yet are the repairs made on the return from captivity; while lowest of all on the bed rock of Mount Moriah, seventy feet beneath the surface, are the foundation stones that were laid by Solomon. Thus, from beneath the work may be traced through the centuries to the very top stone of the corner. But here the analogy fails, for the Christian Church is not completed. We note a constant progress from the beginning, with some periods of rough work indeed, but never aught but progress; nevertheless we still await the day when the top stone shall be laid with shouts of "Grace, grace unto it!"

In the eleventh year of the reign of Solomon the temple was dedicated to the Lord. The priests and Levites, with the hereditary heads of all the tribes, assembled in the holy city. The tabernacle was brought from Gibeon, old and worn and weather-beaten. With much pomp and circumstance the boards and pillars and curtains were carried upon the shoulders of the Levites up the slopes of the holy hill. Yonder came a group of Levites bearing the brazen altar; yonder another with the table of shew bread; another with the golden candlestick upon their shoulders. Loud hosannas gave welcome to these historic memorials of God's providence and grace. "O that men would praise the Lord for his goodness and for his wonderful works to the children of men." Yonder they came bringing the Ark of the Covenant, the visible token of the divine presence; priests and Levites sang together in welcome : "Lift up your heads, O ye gates ; and be ye lifted up, ye everlasting doors, and the King of glory shall come in!" The choirs in the great galleries of the temple responded one to another: "Who is this King of glory? The Lord of hosts, he is the King of glory." In the midst sat Solomon upon his throne, his archers about him with golden shields and clad in Tyrian purple. Then something occurred in the midst of the festivities, whereat all were instantly silent. Out from the curtain of fine twined linen hanging before the Holiest of All came a fleece of golden mist that flowed outward and upward, expanding until it obscured and enveloped all. It was the Shekinah, the glory of the Lord. Deep silence! And the king knelt with his face toward heaven, and blessed the people.

The time is approaching when Christ shall come in like manner, appearing in the open heavens, and making his influence felt throughout the earth, when the great angel shall proclaim "The tabernacle of God is among men, and he shall dwell among them and be their God, and they shall be his people."

> Arise, O King of saints, arise,
>   And enter to Thy rest;
> Lo, Thy Church waits with longing eyes,
>   Thus to be owned and blest.
> Enter with all Thy glorious train,
>   Thy Spirit and Thy word;
> All that the ark did once contain
>   Could no such peace afford.
> Here let the Son of David reign,
>   Let God's anointed shine,
> Justice and truth His court maintain,
>   With love and power divine.

The Lord is in his holy temple; let all the earth keep silence before him!

IN THE FIELDS AT EVENTIDE.

"And Isaac went out to meditate in the fields at eventide."—GEN. xxiv. 63.

We know little of Isaac. He was one of the ancient nobodies, the son of one great man and the father of another, and he lived a hundred and eighty years. Two things, however, make him illustrious: one is, he was the Child of the Covenant, of whom God had said to Abraham, "In thy seed shall all the nations of the earth be blessed." The other is an incident that occurred in his youth. One morning his father awakened him early, laid a bundle of sticks upon his arms, and himself took a knife and a brazier full of coals; and as they set forth, he said, "We go to sacrifice." The two climbed the slopes of Mount Moriah, and after a time the lad asked, "Where is the lamb for a burnt offering?" The question must have pierced the father's heart like a knife, for he had received a command from heaven to slay his only son; but he answered, "God will provide himself a lamb for a burnt offering." As they neared their destination, however, he told Isaac the truth. The lad acquiesced and suffered himself to be bound and made ready for the altar. In all this he was a living type of the victim of the cross. It may be that his vision was dim, yet he must have learned that this was a prophetic silhouette of the great atonement in which Christ was to be led as a lamb to the slaughter:—"God so loved the world that he gave his only-begotten Son, that whosoever believeth in him should not perish, but have everlasting life."

This was enough for a single life. His one hundred and eighty years were otherwise uneventful. He was a loving son, an affectionate husband, a kind and perhaps over-indulgent father. He was of a sunny and hopeful disposition, worthy of his name, "The Son of Laughter." He lived a busy, honest, humble life.

And here we see him meditating in the fields at eventide. Meditating of what? Of his broad acres? For his was a great inheritance and he showed himself wise to turn an honest penny. Or was he thinking of the covenant and the coming of the Christ? Or was he dreaming of wedlock? For his father's servant had recently gone to Mesopotamia to bring from thence a wife for Isaac, and even at this hour the young Rebekah was approaching, in whose breast were throbbing the uncertain hopes and fears of an Oriental bride. Up and down over his fields he walked and thought. The sun was going down, the birds were seeking their nests. He was alone with himself and God.

A man is at his very best in such an attitude as this, meditating in the fields at eventide. This is our theme, the importance of thoughtfulness.

I. *Think.* Think for yourself; let no man do your thinking for you. We are bipartite beings, made up of body and mind,—mind here including the will and conscience as well as the reasoning powers. The mind is larger than the body, though in point of fact we do not make it so. We are all the while asking, "What shall I eat?" and, "What shall I drink?" and, "Wherewithal shall I be clothed?" The body keeps us busy most of our time, while in reality the mind is its master and incessantly clamors for the crown.

We are much given in these times to an investigation of psycho-physical phenomena, that is, the influence of the mind over the body; and it is scarcely possible to overestimate its influence. A butcher on First Avenue, not long ago, while on a step-ladder under his awning, fell against a meat hook, and as he heard it tear, shrieked out in anguish. He was taken into his shop and laid upon the floor, begging all the while for a priest to shrive him ere he died. On examination it was found that the hook had torn his outer garments, not penetrating to the flesh at all. As soon as he knew the fact, he arose, picked up his cleaver and proceeded to his common task. Thus all the while the mind is asserting its domination over the body. The mind has a right to govern, for it is as much larger than the body as the sun is vaster than the mote that flies in a sunbeam. How important is it then that we should cease to be servants of the flesh, and give our mind, that is, the divine and immortal part, a chance to live.

The underlying sin of all sins is thoughtlessness. Our vices and blunders are for the most part due to thoughtlessness. Our prisons and asylums are full of thoughtless people. You voted, perhaps, the wrong ticket at the last election, because you did not think. You have invested your money in losing ventures, because you did not think. You bought a Sunday newspaper this morning because you did not think, though in fact God had admonished you in particular to remember the Sabbath day to keep it holy. I could suggest a law that would empty one-half of our jails and reformatories, if only our legislators could be persuaded to enact it; to wit, a law requiring every man to meditate alone one hour every day. The observance of such a law as that would mean disaster to the prince of darkness; for men go to perdition in eager procession, lock-step, quick-step, for want of thought. No man intends to die; no man purposes to spend eternity in the outer darkness. Men die inadvertently; but, alas, at the judgment there will be no room for the plea, "I didn't think."

II. *Go apart by yourself to think.* We do not love solitude. The best two friends for me are God and myself; it is strange that I should be so reluctant to look them in the face. It was a clear discernment of human nature that led Cowper to sing:

> I praise the Frenchman; his remark was shrewd:
> " How sweet, how passing sweet is solitude!
> But grant me still a friend in my retreat,
> Whom I may whisper, 'Solitude is sweet.'"

We are living in a busy world and in a busy age. We hurry to our tasks, and hurry away from them. We bolt our food, read a book in an evening, and abbreviate our rest. We want quick transit, steam and electricity; the art of ultimate arrival is the practical art of these days. We care to see nothing and hear nothing, but only to reach our destination. Yet there is something to be said for pedestrianism. The man who goes afoot alone may catch a glimpse of the fields, of the heavens above, and may hear the lark singing as it cleaves the air. But we cannot take time for this. We are too busy with the muck-rake. The sound of the city's life comes this way and we are impatient to reach it. Alas for us!

> " The world is too much with us; late and soon,
> Getting and spending, we lay waste our powers!
> Little we see in Nature that is ours;
> We have given our lives away, a sordid boon!
> The sea, that bares her bosom to the moon,
> The winds, that will be howling at all hours,
> And are regathered now like sleeping flowers;
> For this, for everything, we are out of tune.
> It moves us not. Great God! I'd rather be
> A pagan, suckled in a creed outworn;
> So might I, standing on this pleasant lea,
> Have glimpses that would make me less forlorn;
> Have sight of Proteus, rising from the sea;
> Or hear old Triton blow his wreathéd horn."

Our English cousins are wont to speak of "an uncomfortable individuality" which they have discovered among us. So far, so good. There is nothing better than a true egoism. *Ich bin ich.* Barbarians all think alike. If we would rise to higher levels, if we would breathe a clearer air, we must cut loose from the bondage of tradition, of authority, and of fashion, and be ourselves. We cannot run with the multitude, and be true men. It is one thing to lift our voices in the general clamor, and another to be able to give a reason for the faith that is in us. The design of the seal of Vespasian was an anchor and a dolphin. He was asked what it meant. He said, "Fixed opinion and swift execution." What better could you find than that? Convictions, that like an anchor grip the rock, and a swift spirit that speeds to its purpose as a fish cleaves the waters of the sea. But men never reach such distinction except as they enter the closet, and shut to the door. Truth comes to the man who sets out by himself upon the noble quest, with no light but the light of revelation, and no restraint save in the authority of God.

III. *Think to some purpose.* For what profit is it that a man should go apart and dream dreams and build castles in the air? Or what profit is it that a man should lie in the night-watches brooding over old grudges, or walk in the fields at eventide speculating as to the unknowable? A man may think he is thinking without thinking at all.

It is impossible to exaggerate the importance of governing the thoughts. But can we govern them? Aye; the will is sovereign in this province as elsewhere. He is a foolish man who complains that his thoughts run away with him. It was a wise saying of Luther, "We cannot prevent the birds flying over us, but we can prevent their building nests in our hair." The Scotch have a proverb, "Do wi' your ill thoughts as wi' your ill neebor; dinna gie him a stool to sit on." It is important here that we should choose our guests, for as a man thinketh in his heart, so is he.

The objective point of profitable thinking is an idea. To get an idea is to find a bonanza. I remember meeting, in my college days, an old man with long white hair, who was pre-eminently a man of one idea. While a workman in a mechanic's shop at nine dollars a week, he heard a conversation in which his employer said, "Why does not some one invent a sewing machine?" The thought took hold of Elias Howe, and he meditated for years upon it. The thing could be done if only a needle could be threaded at its point. At last he evolved the sewing machine, and became thereby the benefactor of the race.

One secret of success is attention. Our failures

are largely due to a dissipation of energy. It is wise, therefore, in our seasons of meditation to converge our faculties, and so arrive at something definite. Life is too short for the scattering and squandering of strength.

IV. *Let us approach the highest themes.* The highest themes are not such as concern our temporal good or the world's material welfare. There are truths that ever knock at our doors demanding our attention, yet likely to be disregarded amid the hurrying cares of earthly life.

(1) There is *the past.* Take time, my friend, to look over your shoulder, and one thing you will be sure to see :—Sin. Sin upon sin ; neglect of duty, violation of law. Sin—and what is this that follows after? A man committed a murder yesterday and escaped. Where is he now? In hiding somewhere, crouching behind a wall and trembling at every footfall. Will he sleep to-night? No. Retribution like a bloodhound will be baying after him ; remorse like a nightmare will bestride him ; the furies will stand about his hard bed and leer at him ; his heart will beat like a trip-hammer and awake him ; he will sit up, staring before him, and see a white face with wild reproachful eyes. Ah, he remembers ! These hands,— will all great Neptune's ocean wash this blood away? So it is written, "Sin, and death following after"; the death of an endless shame and despair. This is what a man sees when he looks over his shoulder.

But something else. A cross lifted in the midst of his past and throwing its resplendent shadow on every side, and a voice pleading with every man who will hearken, "Come now, let us reason together," saith the Lord ; "though your sins be as scarlet, they shall be white as snow : though they be red like crimson, they shall be as wool." Look back and meditate upon that. Get a right view of the past and set your past right before God.

(2) *The present hour;* the present responsibility, the present duty. Let nothing divert your attention from that. Æsop, in one of his fables, tells of a philosopher, who, while dreamily looking toward the heavens, fell into a pit and cried aloud for help. A shepherd who had been watching his flocks near by, ran to his relief, reached down his crook and saved him. "What can I do for thee?" asked the philosopher. "Nothing," said the shepherd, "but this; give more heed to the things that lie about thy feet and less to the skies above thee, and thou wilt save thyself much trouble." To live for to-day is in the noblest sense to live for eternity. To be my very best this very hour, to do the very best for those about me, and to spend this moment in a spirit of absolute consecration to God's glory ; this is the duty that confronts me.

(3) *The future.* What lies behind this veil? Some things, to a certainty. Death, I know, awaits me. Why shall I shudder to think of it? *Memento mori.* A wise man will not shut his eyes to the inevitable, but will prepare for it. And after death, eternity. I live forever. Time is a handbreadth. Eternity! eternity! how long art thou? And between death and eternity, the judgment day. This also is bound to be. We must all appear before the judgment-seat of God. "Rejoice, O young man, in thy youth ; but remember ! remember ! remember ! that for all these things God will bring thee into judgment." Let that tremendous thought cast its light continually over you.

The age we are living in calls for thoughtful men ; not melancholy, but serious men. It calls for men to solve great problems, to stand against social heresies, to resist the world, the flesh and the devil, to champion the just cause, to evangelize, to press hard on the long arm of the lever which is to lift this old world of ours into the light of God. This is no age for Don Quixotes, no age for Harry Hotspurs, no age for dreamers.

> " There's a fount about to stream,
> There's a light about to gleam,
> There's a midnight darkness changing into day ;
> Men of thought and men of action,
> Clear the way !"

And Isaac went out to meditate in the fields at eventide and he lifted up his eyes, and, behold, the camels were coming. Yonder was the fairest sight that ever greeted his eyes. Rebekah alighted from the camel and lifted her veil ; his bride came to him there in the eventide and he opened his arms to welcome her. O ! companies of angels come to us thus in our hours of meditation ; angels of life and happiness and peace. Hither come troops of promises and bright hopes and aspirations. Hither comes Christ himself to greet the thoughtful man ; he lifts his hands in blessing, " Peace be unto you." Lift up your eyes, good friend, as Isaac did, and go to meet him.

"SHIBBOLETH."

A SERMON PREACHED BY DR. BURRELL, SUNDAY, MAY 30, 1897.

"Then said he unto him, Say now Shibboleth; and he said Sibboleth: for he could not frame to pronounce it right."—JUDGES xii. 6.

Jephthah was a bandit. He had been driven out of Gilead by his brethren because he was the son of a harlot. He fled to the hill country and gathered a band of "vain fellows" about him. He was sent for, however, in the time of Gilead's extremity and proved himself a great captain. In battle with the Ephraimites he smote them hip and thigh. He placed guards at the fords of the Jordan to head off the retreating fugitives. The Gileadites and Ephraimites were cousins, and could only be distinguished by their articulation. The Ephraimites used no aspirate. So, as Milton says, they fell

——without reprieve, adjudged to death
For want of well pronouncing Shibboleth.

The two peoples, divided only by the width of the Jordan, were clearly differentiated in this manner; just as we detect a Frenchman nowadays by his inability to say "thin" or "thistle."

We think of "Shibboleth" as the watchword of a party. In fact, however, its significance goes deeper. The unctuous phrases with which the Reverend

Messrs. Pecksniff and Chadband are wont to interlard their discourses—these are not Shibboleths. Nor yet those non-essential truths and dogmas which separate between our modern tribes of Israel. Nor mere party names of any sort, as Luther, Calvin and Wesley. These are relatively of little worth. The power of life and death is not in them. But there are Shibboleths of tremendous import. There are words which represent facts—facts essential to the being of the church and of religion itself—words which the unregenerate cannot speak because they cannot apprehend the truths within them.

I. Such is *that great word God.* Those who have not entered upon the spiritual life can say Law, Force, Energy, "Something not ourselves that maketh for Righteousness;" but they cannot apprehend the Deity as he is and as he has revealed himself to us.

He is the one God. Not multitudinous as polytheists make him, nor yet an all-pervasive, nitrous-oxide, unconscious entity, or non-entity as Pantheists make him; but one great, living, thinking, reigning, personal Sun at the centre of the universe. Allah il Allah!

He is the triune God: that is, Father, Son and Holy Ghost. "These three are one." There are foolish folk who deride the doctrine of the Trinity as contra-rational. By the same token they must reject some of the simplest facts within the range of our observation. I myself am a tripartite being,—body, soul and spirit,—and these three are one. Will you deride that? The flame of a candle is light, heat and electricity; these three are one. Will you deride that? These are but imperfect analogies, for the finite can never perfectly analogize the infinite; but they suffice to show that the Trinity, while mysterious, is not therefore to be thrown out.

We believe also in the incarnate God. A God in swaddling bands! "Behold, I show you a mystery." The world rejects it. Yet the same truth finds expression in the Greek and Roman mythologies and in the Oriental religions. Why should it be thought a thing incredible that God should take flesh upon him? This is as easy for him as for me to put on a domino. And if the Scriptures are true, if our religion stands, he has done it. As it is written: "The Word was made flesh and dwelt among us."

II. *Faith is another* of the Shibboleths which the unconverted cannot articulate. By faith we mean the apprehension of facts in the province of the unseen.

All knowledge is covered by two terms: Science and faith.

(1) Science covers the field of visible things. True science is always exact because it deals only with facts. But much the larger part of current science deals with hypotheses. And exactness itself is frequently a relative term. A young man in Divinity Hall at Yale was practicing with an air-gun. His aim being poor, he sent a bullet through the window of a Professor's room. It chanced that this man was a Professor of Science. Now was his opportunity. He computed the parabola. For are not the data here? the bullet imbedded in yonder wall, the round hole in the window? Thus, knowing the exact curve, he was able to trace the course of the projectile to the room of a young theologue, who, in fact, did not know an air-gun from an earthquake. In vain did the poor culprit deny all knowledge of it. Exact science sealed his doom. At this juncture, however, the real male-

factor walked in and confessed his guilt. And, behold, his room was two hundred feet beyond the line of the computed parabola! The matter was dropped on the spot. Not all science is true science. But true science is exact with respect to all things which can be touched with fleshly hands or seen with fleshly eyes.

(2) Faith covers the entire field of the unseen and eternal. This is an infinitely larger field than the seen and temporal. And true faith is just as exact as true science. Let us not confound it with credulity, which rests on mere hearsay. Faith is the most substantial thing in the world. "Faith is the substance of things hoped for, the evidence of things not seen."

The sources of faith's evidence are prayer and Scripture and personal experience. In prayer the Lord speaks directly to the soul. Science can furnish no such evidence as that which the Magdalene had after the Lord had said, "Thy sins be forgiven thee." This great spiritual fact, the pardon of sin, is as real as a stone or a planet, but logarithms cannot demonstrate it.

God speaks also to the soul through Scripture. We who have professed to follow Christ have taken Scripture to be our rule of faith and practice. The question as to its authenticity and credibility was prior to our religious confession. The helmsman steers by his chart. He went to the Admiralty Office and provided himself with it at the beginning of the voyage. He made sure then that it had the proper seal and signature. He asks no more questions. This man at the wheel would be a fool if at every flurry of wind, when the ship begins to reel and toss, he should begin to question the authenticity of his chart. He believes it; he consults it.

And then Personal Experience; "That which mine eyes have seen and my hands have handled of the word of life declare I unto you." If Christ has passed my way and transformed my life, you may say to me with all the possible power of logic, "Is not this the son of Joseph?" and I must answer, "No; he is the chiefest among ten thousand, the one altogether lovely! He has led me into his banquet hall and his banner over me is Love. Not to mine eyes is light so dear nor friendship half so sweet!" Such conviction as this is impossible to those who have not known him. Can you send a man to see Chamounix for you? Can you listen to the Oratorio of the Messiah by proxy?

So the infinite world of invisible facts is open to faith only. You look at the stars and bless the telescope; but look through the interstellar spaces, on and on, and say, "Somewhere yonder are heaven and the great white throne!" This is a path which no fowl knoweth, and the eagle's eye hath not seen. Here is no use for the telescope nor for fleshly sight. Faith alone can apprehend the unseen and eternal.

III. The world *cannot say Providence.* It can say "Kismet!" It believes in Fortune; dreads a mysterious, supernatural Something; is afraid to sail on Friday, dare not sit down at table with thirteen; carries a crooked sixpence in its pocket; nails a horseshoe to its mast. But we believe in God at the centre, ruling all. We believe in a vast, eternal Providence, in which are comprehended all the details of the universal and harmonious plan. Here are involved three truths, covering the past, the present, and the future.

(1) Predestination. Ah, you will have none of that! Predestination is a repellent "dogma." The world refuses to articulate it. But see how simple : If there is a God, he must foreknow; if he foreknows, then the ultimate fact is an absolute certainty; but a fact which was eternally known and certain to the divine mind, was obviously predestinated. The word is of no particular value; the fact itself is undeniable. An objection is interposed, "What, then, about man's freedom?" Man is just as free as if there had never been a decree at all. It does not interfere with the freedom of your choice that your wife is preparing dinner for you, that she knows what you are going to eat, and ordains that you shall eat just that and nothing else. Neither does the fact that whatever I do has been eternally clear to the divine mind, affect my doing as I will.

(2) Government. I am held in the supervision and control of Providence. God watched over me all last night. I laid my head upon my pillow, and presently there came a voice of singing far away,—lower,—fainter,—and I was gone; that was God's lullaby. This morning I stirred in my sleep, there was a twitter outside my window,—a glimmering under my eyelids—and slowly, sweetly, I came back from the land of forgetfulness. Then God took my hand, and all day long he has been leading me. Some people are praising him because in dreadful accidents they have escaped. Let us praise God that we have been in no accident. O, the depth of the riches both of the wisdom and knowledge of God!

(3) Grace. We speak of "Providence and Grace." In point of fact, however, Grace is within the sphere of Providence. It is, indeed, the most special of all

"special providences." The world can see, with fleshly eyes, sin and its penalty. "The soul that sinneth it shall die." But the man who has learned grace sees one thing further; the interposition of a divine Father, in the redemption of the cross. The world believes in *Karma*, the doctrine of consequences; but those who have learned the language of Canaan can say, "God so loved the world, that he gave his only begotten Son, that whosoever believeth in him should not perish, but have everlasting life."

IV. *Righteousness.* The world can say Morality, but there is a difference; there is a difference as wide as the gulf between life and death. Morality is personal merit. Righteousness is godliness, that is, Godlikeness. Righteousness is a vast word and comprehends a trio of doctrines.

(1) Regeneration. This is the beginning of it. It means not outward seeming, not resolving or "reforming," but an inward change. For a lion in a cage is a lion still. Nicodemus came to Jesus with some conception of morality, but none whatever of the great mystery wherein a man is turned about from facing hell to facing heaven. "Verily, verily, I say unto thee," said Jesus, "except a man be born again, he cannot see the kingdom of God." And Nicodemus answered, "How can these things be?" He could understand reformation; but a new heart, a new conscience, a new mind, a new man,—"How can these things be?"

(2) Sanctification. The Holy Spirit takes us in hand, if we will. He points to Jesus as the ideal of character and says, "Imitate him," and helps us do it. This is something better than "ethical culture." Not that ethical culture is not good as far as it goes. But

you can buy carpet made that way, printed on one side, for a quarter dollar a yard. Sanctification, however, is ingrained. True character is dyed in the wool; and it wears.

(3) Imputation. This makes a man perfect, and nothing else can. The world wants to "make merit." A Christian prays that Christ will impute his righteousness unto him. Be as good as you can, in the name of God and manhood, but then confess, in all honesty, that you are not as good as you should be. The last touch is put upon character when Christ throws about us the white robe of his own obedience, his absolute righteousness, his infinite merit.

> Jesus, Thy blood and righteousness
> My beauty are, my glorious dress;
> 'Mid flaming worlds in these arrayed,
> With joy shall I lift up my head.

V. *The Kingdom of Christ.* Those who take no interest in religion are wont to speak of "the philosophy of history," "the logic of events," "the evolution of the race;" but a Christian must go further and find an ultimate consummation of all these in the setting up of the Kingdom of Christ. This is nothing to the multitude. They can say "gold," "pleasure," "personal emolument,"—"Let us eat and drink and be merry,"—but here is something they can neither understand nor clearly articulate, "Seek ye first the kingdom of God."

This kingdom has its beginning in the subjugation of the individual soul to the authority of Christ. It is written, "The kingdom of God is within you." We are not in the kingdom until the kingdom is in us. We are not a part of the kingdom until we have brought every thought into subjection to the king.

The kingdom, furthermore, is about us. It grows in the multiplication of those who acknowledge the King. We serve him whenever we awaken a new song, or bring the hopeless into the beneficent light of salvation. Let others set their hearts wherever they will, we can have but one supreme ambition, to honor the King.

This is ultimate; the setting up of our Lord's sovereignty on earth. For every knee shall bow before him and every tongue shall confess that he is worthy. The remarkable work of Saint Augustine, *De Civitate Dei* was written about the beginning of the fifth century, during the fires and disasters under which the Roman Empire tottered to its fall. A flood of Teutonic barbarians swept in, bringing darkness and chaos with them. Just then Augustine made his wonderful picture of "The City of God." It was a prophecy of that which shall be. The world cares nothing for this splendid restitution of all things. Ah, but the followers of Christ love his appearing, and long for the day when he shall reign among them. This is their dream: "I saw the Holy City, New Jerusalem, coming down from God out of heaven, prepared as a bride adorned for her husband. And I heard a voice say, He shall dwell among them and they shall be his people and God himself shall be their God."

But these things are addressed to many in an unknown tongue. They say, "Doth he not speak in parables?" Alas, that the present order should be for multitudes the eternal order. Alas, that those who are born to live forever should not learn the language of the heavenly Canaan.

One watchword we must be prepared to utter when we stand at heaven's gate. All other Shibboleths will fail; this will give us entrance into life, *"In His Name!"* It was the watchword of the old crusaders. A knight, pursued, and hard bestead drew near the castle, riding hot and fast; "In Christ's Name!" he cried. Up went the draw-bridge, open flew the gates; and he was safe. Friend, have you learned it? Can you give the countersign? Can you say, "Jesus," not with your lips only, but with heart and conscience and will? For this is his own word, "No man cometh unto the Father but by me."

"SON, REMEMBER."

A SERMON PREACHED BY DR. BURRELL, SUNDAY, JUNE 6, 1897.

"But Abraham said, Son, remember that thou in thy lifetime receivedst thy good things, and likewise Lazarus evil things."—LUKE xvi. 25.

We speak of the parable of Dives and Lazarus. But why "parable"? In other cases a parable is introduced by some such phrase as, "He spake a parable unto them, saying." But here the narrative begins abruptly,—"And there was a certain rich man." Moreover, there is a tone of verisimilitude from beginning to end. It sounds like common life. The beggar here is just such as you will find at the doorways of the more opulent homes of the Oriental cities of this day. His sores were real sores; his hunger was a real hunger. Light is thrown upon his character in the name Lazarus, which means "My helper is God."

And the rich man is like the rich man of to-day. Hss real name is not given, for obvious reasons.* We have no reason to suppose that he was notoriously wicked in any way. So far as we are aware, he was not a thief, a usurer, an extortioner. He was rich, to be sure; but many of the wealthy are true servants of God. He was an aristocrat, but that is not so bad, if

---

* The meaning of "Dives" is, "A rich man."

you stick to the root-meaning of the word. He was arrayed in purple and fine linen, and fared sumptuously every day. But before passing an adverse criticism at this point, we should know whether he was able to foot his bills. He was a prominent citizen, genial, hospitable, and probably well thought of. Nor was he without kindly feeling We would think twice before allowing a beggar like Lazarus to lie before our gate. He not only permitted this, but said to a servant when the banquet was over, "Gather up some of the cold bits and carry them to yon beggar at the gate."

What then was the trouble with this rich man? Selfishness. He lived a self-centred life. He was sordid; of the earth, earthy. Luther says, *"Lebte herrlich und in Freuden"*: that is, his life was environed by sense and time. The great questions to him were not "What shall I do to be saved?" or, "How shall I be just before God?" or, "What can I do to help my fellow-man?" But, "What shall I eat and drink, and wherewithal shall I be clothed?" Do not hastily condemn him, however, for multitudes of eminently respectable people are spending their lives that way.

And the sequel. "The beggar died." Of course he died. All beggars die. No note is made, however, of any imposing obsequies.

> Rattle his bones over the stones;
> He's only a pauper, whom nobody owns.

But while they were carrying his poor body out to the potter's field, a retinue of angels took charge of the man who had passed out of that frail tabernacle and bore him to Abraham's bosom; that is, to the innermost place of heavenly glory. And they said, "Here is the beggar who lay at Dives' gate, whose name was 'My helper is God.'"

But what about Dives? It is written, "The rich man also died." Do rich men die, then? They think not. But the black camel waits at their door too. One day Dives was ill; his pulse was too rapid, his temperature too high. The physician was summoned and the nurse; the light burned low. Dives was dead. Mention is made of his funeral. No doubt it was a great occasion in the city. There were trappings of woe on every side. An eloquent eulogium was pronounced upon him in the synagogue which he was accustomed to attend. Hired mourners went wailing before the bier; friends and kinsfolk wept as they carried Dives out to the ancestral vault; a splendid epitaph was inscribed above him.

Was that the end? O, no! "In hell he lifted up his eyes, being in torments." I am not going to defend God in these premises; he can take care of his own administration. It is enough to say that the veil is lifted, and we have a momentary glimpse of the eternal world. There is a separation there,—a great gulf fixed. Fixed! Let us not trifle with that word, but take it as Christ gives it. And another thing we see in this brief lifting of the veil is the fact that memory abides in the other world. Let us stop right here and think. This is our theme, *Memory in the eternal world.*

I. *There is no forgetting, here, or there, or anywhere.* The ancients spoke of a river flowing between time and eternity, in which the souls of the departed bathed seven times, and remembered no more. But Lethe is a fable. There is no oblivion. Memory is like the Great Salt Lake, fed by streams from the plateaus and Wasatch hills, but with no outlet. Sir William Hamilton defines memory as the retentive faculty. It is purely mechanical; quite automatic; as irrational as a magpie, to which it has been likened; it steals your spoons and your silver pencil, and hides them away without rhyme or reason. We used to say, when we were children, "I know, but I can't remember." Our teachers called it a poor excuse; but they were wrong, and we were right. The things we had learned were stored away in memory, but recollection, which is the disbursing faculty, could not on the instant produce them. The money was on deposit, but the paying teller could not lay his hand upon it.

In 1804, Benedict Arnold lay dying in London. A quarter of a century had passed since his treason; he had tried to forget, his friends had been forbidden to mention it. But as death approached, he called for his faded Continental uniform, and put it on—buff waistcoat and cocked hat; and thus, sitting erect in bed, he faced the King of Terrors. Then his honor came back to him. He was again at Ticonderoga. He was on his black horse, driving the savages before him; he was pushing his way through the trackless forests; he was again under the walls of Quebec, and his voice rang forth in one clear word, "Surrender!" The things of the past had never died; they were but sleeping. And so it ever is.

II. A step further: *The hidden things shall ultimately be brought to light.* In other words, the book of remembrance shall be opened.

The record of our lives is kept in "double entry."

Omniscience is the ledger. Nothing is lost out of the divine mind.

> Eternity with all its years
> Stands present to Thy view;
> To Thee there's nothing old appears,
> Great God! there's nothing new.

Our memory is the day book; the complement and correspondence of Omniscience. The opening of the record is indicated in these words, "Son, remember." It is well-known that a sailor falling from the masthead sees his whole life pass before him in panoramic scenes before he strikes the water. A fact like this demonstrates the possibility that the soul in its flight from time to eternity may see the unrolling of the entire past. The memory may be vivified and all things revealed, in a moment, in the twinkling of an eye.

III. Observe now *the bearing of these facts upon the sorrows of the lost.* What possibilities are here.

"Son, remember that thou in thy lifetime receivedst thy good things." The man whose lips are parched with an unquenchable thirst sits again at the table spread with luscious viands. Here are music and laughter, and servants flitting to and fro. He lifts from the table the deep, cooling draught, and awakes. He did but remember, and, alas! "Sorrow's crown of sorrow is remembering happier things."

He must needs remember also his past sins. Time was when he could drown the remembrance of them in the flowing bowl, but he cannot now. The open page covered with sins, unexpiated and unforgiven, stares him in the face. On the fly-leaf of Campbell's copy of "The Pleasures of Memory" were written these words:

> Alone at midnight's haunted hour,
>   When nature woos repose in vain,
> Remembrance wakes her penal power,
>   The tyrant of the burning brain.
> She tells of time misspent; of comforts lost;
>   Of fair occasions gone forever by;
> Of hopes too fondly nursed, too rudely crossed
>   Of many a cause to wish, yet fear to die!
> For what, except the instinctive fear
>   Lest she survive, detains me here,
> When all the life of life is fled?
>   What but the deep, inherent dread,
> Lest she beyond the grave resume her reign,
>   And realize the hell that priests and beldames feign?

The one sin—the one preüminent, tremendous sin—standing forth above and beyond all others—will be the rejection of Christ. "They shall look on him whom they have pierced." Calvary will be reproduced, and the cross with its outstretched arms will cast its shadow forever. The lost soul will remember the day in early youth when Christ for the first time came with his overtures of mercy; the day later on when the minister in the village church preached, perhaps, on the words, " Behold, I stand at the door and knock; if any man hear my voice and open the door, I will come in to him and will sup with him;" and the soul made answer, "Go thy way for this time; when I have a more convenient season, I will come unto thee"; the day when he looked down into the cold face of his mother, and her silent lips seemed to move again, as if pleading in the Master's name, "Come unto me, and I will give you rest"; the day when life seemed dreary and purposeless, when he said to himself there must be something better than this toiling with the muck-rake, this chasing of thistle-down, this grasping after faded wreaths; when the voice of the reapers came from the distant field and one standing near by, and said, "Go thou and thrust in thy sickle and reap." Alas, alas, it might have been! This is the sorrow of it, "The harvest is past, the summer is ended, and I am not saved." Privileges wasted, opportunities thrown away. O fool that I am! Self-convicted, openly confessed, eternally pilloried fool that I am!

Do you say "This is old-fashioned preaching. This is much like preaching hell"? But I have not said the word. The thing is so true that the Master, kindest and most loving of all friends, must needs speak of it. The "outer darkness," the "fire that is not quenched," the "worm that dieth not," shame, remorse, forever and ever; if these are true, no faithful minister can fail to present them. It is better to admonish now, while there is time to purge the memory and prepare for eternity. "The blood of Jesus Christ cleanseth from all sin."

IV. We turn now to brighter thoughts. Consider *the part which memory takes in the felicity of the saints.*

They, too, will remember their sins, but not like those who know no pardoning grace. They will look on the hole out of which they were digged, and will praise the Lord who delivered them. They will remember the dismal past as the prodigal son did when he sat again at the table in his father's house. He could not but recall the rags and tatters, the hunger, the shame, and the swine-field. But he looked on his robe—"the best robe"—the shoes upon his feet—a freedman's shoes—and the signet ring on his finger; and he must have said to his father, in a voice broken with grateful emotion, "My father, I thank thee that thou didst not cast me utterly off, but didst patiently wait and watch for me, and didst come out to meet me when I was yet a great way off."

I feel sure we shall forever remember the day of our conversion, when Christ came and said, "Thy sins be forgiven thee." I see a man in princely garments standing by a ruined altar. A retinue of slaves and dependents are gathered about him. They would help him to rebuild the shrine, but he refuses their aid, and with his own hands gathers the stones and replaces them one upon another. Then he pours the anointing oil upon this rebuilt altar, kneels beside it, and uplifts toward heaven a face suffused with tears. His memory runs back. He speaks: "I thank thee, O gracious God, for that day, for that day thirty years ago, when homeless, hopeless, godless, a fugitive from a wronged and infuriated brother, I laid my head upon a stone just here and slept. I thank thee for the vision that came to me; the ladder let down from thy throne to my very feet, whereon I saw the angels carrying up to thee my poor broken prayers and bringing down to me thy richest benediction. I thank thee for the covenant which was sealed, when I awoke, between my soul and thee; 'This God shall be my God forever.'"

> O happy day that fixed my choice
> On Thee my Saviour and my God!

We shall recall the sorrows of the past, the dark days when we passed through the vale of weeping, our pains, adversities, disappointments, bereavements. We shall remember how friends came to us with their well-intended sympathy, like vinegar on nitre, saying, "It is the Lord, and he doeth all things well." And we answered in our hearts, "That is but cold comfort." And they said, "No affliction for the present seemeth to be joyous, but grievous; nevertheless, afterward it yieldeth the peaceable fruit of righteousness unto them which are exercised thereby." And again we said in our hearts, "It is cold comfort." But the Lord has promised us, "In that day ye shall know." We shall then see face to face, and eye to eye, and understand how all things were working together for our good.

We shall remember our struggles too. I have seen one of Sherman's men, with a map on his knees, pointing out with pride the memorable march to the sea: "Here, just beyond Chattanooga, we were driven back. Here, as we came in sight of Atlanta, I was wounded. And here is Savannah,—and the taking of Savannah was worth it all." So shall we recall our conflicts with the world and the flesh and the devil. We shall show our honorable scars. We shall rejoice that on occasion we could say, "No," under trial and were brave enough to stand by our convictions. We shall know then that we never did a more valorous thing than when we got the better of an evil habit or slew a darling sin. *Haec olim meminisse juvabit.*

And we shall surely remember the day of our death, that strange day of which we stood in constant terror before it came. How we dreaded to meet the King of Terrors! But in the moment of our need, dying grace was given us. Friends wept at the bedside. Some one read, "Yea though I walk through the valley of the shadow of death, I will fear no evil, for thou art with me." But they could not know how true that was for us. Then the farewell. Yonder, in a moment, was heaven's gate, and hands were beckoning.

> The world recedes, it disappears,
> Heaven opens on mine eyes; my ears
>   With sounds seraphic ring.
> Lend, lend your wings! I mount! I fly!
> O grave, where is thy victory!
>   O death, where is thy sting!

Then the first hour in heaven,—light, glory, effulgence, and one Face shining over all. O the light of his countenance! There is no need of the sun or the moon. And other faces! Faces everywhere. In the joy of that first greeting you scarcely think of the beauty of the city. But with every hour the words of the Queen of Sheba come to us, "The half was never told!"

What then? Let us hear the conclusion of the whole matter: "Live for eternity." The thought of eternal remembrance invests our life with solemnity. We are writing with a diamond on a rock We are writing in the Book of Remembrance with invisible ink. We are accumulating for the future. What we do, is done forever. The thoughts we think, the words we speak, the kindly and unkindly acts of daily life, we must face them again. Take heed therefore. Live for eternity. And the way to live for eternity is to concentrate all the energies of our life upon the discharge of present duty. Therefore, live to-day!

SUNDAY PLEASURES.

"If thou turn away thy foot from the sabbath, from doing thy pleasure on my holy day; and call the sabbath a delight, the holy of the LORD, honorable; and shalt honor him, not doing thine own ways, nor finding thine own pleasure, nor speaking thine own words: then shalt thou delight thyse f in the LORD; and I will cause thee to ride upon the high places of the earth, and feed thee with the heritage of Jacob thy father: for the mouth of the LORD hath spoken it."—ISA. lviii. 13, 14.

A portentous sin of our time is Sabbath desecration. What inroads and encroachments have been made upon the sanctions of the Fourth Commandment within the memory of the youngest among us. Not many years ago it was customary to stretch a chain across the avenues in the neighborhood of churches while worship was going on. Now we hear the rattle of chariot wheels and the rumble of the horse-car. The ranks of the Sabbath workers are being reënforced, slowly but surely, as the years pass. Observe, also, the multiplication of Sunday pleasures. The theatres are thrown open; the athletic parks are filled with ball-players; the boulevards are thronged with wheelmen taking their Sunday spin. A great change truly! In my boyhood I was never allowed to walk abroad on Sunday, unless it were hand in hand with my father to the graveyard, where we read the epitaphs together. The good man doubtless made a melancholy mistake at this point, but indeed it was a thousandfold better to err in the direction of an extreme observance than to run, in secular dissipations, upon the bosses of the shield of God.

It will be an evil day for our country, for the community, for our home-life when the Sabbath loses its solemn and splendid significance. The destiny of nations is bound up with Sabbath observance. We are accustomed to say of America "God has not dealt so with any people." Let it be said, also, that as a nation we have hitherto been singularly true to the obligations of the Fourth Commandment. But now the pendulum is swinging fast the other way. The children of Israel were sent into a wretched captivity of forty years to expiate their disobedience of Sabbath Law. Woe worth the day when our American Sabbath shall pass from us!

It is evident that the moral convictions of many of the American people, with reference to the duty of Sabbath observance, have radically changed in recent times. Loose habits are due to loose views; for as a man thinketh in his heart, so is he. We are fast drifting away from the true philosophy of the Sabbath. A man is not better than his creed. It will be profitable for us, therefore, to enquire, What are the true grounds of Sabbath rest? On what foundations does the Fourth Commandment stand?

I. *It rests on the authority of God.* No man can arrive at a just estimation of the Sabbath or of his personal duty toward it, without beholding the gleaming peak of Sinai dominating the sacred day. We may regard the enactment of Sabbath laws on the part of local councils and legislatures as an infringement of personal liberty, and we may question the right and justice of them; but no man can challenge the right of God Almighty to say to his creatures, "Thou shalt," or "Thou shalt not." For who art thou that repliest against God?

It is said, however, that the Fourth Commandment was abrogated by Jesus Christ. I say that is a libel on the only-begotten Son of God. He would not, if he could, have abrogated it; and, with all reverence I add, he could not if he would. In creating man under the sanctions and conditions of the moral law, God had made it impossible to disannul or amend that law without changing the constitution of man. Is it not strange, that by common consent all other precepts of the moral law are regarded as eternal and unchangeable, save only this Fourth precept of the code? Could Jesus Christ have disannulled the law, "Thou shalt not kill"? Would he, or could he have repealed the edict, "Thou shalt not steal"? Is it thinkable, that he could have reversed the commandment, "Thou shalt not commit adultery"? But let it be observed, the Fourth Commandment is, just as really as these, an essential item of the moral law. The Decalogue was written on tables of stone because it was intended to be eternal. If it ever is repealed, God himself must repeal it. Only he who said, "Remember," may presume to say, "Forget." And he has never said it.

How then did Jesus treat the Sabbath? What was his attitude toward it? He found the Fourth Commandment overlaid with the traditions of the elders. They had made it an intolerable burden by their ceremonial exactions. It was not permitted under the Rabbinical law to kindle a fire on the Sabbath, nor to bandage a wound. A man must not walk on the ripened grain, lest it should be construed as threshing. He must not chase an insect, lest the ungodly say he had gone a-hunting. If he fed his fowls, he must leave no grain on the ground, lest it should seem like sowing. If he dipped a radish in salt, he must not leave it there, for some man might say he was pickling. There were hundreds and thousands of such minute prescriptions as these. The Sabbath had thus come to be an intolerable burden and weariness. The Lord Jesus Christ tore away these unwarranted and pernicious precepts, and bade the people return to the original form of the Sabbath law. He did not destroy, he restored it. A ship comes laboring into port, unable to make headway because her hulk is covered with barnacles. The skipper hastens to put her into dry dock, that she may be scraped and made ready to "sail free." He would be a foolish man who would say that this was equivalent to scuttling the ship. The Lord stripped the Fourth Commandment of its burdensome and unpermitted trappings, and left it to the people as God originally gave it.

II. *It rests also on our filial relation with God.* We are his sons and daughters. He made us in his likeness and after his image and he appeals to this relationship in giving the Sabbath law; "for in six days the Lord made heaven and earth, the sea and all that in them is, and rested the seventh day; wherefore the Lord blessed the Sabbath day and hallowed it." In that "for" and that "wherefore" he distinctly brings us into copartnership with himself in the observance of this rest day.

In our observance of the Sabbath we recognize and perpetuate this blessed relation with him. Here is one test of our sonship. When James II. of England heard of the approach of Dutch William, he fled with all possible haste in a little boat; as he passed Lambeth Palace, he dropped the Stuarts' seal over into the Thames. It was counted an irreparable loss; but the officers of the crown afterwards dredged the river and found it. The Sabbath is like the Stuarts' seal; it keeps up our lineage with the great Father. To disregard it, is to show our indifference or disloyalty toward him. One purpose of this ordinance was to keep in mind our descent from God. The ox and the horse know no difference between the Sabbath and any other day; it belongs to our Father and us. He claims a property right in it, saying, "The Seventh Day is the Sabbath of the Lord thy God." But he also gives us a distinct right in it, saying, "The Sabbath was made for man."

III. *It is interwoven with the fibres of our physical constitution.* It is a scientific fact, that we cannot preserve the best measure of health and vigor without just observance of this law.

Not long ago Dr. Haegler of Basle, in a work on "The Expenditure and Repair of Vital Force," called special attention to the relation of sleep and Sabbath rest. His proposition is one that is generally known and universally conceded among scientists, to-wit: "The night rest after a day's work does not afford a complete recuperation of vital force." He illustrates in a series of zigzag lines.*

The Monday line representing the reservoir of

---

* "Beginning on Monday morning, each downward stroke marks the daily expenditure of energy, and the upward stroke the nightly recovery, which does not rise quite to the height of the previous morning; so that there is a gradual decline during the week, which only the prolonged rest of the Sabbath repairs. The downward lines show the continued decline of the forces when they are not renewed by the weekly rest."—*Craft's* "*Sabbath for Man.*"

vigor, after the Sabbath rest, is the longest line and shows the maximum of strength. On each succeeding day the line is shortened a little. On Tuesday morning the workman refreshed by sleep has regained most of his lost energy, but not all; there is a margin of loss. On Wednesday the line is still shorter; that is, there is a larger margin of loss. On Thursday, Friday and Saturday the lines are shortened more and more. On Saturday night the man has reached his minimum of strength. Now comes Sunday. If he observes it, he regains his full normal vigor and begins again where he began a week ago. If he refuses to observe it, he will never reach his full normal standard of vital force, but will suffer a constant drain more

HAEGLER'S CHART — Level of vital force preserved by Sabbath rest; Deterioration without Sab. rest.

and more until he ends in debility and breakdown. Thus it is made to appear, as a scientific fact which is disputed in no quarter worthy of consideration, that a man who habitually refuses to observe the Sabbath in rest, is living constantly on his reserve of vital force. This means that the Sabbath is necessary for our physical health. The Sabbath was made for the body of man.

IV. *It is grounded in the necessities of our spiritual life.* We are something more than bodies. Our life is not an handbreadth; we live for eternity, and the Sabbath is given in order that we may have opportunity to prepare for it.

What is a man? Is he, as somebody has said, "A stomach with its appendages"? Or, is he indeed an immortal soul? What a story is this which the telegraph brings of Barney Barnato, the diamond king. He set out in conquest of material wealth. He won five hundred millions. He would make it a thousand and be the prince of multi-millionaires. But the other day he leaped over the taffrail into the sea, and all that is left is a white face, a silent pulse, lustreless eyes. O what shall it profit a man if he gain the whole world and forget his life and lose it?

The words of the original precept are significant: "The Lord blessed the Sabbath day and hallowed it"; that is, he set it apart for spiritual uses. He knew that we are too bound up and harassed and overburdened in our six days of secular life. He knew that if the galley-slave should ever know the delights of freedom, it must be because his chains are broken by an Almighty Hand. The Sabbath is our emancipation from the world. It is the day on which a thoughtful man will give his soul a chance to soar aloft, gaze at the great verities, and commune with God.

Let us turn now to certain specific questions with reference to the proper observance of the day.*

---

*This sermon was preached by request of a number of young people who desired light as to lawful pleasures and recreations on the Lord's Day.

(1) *What manner of work are we permitted to do?* The commandment reads: "In it thou shalt not do any work, thou nor thy son, nor thy daughter, thy manservant nor thy maid-servant, nor thy cattle, nor the stranger that is within thy gates." The Lord, interpreting this in the light of reason and common sense, makes two specific exceptions with reference to works of necessity and works of mercy, which indeed in the last reduction can scarcely be regarded as "works" at all. As he passed through the wheat-field with his disciples, he permitted them to pluck the ears of wheat and rub them in their hands and eat the grains. For this the Pharisees rebuked him. And he defended his disciples on the ground that what they had done was in the nature of necessity; that is, for the sustenance of life. And then seven of his most notable miracles of healing were wrought on the Sabbath; clearly indicating the right of his followers to perform deeds on mercy on that day.

We may indeed go so far as to say that it is not only the right of Christians, but their duty, to do good as they have opportunity on the Sabbath. Go down into the slums and teach the Gospel. Go to the hospitals and smooth the pillow of the weary. Give the cup of water to thirsty lips; stretch forth the helping hand. This is to rest according to the divine ordinance; to find the sweetest possible rest in the service of the Lord and of our fellow-men. But, apart from works of necessity and mercy, there is a clear prohibition. We are to reduce our labor to the lowest minimum on that day.

(2) *What pleasures are we permitted to indulge in?* Only such as conform to the original Sabbath law

and are consistent with the general principles which furnish the foundation of it.

What shall you read on Sunday? Not light fiction; not such secular literature as will distract your heart from the just consideration of spiritual things. Not the Sunday newspapers; for apart from the fact that you deliberately break the Sabbath in purchasing one, and that in doing so you become a contributing supporter to the ungodly enterprise, you know that the contents of that Sunday newspaper will not make for truth and righteousness in the education of your soul and in preparation for an eternity with God.

But what about golf? And what about the Sunday spin? I know the specious arguments which young people are accustomed to offer in defense of it. "I am busy all through the week and have no other day for recreation." Yours is a pitiful case, my friend; but unfortunately you prove too much. Are not all honest people in this world busy through the six days? If your argument holds, it will let the whole world of busy people loose on wheels, with golf clubs, and otherwise intent upon secular recreation, on the Lord's Day. In point of fact, the great multitude of those who are seen spinning along the boulevards on the Sabbath, are not the busy, thrifty handicraftsmen at all. A casual glance is enough to reveal that fact. But suppose that all these Sunday pleasurers could cry with a single voice, "We have no other day for our recreations," one word would answer them:— "You have no other day for the culture of your souls. You have no other day to read your Bibles, to worship in the sanctuary, to meditate on holy things, to blend your praises with the hallelujahs of the angels and to get ready for the endless life."

Now read the text again and see if it does not appear as if it had been written especially for wheelmen. "If thou turn away thy foot from the Sabbath"—thy foot, the foot upon this pedal; take heed, turn it away!—"from doing thy pleasure on my holy day, and call the Sabbath a delight"—the Sabbath itself, in and of itself, with its own peculiar uplifting joys—"the holy of the LORD, honorable, not doing thine own ways nor finding thine own pleasure, nor speaking thine own words: then"—then what pleasures shalt thou have to compensate for all?—"then shalt thou delight thyself in the LORD, and I shall cause thee to ride upon the high places of the earth"—ah, there is something infinitely better than a Sunday spin; to ride upon the high places of the earth!— "and I will feed thee with the heritage of Jacob thy father; for the mouth of the LORD hath spoken it."

It is probable that some in this audience do not recognize the binding authority of the Fourth Commandment, nor confess themselves to be the followers of Christ. May I venture to say this word to all such, as to thoughtful men: You mean to do right; you love your country; you love the Christian home; and you would fain make the most of yourselves here and hereafter. You will probably admit that with these ends in view the Sabbath, quite apart from its religious sanctions, is of vital importance. You would deplore the loss of the American Sabbath almost as much as any of us. May I not, therefore, ask you, What you are doing personally to preserve it? Are you joining in the clamor for larger liberty of work and recreation on this day? Will you not think twice, and join us in doing what you can to strengthen the things that remain?

But to those who revere the Decalogue and have made of themselves, body and soul, an unconditional surrender to the Lord Christ, the Sabbath argument makes a tremendous, an unanswerable appeal. Here we get our foretastes of heaven. Shall it be to us a burden or a weariness? Can we not call it "a delight, holy of the LORD, honorable"?

> The Sabbaths of man's life
> Threaded together on time's string
> Make bracelets to adorn the wife
> Of the Celestial King.

For all such people there is one answer to every question that bears on Sabbath observance. Why come to your minister, asking, "Shall I do this?" or, "Shall I do that?" We are not popes or bishops to make minute prescriptions in ethics. It is for us to hold you to your responsibilities in the freedom of a quick and educated conscience. "If any of you lack wisdom, let him ask of God and it shall be given him."

A Scotch minister one day met a parishioner looking downcast. "How is it wi' you the day?"—"The adversary's been at me again."—"And what's he been saying to you, Janet?"—"He's been sayin', It's a' a delusion; that the Bible's a tissue o' lees, that there is no heaven, that there's no hell, that there's no Saviour, that it's a' a delusion."—"And what did you say to him?"—"Ah, minister, I kent better than that. I kent it was no use to argy wi' him; I just referred him to the Lord." Here is the secret of a definite and comfortable decision in all questions of casuistry. Would you know what work you would do, what pleasures you may indulge in, on the Lord's

Day? Pray over it. God will give you wisdom. Pray over it whenever a doubt comes to you; no matter what the question is, refer it to the Lord. If you are afraid to pray over any question, take heed, for danger lies that way.

OUR CONFIDANT.

"And they went and told Jesus."—MATT. xiv. 12.

At first glance there is no more repellent figure than that of John the Baptist. Gaunt, cadaverous, clothed in camel's hair and bound about the loins with a hempen girdle, a face browned by the suns of the wilderness, deep eyes flaming in cavernous sockets, a voice with the roll of muffled thunder in it. Yet not infrequently such men as he are the centre of a coterie of most devoted friends. Their very sternness has a strange attractive power. So it was with Peter the Hermit; so with Savonarola. No leader ever had a more devoted following than John the Baptist. His disciples were bound to him as with hooks of steel.

Then came Jesus of Nazareth, to whom John himself pointed with the words, "Behold the Lamb of God!" The tide of popularity turned thereupon from John to Jesus, and the Man of Nazareth was followed by an ever-increasing multitude who heard him gladly. John's disciples were filled with envy, and said, "Master, behold, he to whom thou didst bear witness baptizeth, and all men come unto him." John replied, in a rare spirit of abnegation, "The friend of the bridegroom rejoiceth greatly because he heareth the bridegroom's voice. Said I not, I am not the

Christ? He must increase and I must decrease." So John grew smaller and smaller as time passed and the figure of the Nazarene Prophet filled an ever greater place in current events.

Then John was arrested and thrust into the castle of Machærus. His disciples still clung to him. To and fro they passed between Machærus and the Jordan where Jesus was teaching. One day beneath the castle walls they called their master's name, and there was no answer. "Where is he?" "Dead!"

Dead? It was a hideous tale. It seems Herod had a wife who did not belong to him, and John had reproved him, saying plainly, "It is not lawful for thee to have thy brother's wife." John knew Herod for a coward, but he must reckon with Herodias. Hell hath no fury like a woman scorned. She nursed the adder in her breast and bided her time. There came a banquet, and her daughter Salome danced before the court. O shame! a descendant of the Asmonæan princes! And she danced their senses away. Herod in his drunken enthusiasm cried, "Ask what thou wilt, even to the half of my kingdom, and thou shalt have it." She ran to her mother and returning said, "Here, forthwith, the head of John the Baptist on a charger!"

It is written, "the king was exceedingly sorry"; but, alas! he was frenzied with drink. The order was given. It was night. Up the stone stairway, lantern in hand, went the executioner; John heard his footsteps approaching. The deed was done in secrecy. The executioner lifted the head by its sable hair and, placing it on a royal dish, brought it into the audience hall. It was a sight to haunt one's dreams. The tongue was still, and yet it seemed to say with a voice that nevermore would be hushed, "It is not lawful for thee to have thy brother's wife." The light in those fierce eyes was quenched, but Herod saw them many and many a time, in the watches of the night, flaming down upon him. Mene! Tekel! Upharsin! Conscience makes cowards of us all. Away with the gory thing, and fling the body over the battlements to the dogs!

But the disciples of John came and took up the body—the poor thin body, so lean with long fasting—lifted it tenderly, saying one to another "So true, so fearless! alas! alas!" and they buried it. Then what? Did they go to Herod complaining of his tyranny? Too late; the deed was done. Did they meet by the banks of Jordan to mingle their tears? Nay, every familiar spot by the Jordan spoke to them of the hushed voice and the vanished presence. Whither should they go? "They went and told Jesus." They had learned his truth and tenderness. They could confide in him.

Are you in trouble? There is one that sticketh closer than a brother. He is a friend in fair weather and foul. Our religion is in its last reduction a personal relation to him. Hear his word of promise, "I will not leave you comfortless. Lo, I am with you alway, even unto the end of the world."

Are you brought down into the valley of tears? Is there crape on the door?

> Enters to-day
>   Another body in churchyard sod,
>   Another soul on the life in God?
> His Christ was buried—and lives alway:
> Trust Him, and go your way.

A man can bear any sorrow when his Lord Jesus

stands by. It was a dark night when Oliver Cromwell lay dying; the tempest shook the windows of his room. He said to his wife, "Read me Paul to the Philippians." When she came to the place where it is written, "I know how to be full and how to be hungry, both to abound and to suffer want. I can do all things through Christ which strengtheneth me," he said, "Stop there. That was the word that saved me when our lad Oliver went his way; that is the word that, above the roar of the tempest, shall cheer me now." There are times indeed when nothing else will answer; when the sympathy of earthly friends is but as vinegar on nitre. But the compassion of Jesus is infinitely helpful, for it has omnipotence behind it.

But there are sorrows deeper and darker than death. There are home troubles with which no stranger may intermeddle,—so black and bitter that wife and husband can scarcely speak of them to each other. The "skeleton in the closet"! What a significant phrase that is! A locked door, a white, ghastly, rattling thing behind it; never dragged to light, but always there, always there. A scapegrace boy, a scandal touching the family name, the memory of an unexpiated crime; these are experiences that human friendship cannot touch. To bear them alone is to eat one's heart out. There is only One who can help now. Go, tell it to Jesus. He not only asks us to take his yoke upon us, but he promises also to take our yoke upon him.

Or is yours a more sordid trouble? We are living in hard times, when the rich and the poor draw near together and adversity is master of all. I know of no sadder sight than a pawnbroker's window in these days. We laugh and speak slightingly about "our uncle." But, O, it is a frightful pleasantry. I stood before such a window yesterday and this is what I saw: a ring, among others, and two names within it; a mandolin; a life-saver's medal; diamonds; a case of surgical instruments; a gambler's outfit; a revolver; an India shawl. It is an easy matter to read the story between the lines,—shame and anguish, broken vows, the wolf howling at the door, vice and misery. God pity us, these are everywhere in these days. And blessed is the man who has a helpful friend. "We should have gone under long ago," said a merchant to me recently, "had it not been that our senior partner has resources to draw on." It is an excellent thing to have such a partner in times like these. The Lord Christ has infinite resources to draw on.

But there is another side. There are some who have never tasted sorrow. Do they need him? Dr. William Jay was once surprised to receive in his pulpit a note asking for "prayers for a man in prosperity." If the prosperous knew the dangers that beset their path, such requests would be more common than they are. Near the head of Wall Street the other day, I saw a placard hanging from a beggar's neck, and read its legend, "Pity the poor." But what about these men going up and down the busy thoroughfare bearing the marks of good fortune? Ah, pity the rich! They are so absorbed in the cares of this present world that they hear no songs over their heads. Their eyes are so intent upon the yellow dust at their feet that they see not the gates of pearl open above them. Pity the prosperous! If you are blest with an abundance of this world's goods, if adversity has never transfixed you, by all means make now the acquaintance of this Confidant. Tell him your pleasures and let him participate in them.

It is not fair to shut him out. If you expect him to weep with you in sorrow, shall you not also invite him to make merry with you? It is but a one-sided covenant that covers the night and not the day. If there is a funeral at your home, he knocks, and you say, "Come in, Lord ; come in and condole with me." If the meal is low in the barrel and the cruse is empty of oil, he knocks and you say, "Come in, Lord, and supply my need." But if there is the sound of merry voices and tinkling feet, what then? He draws near and cries, "Behold, I stand at the door and knock ; if any man open to me, I will come in and sup with him." But the music and laughter are ringing in your ears and you cannot hear him !

There never was a marriage like that of Cana of Galilee at which Jesus was a guest. He did not glower on their pleasures that day. Jesus is no kill-joy. His pure heart was full of the sweetness of the hour; and when the bride and bridegroom joined their hands amid congratulations and good wishes, no guest had cheerier words to say than this friend from Nazareth who lifted his hands and laid his blessing upon them. What promise was theirs as they passed under the rainbow arch bearing this benediction of the Son of God !

One reason why we hesitate to receive this divine friend into our pleasures is because we have our misgivings as to their quality oftentimes. Yet this is the way to solve the "amusement question." Do nothing that you cannot pray over. You need the Lord Christ always and everywhere.

It is not wise to shut him out, our pleasures are so

near to pain. The élite of Paris who gathered in the charity bazaar a few days since, arrayed in their laces and broadcloth, had no thought of calamity. What means the clanging of yonder bell? The cry is heard, "Fire! Fire!" and in scarcely more time than we have taken to relate it, the frail structure is consumed. The laughter is turned into mourning. Summon the ambulance; gather up the ashes; scores on scores have rushed into eternity. So close together lie pain and pleasure, on the border line of eternity.

But there is another hour in human experience when none but Christ can help us,— the hour of spiritual doubt. I suppose there are some who have no doubts; who live in such a serene and blessed atmosphere that they entertain no question as to the eternal verities. They are like birds that fly so high above the earth that the dust never falls upon their wings. But I confess to another experience. There are moments when sweetest spiritual communion is broken in upon as if by the voice of the adversary with such suggestions as, "Are you sure there is a God? Are you sure that death does not end all?" These are but momentary interruptions of the blessed life of faith; but while they last they are unspeakably painful. I can recall one period in my life when for weeks together I could make no prayer but this, "Lord, I believe; help thou mine unbelief." But alas for a man who in such moments cannot speak with the Lord of life, who cannot look upward out of his deep midnight into the clear shining of the sky above him.

If you have doubts, go tell them to Jesus. Do not confer with other doubters. Do not seek counsel of skeptics and scoffers. Do not plunge into your books of radical philosophy. Go make a clean breast of all to him who said, "I am the light of the world." He can dispel doubt. As our spiritual physician he can meet our case, but we must tell him all. If having a dreadful sinking of the heart, I go to an earthly physician, he will feel my pulse and take my temperature and ask me one question after another until I say, "I have a strange sinking of the heart"; then he exclaims, "That alters the case; why did you not tell me? I know now what ails you." If we are going to the mercy-seat at all, let us not go wearing a false face. Let us not try to make it appear to our Lord Jesus that we are better than we really are. The only way to get the blessing is to tell him all. We speak of "Doubting Thomas." I see no reason for that appellative. He was no more a doubter than the other disciples; his fault lay, not in refusing to believe, for they all had declined to believe until they saw the risen Christ, but in being absent from the prayer-meeting on a certain night. They told him they had seen the Christ with the marks of his anguish upon him. "I will not believe until I also have seen him; until I have seen his wounds and thrust my hand into his side." The time came when the Lord met him upon that very basis of faith. As the disciples were met in the upper room, he stood suddenly in the midst, and turning to Thomas said, "Behold, the nail-prints in my palms; reach hither thy hand and thrust it into my side, and be not faithless but believing." And Thomas cried, "My Lord and my God!"

So long as we walk by faith, there must be a possibility of doubt; but when the moment comes and we stand in the night surrounded by doubts that taunt and hiss at us, let us remember that we have a Friend who dwells in the glory of absolute verity and who is ready at our call to help us. Meanwhile, stand fast! You are a foolish man if you leap from the carriage when your horses are running away. Get hold of the lines if you can, but in any case stay there. Do not give way in the stress of the adversary's assault, but abide the coming of your Friend; he will bring the morning with him.

But there is another experience, deepest and most dismal of all,—conviction of sin. At this point we are all alike. As the Scotch say "We are a' John Thompson's bairns." Or as Paul says, "We have all sinned and come short of the glory of God."

Sin is an awful thing. Let us not minimize it. The possibility of hell-fire is in it; the fire that is never quenched, the worm that dieth not, the outer darkness, exile from God.

We have repeatedly been told by Biblical scholars that there is a question as to the authenticity of the story of the woman taken in adultery. I am glad that narrative is in the new version. The revisers, among whom were the most learned of Biblical expositors, weighed the question pro and con exhaustively and concluded that the story should remain. For this many souls will rejoice. No part of Scripture comes closer to personal experience. The Rabbis hurled her down upon the marble floor of the temple and looking to Jesus said, "Moses in the law requireth that such as she shall be stoned; but what sayest thou?" All clamored for her death; two only in that company were silent, Jesus—who wrote with his finger in the dust "Let him that is without sin cast the first stone at her"—and the woman herself. Was she penitent for her sin? Her crouching form that shook with sobs cried, *Peccavi*. Her crimson face, which she vainly sought to cover with her hands cried, *Miserere! Miserere!* Her whole attitude was confession; his whole attitude was compassion. "Go and sin no more!" So he sent her forth into a new life of hope and virtue.

Aye, but we are not like her. No? "God, I thank thee that I am not like other people, or even as this woman." Ah, "we are a' John Thompson's bairns." There is no difference. It is the fact of sin and neither its quality nor its quantity that brings us into enmity against law. And there is only One who can heal and comfort us. There is only One in all the world who can say "Son, daughter, thy sins be forgiven thee."

I want a friend, you want a friend. There is no sorrow deeper than friendlessness. An old writer says, "Friends are like shadows; some like the shadow cast by the sun, and others like the shadows cast by moon and stars." But there are times when there is no shadow. There are nights when the moon and stars go out. Then there is one Friend who stands by us in the blackness of darkness.

At this moment there is a man somewhere sitting at his desk with his face in his hands, a half-written note beside him, and a pistol. The papers will tell it to-morrow. And somewhere there is a wild-eyed woman walking by the river side, the fire of despair burning in her eyes; and from the still depths of the river the sirens sing and beckon. The papers will tell it to-morrow. O that they knew! O that the friendless knew the comfort that the Lord Christ can give!

>   I've found a Friend; O, such a Friend!
>   So kind, and true, and tender,
>   So wise a Counselor and Guide,
>   So mighty a Defender!
>   From Him who loves me now so well,
>   What power my soul can sever?
>   Shall life or death, or earth or hell
>   No; I am His forever.

VANDALS IN THE TEMPLE.

"A man was famous according as he had lifted up axes upon the thick trees; but now they break down the carved work thereof with axes and hammers."—Ps. lxxiv. 5, 6.

An unknown minstrel in the time of the captivity sings in a minor key. It has come to him that the Holy City is made desolate, and the temple with its magnificent furnishings is under the ruthless hand of the spoiler. His harp is hung upon the willows, and he weeps when he remembers Zion. The singer sees the axeman felling the cedars of the forest and shaping them to their places as beams and pillars in the sanctuary. Ah, the builder was a famous man; but now the Vandal wields the axe. He ruthlessly smites the carved work on which the cunning artificers of Tyre and Sidon had expended their most consummate skill. "Alas," the minstrel wails, "we are fallen on evil times! The waster is in fashion now!"

The song of Whittier, called "The Reformer," sounds like an echo of this Babylonish hymn, though in a far more cheerful strain:

>All grim and soiled and brown with tan,
> I saw a Strong One, in his wrath,
>Smiting the godless shrines of man
> Along his path.
>
>The Church beneath her trembling dome
> Essayed in vain her ghostly charm:
>Wealth shook within his gilded home
> With strange alarm.

Fraud from his secret chambers fled
  Before the sunlight bursting in:
Sloth drew her pillow o'er her head
  To drown the din.

"Spare," Art implored, " yon holy pile;
  That grand old time-worn turret spare":
Meek Reverence, kneeling in the aisle,
  Cried out "Forbear!"

Gray-bearded Use, who, deaf and blind,
  Groped for his old accustomed stone,
Leaned on his staff, and wept to find
  His seat o'erthrown.

Young Romance raised his dreamy eyes,
  O'erhung with paly locks of gold,—
"Why smite," he asked, in sad surprise,
  "The fair, the old?"

Yet louder rang the Strong One's stroke,
  Yet nearer flashed his axe's gleam;
Shuddering and sick of heart I woke,
  As from a dream.

I looked: aside the dust-cloud rolled,—
  The Waster seemed the Builder too;
Up springing from the ruined Old
  I saw the New.

*   *   *   *   *   *   *

For life shall on and upward go;
  Th' eternal step of progress beats
To that great anthem, calm and slow,
  Which God repeats.

Take heart!—the Waster builds again,—
  A charmèd life old Goodness hath;
The tares may perish,—but the grain
  Is not for death.

God works in all things; all obey
  His first propulsion from the night:
Wake thou and watch!—the world is gray
  With morning light!

God bless the axe,—the axe that is wielded upon the thick trees of the forest for the building up of homes and legislative halls and sanctuaries. God bless the axe that is laid at the root of all trees of oppression and wrong. As everybody knows, Gladstone, wreathed with his honorable garland of almond blossoms, still loves to swing his axe in the woods of Hawarden. Many a beam and pillar has he hewn for their places in the fabric of civil and ecclesiastical freedom. O that his right hand might be strengthened still, to cut up by the roots the upas-tree of English protection, under which the Sultan and his Moslem assassins have so long sheltered the religion of war and lust and slavery!

But there is a sharp contrast here between the work of the builder and that of the destroyer: the one lifting his axe against the thick trees of the forest, the other against the carved work of the sanctuary. There is a contrast sharp and distinct between the Vandal, who glories in mere destruction for destruction's sake, and the reformer, whose ambition is to add to the sum total of the public weal and contribute somewhat to the glory of God.

The Vandal is a familiar figure in political life. He hates the present order of things and thrusts out his lip at every citizen, except himself, who presumes to take a practical interest in public affairs. "Down with parties! Down with political platforms! Down with the administration!" You heard this Vandal speaking from the tail-end of trucks and bandwagons in our last presidential campaign; you will see him again when the issue is joined for a just administration in the greater and better New York. He is a most vociferous critic, but has no suggestion to make as to practical reform. Trust him not! The Germans have a homely proverb which meets his case: "See to it that in washing the bath tub, you do not empty the infant into the brook."

The Vandal makes himself conspicuous also in all the current controversies of society. He will solve for you the problem of labor *versus* capital in a trice. He poses as an anarchist, a socialist, at times a walking delegate, but always a reformer. He denounces trusts and corporations without being able to give a reason for the faith that is in him. He is against employers and millionaires. To his mind, the issue is between the bomb and the ballot; between dynamite and the trowel. This man is of no perceptible use in the social fabric. Anybody can tear down; but where is your builder? Anybody can be an iconoclast; but where is your sculptor? Anybody can destroy the carved work; but who will hew us the beams of cedar from the forests of Lebanon?

This philosophy of destruction found expression in the French Revolution. So vain an outpouring of life and treasure in the mere passion for overthrow had never been seen before, and, please God, shall never be seen again. The Bastile was torn down from turret to foundation. So far, so good. But homes and palaces, churches and legislative halls, followed fast. The cry was, "Down with God! Down with wealth and prosperity! Down with government!" The cup filled with the blood of aristocrats was pressed to princely lips. Then the reign of terror! The streets were red. The nights were filled with shrieks and curses. And down from the deadwalls, while the mobs went surging by, gleamed the grim satire; "Liberty, Equality, Fraternity." Chaos and confusion! And then the Little Corporal came marching in, welcomed with cries of " *Vive l' Empereur*," took his place upon a throne of tyranny riveted with such fetters and manacles as France had never dreamed of, and laughed the iconoclasts to scorn. Such is the logical end of social vandalism. Thus it must ever be.

Our chief interest to-day, however, is with the Vandal in the Temple. Religion is a matter of common interest to all the children of men. A neutral attitude is impossible. You must be for or against. You must be a waster or a builder.

The Vandal in this relation sometimes poses as *an atheist*. "The fool hath said in his heart, There is no God"; but this man is not satisfied with his soliloquy; he must needs teach others so. He regards theism as a fable, and cries, "Get rid of this Tyrant who reigns in the skies!"

But, assuming for the moment that theism is a dream, is it not indeed a most beneficent dream? And what will this waster gain, if he dissipates the shadows that walk through it? I know of a man who was left, when an infant, in a basket at a rich man's door. He grew up ignorant of the fact that he was a foundling, rejoicing in all the privileges of sonship in that happy home. But in an evil day a meddling busybody said, "You are not this man's son; you have no father." Who shall estimate the pain and sorrow caused by those words, though indeed they were the very truth? But what wretch is this who would persuade me that I, trained from the mother's knee to lift my voice toward heaven and say, "Abba, Father," have no right to trust him thus; nay, that there is no Father there to answer me.

Or your Vandal is perhaps *an agnostic.* He finds me saying with Job, "I know that my Redeemer liveth"; or with Paul, "I know whom I have believed, and am persuaded that he is able to keep that which I have committed unto him against that day." It grieves him that I should believe anything. He believes only what he can see with fleshly eyes and touch with his finger-tips. He says to me, "You think you know, but in fact your faith is mere credulity. God and immortality and kindred matters are beyond your ken. Address yourself to present tasks and duties. Here is a world that you can see; why dream of the unseen?" Thus the destroyer would cut the earth from beneath my feet.

A dream? A mere dream? A mere illusion? Then leave me alone to die among these beloved shadows. Carlyle never said a truer thing than this: "The saddest case I know, is that of a man who knows nothing which he cannot button in his pocket, and who believes nothing which he cannot eat and digest." To this let us add, the meanest man in the universe is one who would rob a beggar of his crutches without giving him something else to lean on.

And then *the pessimist;* he is a Vandal, too. Optimism is literally *best-ism;* pessimism is literally *worst-ism.* A pessimist is a kill-joy. Not satisfied with taking the darkest possible view of himself, he is not willing that any other should have sunshine in his soul. He regards the church, society, the government, as all wrong. Christians are for the most part deceivers or self-deceived. The world is going to the bad.

But what's the use or where's the gain? Even if the world is going to the bad, we should get the most out of this brief life by making the best of it. The man who whistles at his task, turns out the best job. The secret of Luther's success lay largely in his optimistic views. At the darkest moment of the Reformation, when he was a refugee in the castle of the Wartburg, he was wont to say: "Come, Philip, let us lift our voices in the forty-sixth Psalm—God is our refuge and our strength; therefore we will not fear, though the earth be removed and the mountains be carried into the sea. There is a river, the streams whereof shall make glad the city of God."

There is another Vandal whose passion for destruction is aimed at the moral law. He is an *Antinomian*, and his *bête-noir* is the Decalogue. The Ten Commandments are too Puritanical for him. He would loosen the sanctions of the Sabbath law by permitting many forms of work which God has forbidden, and allowing all common recreations on the Lord's Day. He has liberal views of marriage and divorce, and regards the seventh commandment as a relic of a hide-bound age. The old-fashioned rule of industry, honest work, honest wages, is quite too antiquated for him. He sees nothing wrong in the pool-room or in stock-gambling. His motto is, "Quick transit to a fortune."

And the sorrow of it is, that some who teach these ethical modifications are ministers of the Gospel of Christ. They are not builders, but destroyers. They deceive and mislead. The loose views of social purity, of Sabbath observance, and of the rights of property, which prevail in our time, are largely due to such teaching as this.

We are reminded of the cornet who led the British to Tel-el-Kebir. It was an all-night march through the wilderness. The duty of directing this march was assigned to a young cornet just out of the training school. He rode before the army all night on his camel, watching the stars and consulting the compass, until toward daybreak the neighing of horses was heard. Yonder was Tel-el-Kebir. At the first volley, the young cornet fell. "I am going, General," said he; "but didn't I lead them straight?" Blessed is the man who, being appointed as a teacher, can say, "I led them straight." It must needs be that offenses come, but woe be unto that man by whom they come; it were better for him that a millstone were hanged about his neck, and that he were drowned in the depth of the sea.

The best known vandal of our time, however, is *the neologist*, whose word is, "Ring out the old, ring in the new!" It is enough for him that a truth or a principle belongs to the past. Out upon it! He forgets that all the most gracious things in the universe are old, and that God himself is oldest of all. Do you remember the pathetic words of King Lear, who, when all had forsaken him, turned to the stars and asked compassion of them, "Since ye yourselves are old"? It is too bad that these scholarly gentlemen who clamor against the past cannot refuse to breathe old-fashioned air or drink "traditional" spring water.

We hold to the traditional view of God; that he is an infinite personality, with eyes to see, a heart to pity, and hands stretched forth to help; a God who permits us to say, "Abba, Father." But this view, they say, is superannuated, for God is an all-pervading force, a rare and infinite energy, impersonal law.

We hold to the traditional view of Christ,—with the sinners of past centuries, who have all cried for mercy, and looking toward the cross have seen his hands stretched out, and have heard him say, "Thy sins be forgiven thee." But from Andover comes the word, that there must be a restatement of the doctrine of Christ; the incarnation, the vicarious atonement, the literal resurrection, are to be shelved with the Ptolemaic view of the universe. And we stand bereft like the Magdalene, saying, "Ye have taken away my Lord, and I know not where ye have laid him."

We hold to the traditional view of the Bible; we believe as our fathers have believed from the beginning until now, that the Scriptures were written by holy men as they were moved by the Holy Ghost, and that they are true, and only true from the beginning to the end. But the voice of the Vandal is lifted, to say, "Your Bible is a bundle of fables and folk-lore." God pity us; what then shall we do? And what a sweet and helpful friend is this who takes away our only rule of faith and practice! The wrecker kindles a false light on the shore, but, seeking only plunder, gives decent burial to the dead. Here is a wrecker, however, who tosses back his victims upon the merciless waves of a sea of unbelief. He destroys, and builds not; he curses, and blesses not; he laughs gleefully at the despair of souls.

If the Vandals were to have their way, what then? No God! no Christ! no Bible! Here is a sunless world. When Jean Paul Richter felt himself drifting into a barren and joyless infidelity, his course was momentarily arrested by a vision of a dim figure saying, "God is dead." If these great truths which our fathers have cherished, and which the great multitude of believers cherish still, were to pass from us, the whole world would be at odds and ends. The music of the spheres would cease, and men would relapse into the barbarism from which the Gospel has delivered them.

But these are false forebodings. The Vandal's work is vain. The temple rises despite his work of ruthless and passionate destruction.

> "A charmèd life old Goodness hath;
> The tares may perish,
> But the grain is not for death."

But, friend, look to it that you be a builder and not a destroyer only. The axe is in your hand for weal or woe. Are you lifting it against the carved work or against the thick trees? When we lie upon our death beds, we shall question ourselves like this: "What good have I done in the world? Have I stretched the helping hand? Have I put a cup of cold water to thirsty lips? Have I contributed to the sum total of truth and goodness? Have I revered duty and righteousness? Have I thought and believed and done as conscience bade me? Have I followed in the footsteps of him who went about doing good? Have I cut down beams and pillars and made carved work for the temple? Is the world better for my living in it?"

> "There are lonely hearts to cherish,
> While the days are going by.
> There are weary souls who perish,
> While the days are going by.

> "If a smile we can renew,
> While our journey we pursue,
> O the good we all may do,
> While the days are going by."

www.ingramcontent.com/pod-product-compliance
Lightning Source LLC
Chambersburg PA
CBHW031856220426
43663CB00006B/653